GUNDOG
Health & Welfare

GUNDOG
Health & Welfare

TONY BUCKWELL

THE CROWOOD PRESS

First published in 2018 by
The Crowood Press Ltd
Ramsbury, Marlborough
Wiltshire SN8 2HR

www.crowood.com

British Library Cataloguing-in-Publication Data
A catalogue record for this book is available from the British Library.

ISBN 978 1 78500 387 5

Dedication
To Wendy

Typeset by Jean Cussons Typesetting, Diss, Norfolk

Printed and bound in India by Parksons Graphics

CONTENTS

ACKNOWLEDGEMENTS

I could not have written or illustrated this book without the encouragement, guidance and assistance of many people. I particularly wish to thank my wife Wendy for her support, and to acknowledge the assistance of my colleagues Professor Peter Bedford, Dr Gary Clayton-Jones and Alan Margetts, the professional gundog trainers Mark Bott, Kim Jinks, Tania Stapley and Di Stevens, gamekeepers Bill Gardiner, Stuart Ansell, and Steve Overy, and their beaters and pickers up from the Beech Estate, Brick House, Stone House and Bungehurst Shoots respectively, and my many friends in the South Eastern Gundog Society and the Kent & East Sussex branch of the Utility Gundog Society. I need to thank professional nature photographer Laurie Campbell for generously allowing me to use some of his images, and Andrew Crook for enabling me access to photograph specimens in the anatomy department of the Royal Veterinary College. Last but by no means least, my special thanks to Angela Gilchrist, the consultant clinical psychologist who first encouraged me to take up writing to help overcome the devastating effects of clinical depression.

INTRODUCTION

Man's relationship with dogs is one of the most remarkable examples of domestication and mutual co-operation. It is one that began at least 14,000 years ago when the domestic dog (*Canis familiaris*) was probably derived from the Asiatic wolf (*Canis lupus pallipes*) and various hybrids with other races of wolf. Their increasingly close relationship with early man was facilitated by the suppression of certain fear and stress responses, which having been reduced or tolerated, enabled docility to be increased, whilst the intelligence and special senses inherent in their wild ancestors were retained. Subsequent artificial selection produced dramatic changes to their anatomy and behavioural repertoire, leading to the development of the various pedigree dog breeds that we see today.

Included among those selection criteria was a desire at an early stage to capitalize on, and harness the dogs' natural hunting ability. Initially this was to assist our ancestors to more readily find and bring down game, but more recently, and particularly alongside the development and use of the modern sporting shotgun, we need to use dogs not only to hunt and mark, but also to retrieve game that we have killed or wounded, thereby extending the efficiency of our pursuit of game as a source of food and for sporting purposes.

Associated with interdependency in the process of domestication is a responsibility on our behalf to recognize and provide for the health and welfare needs of our dogs. In the United Kingdom this responsibility has become recognized as a legal obligation, enshrined in British law in the form of the Animal Welfare Act 2006, which makes it an offence either to cause a protected animal such as a dog to suffer, or to omit to take reasonable steps to prevent that animal's suffering. Furthermore the Act, through various associated species-specific codes of practice, recognizes and encompasses the fundamental principles of animal welfare, generally referred to as the 'Five Freedoms', namely:

- Freedom from thirst, hunger and malnutrition
- Freedom from pain, injury and disease
- Freedom from fear and distress
- Freedom from physical and thermal discomfort
- Freedom to perform most normal patterns of behaviour

Ignorance is neither tolerated nor defensible, so whilst we might derive great pleasure and benefit from the dogs that accompany us whilst shooting or when they are capable of competing in the show ring, field trials or working tests, we do need to remember these responsibilities at all times. This book was never intended as a textbook of canine veterinary medicine and surgery, nor is it a comprehensive reference to every facet of canine welfare, behaviour and the law as it relates to shooting with dogs.

What I have attempted to do is provide concise guidance for owners of working gundogs so they might be reasonably informed on how best to ensure their dogs live healthy, active lives, and are able to assure their immediate care should they become injured. To do this I have tried to combine my experience in veterinary clinical practice with owning, training and working my own dogs, together with all that I've gleaned from the many more capable and competent gundog handlers I've had the pleasure and privilege of meeting and knowing over many years.

A healthy and well-cared for gundog can be a friend and companion as well as an invaluable assistant in the field.

1 PUPPY BASICS, PROMOTING HEALTH

ACQUIRING A HEALTHY PUPPY

Acquiring a puppy should never be a matter undertaken lightly, nor should it represent a spur-of-the-moment decision. Acquiring a working gundog means seeking a puppy that will not only become a canine companion, but a dog that is steady to shot, biddable to train, intelligent, particularly in finding game, and of sufficiently robust constitution that it is unlikely to suffer some debilitating illness. Consequently you must be prepared to devote time and attention in the early stages to selecting a suitable puppy, as this will mean you are more likely to enjoy the satisfaction of owning a loyal, healthy, well trained and reliable dog.

A working gundog represents a significant investment, and not just in financial terms. It requires commitment, time and responsibility. A lively young gundog will tax your patience at times, especially during adolescence, so be prepared for a few challenges as well as, hopefully, a great deal of satisfaction.

Before you seek to acquire a working gundog, determine which breed is most suitable for you, and for the type of work you require your dog to perform, and equally importantly, a suitable breeder from whom to purchase the puppy. Don't be tempted to simply obtain a puppy from a friend who happens to have a litter and is looking for homes for the puppies. Do your homework, particularly if this is to be your first dog.

Choice of Breed

Understand that there is no such thing as the perfect dog: each of the working breeds has been developed in an attempt to satisfy certain criteria, and was selectively bred accordingly. No one breed will be perfect in every respect, although

An English Springer Spaniel. Until relatively recently the English Springer Spaniel was far and away the most popular of the working spaniel breeds.

Many people are now finding the working Cocker Spaniel more to their liking, and in recent years the English Springer tends to be less numerous as a result.

certain breeds are significantly more popular than others, the Labrador Retriever perhaps being the most obvious example. This trend reflects the contemporaneous requirements and preferences of the majority of people who choose to work their dogs under current conditions in the shooting field. Circumstances change, however, and the popularity of different breeds tends to wax and wane.

Make sure you understand the type of dog you require, and – just as importantly – the particular nuances of a breed that interests you: each breed has its individual traits and tendencies. It is important to understand these characteristics so that you can anticipate and adapt accordingly to ensure your dog's welfare within an appropriate environment. For instance, a personal favourite

of mine, the Curly-Coated Retriever, is one of the less popular breeds, with a sensitive temperament and very slow to mature. The Curly has a tendency to 'sulk' if reprimanded; it takes a lot of time, patience and perseverance to train a Curly-Coated Retriever, and there's many an occasion when it is better to end a training session there and then and try again another day.

It is not surprising, therefore, that you don't come across many Curly-Coated Retrievers in the shooting field. A large dog with a tendency to be clumsy at times, the Curly will leap straight into the back of a vehicle full of beaters, expecting there to be room. He's not an extrovert and he can be aloof with strangers, but he's a loyal companion. He is content just being with you on the marsh quietly waiting for the evening flight, and is not a breed you expect to see rushing around flushing game from deep covert. He loves water and has a coat to match, which dries easily, albeit with a distinctive aroma that tends to linger in the upholstery after he has returned to the car.

Try to ensure that before you acquire your puppy, you can describe your chosen breed in such terms; then you are less likely to find yourself trying to cope with unexpected surprises.

Breed-Related Diseases

Associated with selective breeding from closely related dogs is an inevitable tendency for there to be breed-related diseases. There are, however, very few breed-specific diseases. Most of the clinical conditions we recognize in different breeds are diseases of dogs (in general) that happen to have a higher incidence in certain breeds. Don't necessarily be put off if you find that the breed you are interested in suffers a variety of reported health problems. It doesn't necessarily imply the breed is particularly unhealthy, because quite often, many breeders will have adopted health testing and selective breeding strategies aimed at reducing the incidence of these conditions within the breed.

Always bear in mind the fact that some diseases may render an affected dog quite unsuitable for work, or require long-term expensive treatment, whilst others may cause the dog little inconvenience or be quite simple to correct. It could be argued that a higher incidence of a disease which has little clinical significance and causes affected dogs little pain or discom-

A Curly-Coated Retriever, the largest of the retriever breeds.

The Labrador Retriever, the most popular retriever in the UK. Although a variety of health conditions are reported, this in part reflects the responsible attitude of breeders in reporting and characterizing any health issues.

The Welsh Springer Spaniel. It is less popular than the English Springer and Cocker Spaniel among the working fraternity; however, in common with many of the so-called 'minor breeds', Welsh Springers can both succeed in the show ring and, in the right hands, be worked on a shoot. WENDY BUCKWELL

fort, might be of less concern than a less common problem that has devastating, long-lasting painful effects in a relatively small number of affected dogs. So seek advice; speak to a variety of owners and breeders, and discuss with a vet any breed health concerns that you may have. Try to understand the relative risks so that you can select a suitable breeder who is more likely to have healthy stock of the type that you want.

Choosing a Breeder

Finding a suitable breeder whom you can trust, and, particularly if this is your first dog, someone who will willingly offer all the necessary further advice as the puppy gets older, can be quite a challenge. In some respects the extent of the challenge can depend on the breed: some breeds are far more numerous than others, so there will be more breeders to choose from and, of course, more litters available from which to choose a puppy. In the case of the less populous breeds, you may even have to select a breeder and expect to wait until a suitable litter becomes available.

In either case you are best achieving a rapport with the breeder so that you can speak openly: explain your circumstances and the type of puppy you are seeking. Expect the breeder to challenge you: a good breeder will be anxious to sell the puppies to good homes, and will need assurance that this is what you offer. You, on the other hand, will want assurances that the breeder has sound, healthy stock of suitable working ability.

Once you have a rapport with one or more breeders, enquire about the health and soundness of their dogs. If they undertake health testing, ask to see copies of the results, don't simply take their word for it. If you have done your homework and understand any health issues in the breed, see how familiar the breeder is with these problems, and how they compare their dogs in these respects. You should find that most reputable breeders will be very well informed, a veritable 'font of knowledge', and in speaking with them your understanding of the breed will improve considerably. Good breeders aren't just there to sell you a puppy: they tend to be the ambassadors of their breed, seeking good working homes where their dogs will be well cared for, well trained, and worked appropriately.

Any reputable breeder and trainer should be able to show you progeny of the 'type' you seek. Ideally both bitch and dog will be health tested so that you are unlikely to pick up any inherited problems.

Choosing a Puppy

So you have decided on the breed of dog you want, and have located a breeder whose dogs you like, someone with whom you have struck up a good relationship and who has a suitable litter of puppies available. So how do you go about choosing one of those puppies as the dog that's going to be right for you?

This purpose-built whelping box has space centrally for the bitch to lie comfortably, and the periphery shelf enables puppies to retreat safely without risk of being squashed when the bitch lies down. Healthy puppies are quiet, sleepy, warm to the touch, plump, round and firm. They should make a contented murmuring noise periodically, and occasionally a sharp yelp if squashed or pushed off a teat.

This litter of Hungarian Vizslas is the result of an intentional 'outcross', where their sire and dam represented genetically distinct types within the breed. Note in particular how this has resulted in different head types among these puppies.

This Hungarian Vizsla bitch remains in fine condition despite the fact that she is nursing a large litter; note the prominent mammary glands.

Ideally visit the breeder as soon as the litter is well established, and the puppies are ready to meet potential new owners. At this stage consider the litter as a whole; ensure they are fit and healthy, and off to a good start in life. The litter should be nice and 'even', with puppies of roughly the same size, although dogs (males) may be slightly bigger and more 'chunky' than bitches, especially as they grow older and start to play with their littermates. If the bitch has a particularly large litter, then there will be competition for the milk bar, and even if the breeder is supplementing the milk supply, it won't be unnatural to see a little unevenness, with maybe one or two smaller puppies, and one or two larger than the rest.

If you have a family, take them with you to meet the breeder and their dogs; many breeders will no doubt insist because, to them, the way your children behave and react to their dogs and puppies will be important. Ideally visit the breeder on more than one occasion so that by the time the puppies are ready to go, you will already have seen them, even if you have not made a final selection.

Once it comes to making a final choice, if you are dealing with a reputable breeder who has many years' experience of breeding, raising and training their gundogs, and particularly if this is your first dog, be inclined to seek and take their advice. In the process of raising and starting to socialize the litter, the breeder will have noticed each puppy's individual idiosyncrasies. Some pups will be bolder and have a more outgoing temperament; others may be more reserved and quieter. The former would probably suit someone with a strong personality who has previously trained a dog,

When you visit a breeder to view puppies always expect to see the bitch with her puppies, and be suspicious if presented with a litter of older weaned puppies and some excuse for the bitch being away from the premises.

Once weaned, Labrador Retriever puppies develop rapidly, and most are able to go to new homes by the time they are six to eight weeks of age.

certainly someone who can most easily cope with the temperament, whilst the latter might be better in a single dog household with an owner seeking a constant companion. Others may be less boisterous and a better choice if there are young children.

Spend time with the litter, handling the puppies and talking with the breeder. If this is your first dog and you are acquiring it from a reputable breeder, maybe one that actively campaigns their dogs in field trials, don't necessarily expect to be offered the 'pick' of the litter. The breeder may already have decided to run on a puppy. He or she will select what they consider to be the best puppy, and if they believe it to show any real promise, they are hardly likely to sell it to a novice with no previous experience either of the breed, or in training a gundog. They should, however, be able to readily compare the puppies with you, and to discuss their various strengths and weaknesses.

A pair of boisterous Vizsla puppies playing together.

If you are seeking a loyal companion and there is any doubt over which to select, let the puppy choose you.

At the end of the day, the breeder will usually want to ensure your satisfaction, and you need to be comfortable that you have made the right decision. If the breeder has chosen a puppy they think is suitable for you, always ask their reason(s) so you can understand their choice. Beware the person who brings out just the one puppy and emphatically announces 'This is yours'. This is not a process that should be rushed, nor should a decision be forced upon you: you always have the option of walking away.

Settling In
Most good breeders can provide you with a list of essential items to acquire in preparation for your new puppy, and will give you small samples of the diet to feed, as well as a feeding guide and some basic instructions on house training and exercise. Typically you will require:

- A dog bed and bedding material that can be washed and dried easily
- A feed bowl
- A separate bowl for drinking water

House Training
Puppies will tend to void urine and pass faeces after each meal so you can take advantage of this tendency for house-training purposes. As soon as the puppy has eaten its food, take it outside and wait until 'all is done' – here there is a distinct advantage in raising puppies in the summer months and not during the winter; praise the puppy immediately it urinates or defecates. In any training regime, always give plenty of praise for a correct outcome, and never scold the puppy for getting something wrong – so always praise the puppy for toileting outside, and you should find that this soon becomes an ingrained behavioural process, the puppy learning to do something that pleases you. It is much more difficult to try to teach the puppy not to urinate or defecate indoors if you simply tell it off for doing so.

The first night in its new home is always one of the most stressful, for new puppy and new owner alike. If you intend the puppy to sleep in a particular room or place at night, it is a good idea to give him something, either to play with or to eat, as you say goodnight. A few biscuits are generally all that are needed just to take his mind off the fact that you are leaving him on his own. He will doubtless cry a little at first, but you must harden your heart: as long as you are sure he is warm enough and not asking to be let outside, then let him cry. If you keep going back to him every time he whines he will quickly learn that by whining and crying he will get your company and consequently cry even more.

Remember that dogs are essentially pack animals and like to be with others, so our domesticated dogs need to be taught to tolerate being alone. Start as you mean to go on, and even if your puppy has the company of another dog at night, always train the puppy to tolerate being left alone. Begin with short sessions when your puppy is young, and build up to longer absences gradually.

Puppies often suffer a mild gut upset after moving to a new home, and pass very loose stools. This is normally transient, however, and will settle down within a day or two. At the first sign of diarrhoea provide only very small amounts of the normal ration but more frequently, and make

ORAL REHYDRATION THERAPY

Mix together:

6 level teaspoonfuls of sugar
½ teaspoonful salt
1 quart (approx 1ltr) water

The water can be boiled or treated with sterilizing tablets, but this is not essential.

sure the puppy drinks plenty of fluid – again, little and often. Use an oral rehydration mixture (see text box) rather than plain tap water. Dose the puppy with a paediatric kaolin 'binding' preparation from the chemist.

Some people would advocate withholding the puppy's normal food for twelve hours, then substituting 'white' meat (chicken, lamb or fish, plus a little rice) for any 'red meat' meals, and giving some natural yoghurt as a 'milk' meal to rebalance the 'friendly' bacteria in its gut. This does, however, represent a change from the norm, and current veterinary advice is to avoid changing the environment any further in an already upset bowel.

Check for dehydration by pinching a fold of loose skin gently between finger and thumb. The fold of skin should collapse immediately; if it remains 'tented' it indicates that the puppy is becoming dehydrated. If the diarrhoea becomes more profuse, or blood-stained, or if the puppy becomes particularly dehydrated, take it to a vet immediately.

TAKING YOUR PUPPY TO THE VET

Once you have your new puppy, register it with a local veterinary practice and make an appointment for an initial consultation so the vet can check it over and advise on vaccination, worming and suchlike.

Visiting a veterinary surgery can be a stressful experience for your dog, especially on the first occasion. There will be lots of sights, smells and sounds in the surgery that will be new and unfa-

miliar to your puppy. There will also be strange people, and most likely other animals of types and sizes that the puppy has never encountered before. There are a number of things you can do, however, that can help make the visit less stressful for the dog and more comfortable and productive for you.

Take your dog for a walk, ideally somewhere safe that is not frequented by other clients' dogs, before entering the reception area and waiting room. This will tend to make the dog calmer and present an opportunity for the pup to empty its bladder. If it's a young puppy think about using a carrier. This prevents the puppy biting or scratching you if you are trying to hold it still whilst waiting, and will protect it from other pets. The last thing you want on the first trip to the vet is for your puppy to suffer any significantly nasty event or highly disturbing experience.

Keep the dog calm and under control in the waiting room by taking control of the situation, and keep him or her relaxed; give plenty of physical and verbal attention, talking softly using a reassuring voice. Make it a pleasant learning experience for your puppy; consider it part of the socialization process that can contribute towards training the puppy – calmness towards strangers in unfamiliar surroundings.

Help in the consulting and examination room. Whilst vets and veterinary nurses will be very experienced in handling nervous and frightened animals, your familiar face and smell, coupled with your tactile presence in helping, will tend to comfort the dog. Vets and nurses often have their own methods of helping puppies become accustomed to the environment in their surgery, so as necessary, expect and allow them to give treats or other forms of reward as part of their examination process.

Allow plenty of time. If possible make an appointment and allow the receptionist to suggest the best time for a first visit. Usually early mornings and evenings are busiest for the vet, so even though it may be less convenient for you, be prepared to avoid these peak periods.

Finally, visit frequently. Regular check-ups will help your dog become more accustomed to the experience, especially if he or she doesn't come to associate the veterinary surgery with pain or some other form of anticipated discomfort. It will also enable the veterinary staff to get to know you and become more familiar with your dog. Obviously you won't wish to incur unnecessary cost, so talk to the veterinary staff, particularly the receptionist and nurses, and see what they suggest. Many vets have weighing scales in the waiting room, and there may be no charge if you simply wish to keep a regular check on your dog's weight as a reason to visit.

Vaccination

Inevitably your dog at some time or other will come across common canine infections, and unless protected, is likely to succumb to those diseases. The seriousness of any consequent illness will depend upon a number of factors, primarily the seriousness of the disease, and the degree of exposure and the effectiveness of the dog's innate protective mechanisms to combat the infection. The latter will vary depending on the age of the dog (puppies and elderly dogs tend to be more susceptible), and his or her general standard of health. Dogs that are otherwise unwell or under-nourished will tend to be more susceptible, and dogs that are under some form of stress, such as from being in unfamiliar surroundings whilst in boarding kennels, will also tend to pick up infection more easily.

'Prevention is better than cure' as the saying goes, and the most effective means of preventing common infections is to have your puppy vaccinated. Effective vaccines are now available to protect against most of the significant infec-

tious diseases of dogs. Most puppies acquired by responsible owners are likely to be vaccinated, but the level of protection will gradually wane. There is evidence to show that many aren't revaccinated as often they should be, particularly as they get older. So do ensure that your dog is given appropriate 'booster' vaccinations at appropriate intervals to maintain his or her level of protection.

How Does Vaccination Work?
Vaccination consists of giving the dog a harmless dose of the infective agent, typically a virus or bacteria. The vaccine is typically rendered harmless either by first killing the agent, the typical method used to prepare bacterial vaccines, or by producing a so-called 'live' vaccine using a modified, non-infectious form of the disease-causing agent; this second method is often adopted when producing viral vaccines. When the dog is given a vaccine, its body will recognize it as something foreign, and this induces an immediate immune response: the body creates what are known as antibodies against the agent in question. Antibodies will continue to be produced and to circulate in the bloodstream, thereby recognizing and attaching to the infectious agent should the dog subsequently be exposed to the infection. The activated antibody attached to the infectious agent will then stimulate other parts of the dog's immune defence mechanism to fight and overcome infection.

There are essentially two means of producing a vaccine. 'Live' vaccines are intended to multiply once administered, mimicking infection and stimulating the immune response to produce antibodies. 'Killed' vaccines need to be administered on more than one occasion and usually as two doses, given two to four weeks apart. The first dose of a killed vaccine will stimulate only a mild immune response, but as soon as the second dose is given, the dog's immune system recognizes the vaccine and responds more vigorously, producing a much higher level of protection.

The immune response to vaccines tends to wane in time; the length of time will depend on the type of vaccine, and, of course, whether or not the dog has subsequently been exposed to infection. The protection given by 'live' vaccines tends to last longer than that from using 'killed' vaccines. Most 'dead' vaccines have to be boosted annually, whereas 'live' vaccines can create a much longer-lasting level of immunity. The need for booster vaccination will depend both on the type of vaccine used, and the risk of exposure to disease within the local environment.

These days the former practice for all dogs needing similar routine annual 'booster' vaccinations has largely been replaced by a more intelligent, risk-assessed approach. When you take your puppy to be vaccinated, discuss your circumstances with your vet and explain your dog's intended lifestyle. Your vet can take into consideration various factors such as how common a particular disease is in your area, and which diseases your dog is most likely to encounter both at home and on a shoot, and can advise you accordingly. By understanding your dog's lifestyle and what it may be exposed to, they can suggest which vaccines are most important, and how frequently those vaccinations need to be repeated.

When to Vaccinate
Puppies are normally given a first vaccination at six to eight weeks of age, and a second at around twelve to fourteen weeks of age, although some

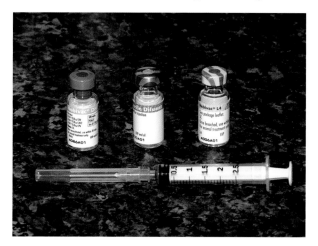

A typical canine vaccine comprises a vial containing a freeze-dried pellet (left), which prior to injection has to be dissolved in either the sterile water provided (centre), or mixed with another agent in liquid form – in this example a leptospirosis vaccine (right).

vets in certain areas may advise delaying the final vaccination until the puppy is sixteen weeks of age. The apparent difference in advice between various veterinary practices is explained by problems arising from the variable persistence of maternal antibody protection – passive temporary protection that puppies receive from their dam through the 'first milk' when they start suckling immediately after birth. The bitch produces a substance called colostrum in her milk, which transfers some of her immunity, as antibodies, in her milk.

Colostrum is only produced by the bitch for twelve to thirty-six hours after whelping, and it is obviously very important that puppies receive the benefit of this 'first milk'. The amount of protection provided to the puppy, and the length of time the colostral milk conveys protection, depends entirely on how much of this milk is consumed. Consequently individual puppies will vary in the amount of protection they receive from their mother, and for how long this protection lasts. The level of protection generally falls off between six to eight weeks of age, but in many puppies, especially those that suckle vigorously after birth and which therefore receive most colostrum, it can persist until twelve to sixteen weeks of age. Maternal antibodies interfere with vaccination, and if the level of maternal antibodies remains high there is a risk that the vaccine won't 'take' and the puppy will be unprotected.

This obviously complicates matters, since ideally the vaccine would be given as soon as the puppy's maternal antibody level declines to the point where the vaccine can stimulate a strong immune response and induce the puppy to produce its own antibodies. Too soon, and the vaccine won't 'take'; too late, and there is a risk that the puppy is unprotected after the protection from its mother falls away, until such time as it is given the vaccine. The problem has been resolved to some extent by modern vaccines that are slightly more virulent and able to overcome low maternal antibody levels.

It will be best to seek, trust and follow the advice of your veterinary surgeon. Your vet will understand the characteristics of the particular vaccines currently used in the practice, and will also be aware of the relative disease risks in your particular area. The diseases that are usually included in most multivalent canine vaccines are described below.

Canine distemper: A disease that affects dogs of all ages, but is particularly common in puppies. It usually results in death, and is characterized by respiratory signs, such as runny eyes and nose, and nervous signs such as fits, which may follow later.

Canine parvovirus: This is a distressing disease, often characterized by severe vomiting and profuse blood-stained diarrhoea, which usually leads to dehydration and death. Again, it is common in puppies, but can affect and be fatal in older, unvaccinated dogs.

Canine viral hepatitis: A very contagious disease. Symptoms include a high fever, jaundice, vomiting and stomach pains. Again, it can be fatal.

Leptospirosis: Dogs infected by the leptospira bacteria can suffer liver and kidney damage, and require prolonged treatment if they are to recover fully.

Infectious bronchitis, or 'kennel cough': Many of the more recent 'multivalent' vaccines include viral antigens that help protect against infectious bronchitis, otherwise known as 'kennel cough'. Kennel cough is frequently complicated by the presence of a bacterium called *Bordetella bronchiseptica*, which causes infection in addition to these common viruses. The combined viral/bacterial infection causes respiratory disease, ranging from a mild cough to severe bronchopneumonia. An intranasal vaccine provides protection against *Bordetella bronchiseptica*, and is strongly recommended for dogs going anywhere where unfamiliar dogs congregate, such as working tests and field trials, and especially into boarding kennels. Any boarding kennel should always ask to see your dog's certificate of vaccination before admitting the dog, and if it doesn't, don't board your dog in the kennels!

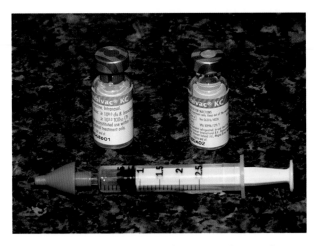

This intranasal vaccine provides protection against Bordetella bronchiseptica, *an important element of kennel cough infection. A special applicator is provided, attached to the syringe, to facilitate administering the vaccine into the nostrils.*

Do also seek your vet's advice on how soon you can take the puppy out after vaccination and allow it to mix with other dogs, and to exercise it in places where other dogs are likely to have been. Owners have a dilemma, in that they must ensure that puppies are kept away from other dogs until they are fully vaccinated, whilst at the same time they need to ensure that the puppy is well socialized whilst very young.

Worming

Worm treatment is simple and inexpensive. Regular worming is recommended not only to ensure no harm can come to the puppy, but also for public health reasons, as some types of worms commonly found in dogs can be passed on to humans.

When you collect your puppy, typically at around six to ten weeks of age, it is likely to have been wormed already by the breeder on more than one occasion, but do check and make sure that you have details of what was used and when, so you can pass on this information to your vet.

How frequently puppies require worming will normally depend on the type of anthelmintic used. An anthelmintic is a product that kills worms: helminth parasites. Some anthelmintics will kill both adult worms and their immature

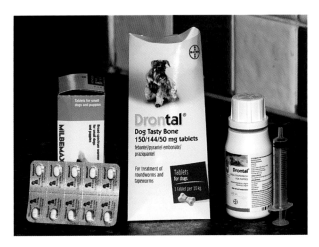

A variety of products is available for worming dogs, some formulated so they can be administered as either tablets or liquids, and even in the form of a tasty bone, as here.

forms (see Chapter 4), and will inactivate worm eggs so they cannot hatch. Most products prescribed by vets will kill both roundworms and tapeworms; most will also be active against hookworms, whipworms and lungworms, although the last three parasites are normally less of a problem. The products that are currently most commonly used are described below.

Fenbendazole: A broad spectrum anthelmintic that can be used to both treat and control adult and immature roundworms. Fenbendazole is also effective in killing roundworm eggs. You should treat your puppy every two weeks with fenbendazole until it is twelve weeks of age. Thereafter it should be treated at three-monthly intervals. Fenbendazole is useful insofar as it is safe to use on very young puppies, and can be used by breeders to worm puppies as young as two weeks of age.

Combinations of Praziquantel, Pyrantel Embonate and Febantel: These have the advantage of being active against ascarids (roundworms, including both adult and late immature forms), hookworms, adult whipworms and tapeworms. Unfortunately they cannot be used to treat pup-

pies that are less than 3kg bodyweight, but once they reach that size, puppies can safely be treated every two weeks until twelve weeks of age, and then at three-monthly intervals thereafter.

When using either of these products, it is not necessary to starve the dog prior to worming, as was often the case previously. Many older worming preparations tended to 'purge' the dog, which then passed worms in its faeces. However, don't be concerned if you don't see worms in the faeces after using most modern anthelmintics, because the worms are killed high up in the gastrointestinal tract and are processed naturally by the digestive juices as they pass down the gut.

A more thorough discussion of the various types of worms, how they persist, and the means of controlling them, will be found in Chapter 4.

Neutering

Neutering is a general term used to describe the surgical removal of the sexual organs from dogs and bitches. Castration describes the removal of the testes from male dogs, and the term 'spaying' describes the removal of the ovaries and uterus (the canine equivalent of the womb) from female dogs.

Be aware that there can be certain consequences following the neutering of puppies, especially bitches; although there is no medical reason not to let a bitch have a litter before spaying, some benefits, such as protection against mammary tumours, can be lost if the operation is delayed. Discuss both the advantages and disadvantages of neutering with your vet (see box below) – though never feel you are under any obligation to decide one way or the other until you are fully conversant with the likely effect(s) on your dog, and you have good reasons to support your final decision.

It is definitely not a good idea to spay a bitch when she is in season or about to come into season. This is because the blood supply to the uterus and ovaries is increased at this time, which increases the risks inherent in surgery.

Another time that vets advise against spaying is around eight weeks after a season, when a bitch will be undergoing hormonal changes that

Castrated at an early age, this Cocker Spaniel has subsequently developed a characteristic dense, fine-textured, woolly coat.

weeks of age and ends when the puppy reaches the age of sixteen weeks. During this period the puppy needs to be exposed to as wide a range of environmental stimuli as possible so that it will develop into a calm, well socialized individual that is easy to train and able to cope with, and tolerate, a wide range of situations and circumstances.

If a puppy isn't properly socialized during this period the likelihood is that it will be prone to suffer a variety of behavioural disorders and/or be much more difficult to otherwise socialize. Deprived of this early experience, dogs will tend to become timid and intolerant, and to develop socially unacceptable patterns of behaviour. Behavioural disorders are not uncommon among the general dog population, and constitute as much of a problem as many of the clinical diseases that vets have to treat. Poorly socialized dogs

can lead to signs of false pregnancy. Spaying a bitch at this time is considered unfair because her hormones make her feel as if she is nursing pups, and the operation would be the equivalent of suddenly removing a litter. She may also be producing milk at around this time as an effect of false pregnancy, and the enlarged milk glands can delay healing of the spay wound.

THE IMPORTANCE OF SOCIALIZATION

Evidence from behavioural studies demonstrates that there is a 'window of opportunity', a prime socialization period, that starts at around three

Beaters' dogs must be well socialized with other dogs as they often have to travel in close proximity.

THE ADVANTAGES AND DISADVANTAGES OF NEUTERING

Advantages of Castration: Castrating male dogs obviously means they are incapable of fertilizing a bitch and producing puppies, although it won't necessarily overcome the characteristic behavioural tendencies around in-season bitches, and castrated dogs might still mount a bitch or another dog. It does, however, remove the risk of prostate problems, and the risk of testicular cancer. It can also reduce some forms of aggressiveness, and can assist in overcoming some hypersexual behaviour.

Disadvantages of Castration: Castrating male dogs may not reliably reduce aggression, and may not reduce dominant behaviour or fighting due to the dominant behaviour of another entire male. It can influence growth rate and maturation, so a castrated dog may grow slightly larger than if it had remained entire. It increases the likelihood that your dog will tend to put on excess fat, unless you take steps to strictly control its food intake and exercise it regularly. Castration will normally affect the growth and texture of your dog's coat, with a tendency for it to grow long and woolly.

Advantages of Spaying: Spaying bitches avoids the risk of them developing ovarian cancer, and reduces the incidence of mammary tumors, if carried out at an early age. The bitch will not subsequently suffer the signs of false pregnancy, and will not develop womb infections (pyometra). Spaying obviously ensures no unwanted pregnancies.

Disadvantages of Spaying: Spaying a bitch can, however, increase the risk of urinary incontinence, especially if the operation is performed before the bitch is fully mature. Like castration, it influences growth rate and maturation, and increases the likelihood of your dog putting on weight. In many breeds it affects the rate of hair growth, and has what most people consider to be a detrimental effect on the texture of the dog's coat.

account for the vast majority of dogs that have to be destroyed at their owners' request because they cannot cope with their pets' behaviour.

A gundog, in particular, benefits from this early socialization so that it becomes accustomed to meeting strange people and other dogs, and to loud, unexpected noises. Socialization will also encourage it to start exploring confidently, so that it doesn't become timid in strange surroundings.

Early Experiences
Although the puppy needs to avoid being exposed to potential infection until it is fully vaccinated, there is no reason why, during this period, it cannot become accustomed to entering your vehicle and being taken on short journeys. If you live in the country where there are few strange dogs, then other than avoiding anywhere where there

is likely to be vermin, the infection risk is far lower than, say, taking the dog to a communal urban park where other dogs are routinely exercised.

Encourage people to visit and meet your puppy, but don't overwhelm it, and don't allow people to bring their dogs with them. Make sure that the puppy meets and interacts with children and older people, and learns to behave accordingly. All such early experience is useful: remember your dog's mental health is as important as its clinical health. It needs to be fit in mind as well as fit and healthy in body – in other words, fit to function as a working gundog, becoming socially acceptable, tolerant and obedient.

Commonly encountered problems in poorly socialized gundogs include a fear of sudden loud noises; what is known as 'separation anxiety', where a dog cannot cope with being left on its own; difficulty entering and travelling in vehi-

A group of beaters with their dogs about to be driven off to the first drive.

cles; and timidity towards strangers, both human and canine. Clearly a dog with such behavioural traits would not constitute the ideal companion to accompany you on a shoot day, no matter how good it might be at finding and retrieving game.

Provide Stimulating Opportunities

Introduce a puppy to strange sights, sounds and smells, and ensure it starts to meet different types of people at the earliest opportunity. Whilst you may not be able to take your puppy out, particularly to places where other dogs congregate, until it is fully vaccinated, don't shut a puppy away in a kennel or leave it in a crate for longer than is necessary during the day: keep it in an environment that best provides it with stimulating opportunities. Many people tend to use the kitchen because this is where there is most human activity, and strange noises and vibrations from domestic appliances such as washing machines and vacuum cleaners.

The kitchen is also one of the most practical places to bring up a new puppy, with floors that are easier to clean up after the occasional 'accident', and being the place where many people will feed their puppy and wash up food bowls. Banging pots and pans will help acclimatize the puppy to the noise of shot, and some

Provide puppies with interesting items that they can safely chew and gnaw. Solid rubber balls are popular as they can also be chased and manipulated.

Take every opportunity to encourage gundog puppies to hunt and explore from an early age by, for instance, providing spaces to exercise that have interesting smells.

owners deliberately use metal food bowls so that a puppy learns to associate noise with pleasant experiences.

You may find it useful to let the puppy see you using long-handled implements, mops, brooms and garden tools. Ensure it becomes used to seeing people using tools and other noisy appliances, and that it doesn't become anxious, but is relaxed and not frightened or nervous in such

situations. Among other advantages, this helps overcome part of the problem that sometimes occurs when introducing a young gundog to the shotgun.

Getting Used to Being Alone

Most importantly, ensure your puppy gets used to being left alone; don't let it follow you around and become too dependent on your company and affection. Leave it on its own for short periods at first, and gradually extend the time and introduce a routine on your return. Always make a fuss of the puppy, but this should include learning a 'controlled greeting' in which it doesn't become too excited. Let the puppy out immediately to relieve itself, which will assist with house training and encourage it into the habit of not emptying its bladder until you return.

If the puppy is very distressed when left alone, try using a DAP (dog-appeasing pheromone) preparation available from your vet or on-line. DAP mimics the odour exuded by the dam and has a calming effect on puppies. It can also be used in other circumstances where you wish to avoid a puppy becoming too distressed, such as when first travelling in the car.

Meeting Strangers

Ensure the puppy is somewhere it knows to be safe when it first meets strangers. Make sure

Dog Appeasing Pheromone (DAP) is available in a variety of forms suitable for use in various different circumstances.

25

it meets a cross-section of people, and not just close family members and friends of your age. It is likely to meet a wide range of people once it is older, so now is the time to start introducing it to members of society in general. Let it become accustomed to meeting, for instance, people in uniform, especially those wearing bright clothing, young children, people wearing spectacles and sunglasses, people with beards and hats, and older people.

Riding in the Car

Getting a puppy accustomed to riding in the car is best done in stages. Start at an early age and first get the puppy used to entering and sitting calmly in a stationary car. Later start the engine,

Having dogs that will willingly and calmly enter, travel and stay in a vehicle is essential in this day and age.

and if all is well, move off. Whilst getting used to travelling in a vehicle, try to ensure that the puppy associates the car with short journeys to places that will provide especially pleasant, positive experiences where it will enjoy itself. If it seems to have problems maintaining its balance in the back of your car, or is restless and won't settle during the journey, try using a DAP collar, and consider investing in a collapsible dog crate or a purpose-made dog transit box to confine it, and provide it with its own space where it can snuggle down whilst travelling.

FEEDING PUPPIES

Puppies need to be fed little and often, rather than in larger amounts infrequently. A typical feeding regime for a young six- to twelve-week-old puppy would be to divide feeds into four small meals given at regular intervals through the day, the first early in the morning and the last before the puppy settles down for the night. The four meals are normally provided as two 'milk' feeds and two 'meat' feeds, although a more robust, rapidly growing puppy may benefit from three solid feeds and just the one lighter 'milk' feed last thing at night.

What to Feed

'Milk' feeds normally comprise more than simply milk. Most people will mix up a baby food, such as 'Farex', with milk, or soak Farley's rusks in the milk, and occasionally beat in a raw egg.

'Meat' meals, again, need not necessarily be restricted to meat and biscuit because these days most 'complete feed' manufacturers (*see* Chapter 2) produce special puppy feeds. These proprietary complete feeds require no further supplementation, as they contain all the essential nutrients, including vitamins and minerals. Indeed it is extremely unwise, particularly for rapidly growing puppies, and especially those of the larger breeds, to exceed the normal daily vitamin and mineral requirement. Avoid over supplementing with calcium and vitamin D in particular: whilst each is essential for bone development, in excess these ingredients can actually cause adverse effects on bone and joints.

If you wish to feed meat, then a more easily digested form such as minced beef or lamb, or minced tripe is preferable, particularly at first until the puppy's adult teeth start to erupt. Alternatively you can choose to feed one of the pre-prepared complete raw foods that can be purchased in the form of frozen blocks or nuggets. Again, these come in 'puppy' varieties specially formulated in appropriately sized particles that are easy for puppies to digest. Importantly, do not feed an all-meat diet or one that is especially rich in meat, liver or bread. Such diets are deficient in calcium and contain an excess of phosphorus, and an incorrect calcium:phosphorus ratio in the diet can lead to abnormal bone growth and lameness.

Most importantly, always feed your puppy the best quality food that you can obtain. This need not necessarily be the most expensive: it is nutrient quality we are considering, not the quality cuts offered at the local butchers. If you get your puppy off to a good start, you can always cut back once he or she is fully mature and needs no more than a maintenance diet.

How Often to Feed

Continue feeding four meals a day until your puppy is around four months of age, when one of the 'milk' meals can be omitted – usually the meal offered last thing at night. Increase the size of the other three meals proportionately. Then at six months of age you can cease feeding the remaining 'milk' meal and provide just the two more substantial meals daily.

When your dog has reached twelve months of age, decide how often you wish to feed him each day, and change accordingly if you decide to feed less frequently. Most dogs do better on two smaller meals each day, rather than on one large one. Twice daily feeding is also an advantage in breeds that are prone to put on weight, especially in middle age and as they get older, since it is easier to control this tendency by simply reducing the size of the meals.

Some people advocate feeding working gundogs six days a week and to 'starve' them on the seventh. Whilst it is true that this more closely mimics the tendency for wild canines to feed irregularly, dependent on the food supply, there is really no other real justification. Certainly it is unwise to submit a dog that has been fasted to prolonged strenuous exercise.

Don't feed your dog immediately prior to performing any amount of strenuous exercise, but do ensure it has adequate reserves to compensate for the calories lost whilst working hard. Remember, wild dogs make every attempt to conserve their energy, and especially when starving will tend to hunt in packs, taking turns to hunt down their prey.

EXERCISING PUPPIES

Puppies need far less exercise than fully grown dogs. If you over-exercise a growing puppy you run the risk of causing significant long-term harm. Understand that until a dog is fully developed, sometime around eighteen to twenty-four months of age depending on the breed, his bones will still be growing, and in some places his bones and joints are more like 'gristle' than typical bone. Long bones in particular have discrete areas, one at each end, from where they continue to grow (called 'growth plates'), and accidental trauma to these plates can damage them, cause them to fuse early, and subsequently distort the bones' growth. Early extensive exercise can also predispose to early arthritic changes, and can exacerbate and worsen the effects of any inherent weakness that the puppy may have – for example, it may contribute towards lameness associated with a tendency towards hip or elbow dysplasia.

How Much Exercise

When you first acquire a puppy the exercise it gets whilst playing and running around with you in the house, plus visits outside for toileting purposes, will be adequate. Thereafter a good rule of thumb is a ratio of five minutes' exercise per month of age (up to twice a day) until the puppy is fully grown: that is, fifteen minutes (up to twice a day) when three months old, twenty minutes when four months old, and so on. From six months your puppy can have twenty minutes' free running and half an hour walking on the lead daily. When he gets to eighteen months old, and rates as a young dog, he should be able to tolerate as much exercise as you are able to give him.

It is important that puppies go out for exercise every day in a safe and secure area. Always check the security of your garden fences, and keep a lookout for any signs of digging and 'tunnelling' under or near your fencing. Realize that simply putting an intelligent gundog puppy into the garden and expecting it to exercise and amuse itself is unrealistic. Make use of the time to encourage positive interactions.

Play and Early Training

It is relatively easy to combine play with early training exercises. Play with the puppy so he starts to bond with you and understands how to please you, by doing what you wish him to do; give him lots of praise and reward for doing things correctly, such as toileting in the garden, and avoid having to scold him for avoidable misdemeanours.

Set up the situation so that you and your puppy have the best chance of succeeding. If you are playing with an old sock and want him to retrieve, do so in a place that presents as a natural 'corridor' or 'alley', where he can either go away to fetch the toy, or return to you having retrieved it,

not where he can circle around you or, worse still, run away. Exercise his mind as well as his body. It is just as important to stimulate his brain as it is to encourage good muscle and joint development.

Exercise as Socialization and Stimulation

See exercise as contributing towards the process of socialization for a young puppy, and later on as an opportunity for mental stimulation that the dog wouldn't otherwise enjoy in his home environment. Time spent in the garden, however large, is no substitute for exploring new environments and socializing with other dogs; but do make sure your puppy is trained to the recall, so that before you let him loose, off the lead, with other dogs, you are confident that he will return to you.

Finally, never exercise your puppy on a full stomach, either after a meal or after having a large drink of water, as this can cause him to vomit, or can contribute to bloat.

CONGENITAL AND DEVELOPMENTAL ABNORMALITIES

There is a variety of relatively common abnormalities that may either be apparent at birth, when they are known as 'congenital' abnormalities, or

Take advantage of every opportunity for your gundog puppy to develop a natural working ability. Encourage the puppy to hunt and retrieve as part of his exercise, whilst ensuring he starts to distinguish the difference between 'work' and 'play' time.

become apparent as the puppy grows and starts its early development, during what is known as the 'neonatal period'. Be aware of these abnormalities; if any are present the breeder should point them out to you, but in any case either check yourself when selecting a puppy, or take your new puppy to a vet so he/she can check them as part of their initial examination.

Many are simply points to be aware of, a few can be more serious, and most can be corrected if necessary as the dog matures.

Cleft Palate

Cleft palate is seen as an abnormal mid-line opening in the roof of the mouth (the palate), and as a consequence there is an abnormal opening between the mouth and the nasal passage. In puppies it results from failure of the two sides of the palate to fuse together during embryonic development; in older dogs accidental trauma to the roof of the mouth can also cause a cleft palate.

Unless the fault is obvious at birth – and it's always a good idea to check each pup as it's born for developmental abnormalities such as these – the first signs that a puppy may have a cleft palate will include the following:

• Difficulty sucking and nursing
• Breathing difficulties due to milk and food passing up into the nasal passage and entering the lungs
• Runny nose
• Coughing

Puppies often develop an aspiration pneumonia resulting from milk and food particles entering the lungs and setting up infection. Later this will lead to lack of appetite, slow growth and weight loss.

Cleft palate is most often a congenital disorder and is likely to be inherited because there are some breed predispositions. Among gundogs, Cocker Spaniels and Labrador Retrievers seem to be more affected, although otherwise it is mainly seen in brachycephalic (short-nosed) breeds.

Cleft palate can also result from exposing pregnant bitches to various chemicals. Feeding excessively high levels of vitamins A or B12 has been known to cause cleft palate in their puppies (never over-supplement pregnant bitches: good quality rations contain all essential nutrients). There is also a risk from giving drugs such as griseofulvin and corticosteroids to bitches during early pregnancy.

Puppies with cleft palate require intensive nursing. They will certainly need hand, if not tube feeding, and appropriate periodic antimicrobial drug therapy to treat any secondary aspiration pneumonia. Surgical closure of the opening is effective when carried out at six to eight weeks of age, before the general health of the puppy starts to become compromised, but only if the defect is small. More severe defects may need grafts or prosthetic implants for repair, and often require multiple surgeries. Obviously there are ethical questions that need to be addressed in such cases, and many would argue that such puppies are better to be humanely euthanased.

Dentition

A variety of anomalies can affect the teeth and jaws of dogs. Breeders will place a lot of emphasis on the mouth (the 'bite', as it is called), and show judges in particular will examine the front teeth to check for a correctly aligned 'scissor' bite. Fed an appropriate diet, domestic dogs will survive and thrive despite anomalously formed mouths, 'shovelling' food into their mouth and swallowing it directly, rather than performing all the functions required of the various teeth in a wild canine. It is advisable, however, to be aware of what is normal, and the terminology used to describe a number of the more common variations.

An adult dog should have forty-two teeth in total, comprising the incisor teeth arranged across the front of the jaw, flanked by the long canine teeth ('fangs'), the premolars at the side of the jaw, and the larger, molar teeth at the back of the jaw. These various types of teeth and their arrangement in the skull of an adult dog are illustrated in the accompanying photographs.

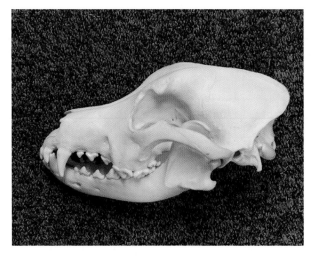

The skull of a Labrador Retriever showing the normal arrangement of teeth.

Puppies are born with slightly fewer teeth, which they lose at around four to six months of age as their adult teeth erupt.

A 'scissor' bite: The normal arrangement, where the incisor teeth in the top and bottom jaws meet and are in contact, the top ones overlapping those in the bottom jaw. The result is a perfectly correct scissor arrangement that would enable the dog to grasp and tear flesh off a carcass.

A 'level' jaw: The upper and lower incisors meet precisely and do not overlap. This is a minor point that appears to have little significance, however there is a possibility that as the dog ages and the teeth wear, the crown of the incisor teeth will be subject to excess wear and subsequently expose the pulp cavity inside the tooth as the overlying enamel wears away.

An 'overshot' jaw: The length of the upper and lower jaws differ, the upper being longer than the lower.

An 'undershot' jaw: The opposite of an 'overshot' jaw. Here the lower jaw is longer, sometimes such that the lower incisors protrude, giving the dog a 'bulldog face' appearance.

Obviously some breeds inherently have a tendency towards one or other of these anomalies

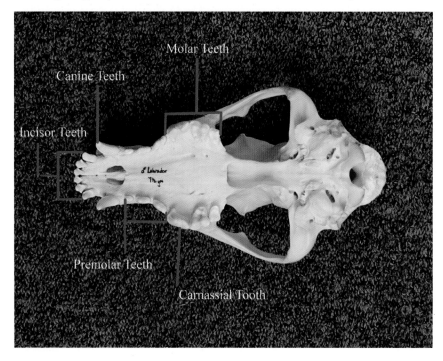

A view of the upper jaw illustrating the normal arrangement of the incisor, canine, premolar and molar teeth respectively, and the prominent fourth premolar, 'carnassial' teeth.

A view of the lower jaw. The first molar tooth in the lower jaw is the 'carnassial' tooth, forming a corresponding shearing edge with the fourth premolar tooth in the upper jaw.

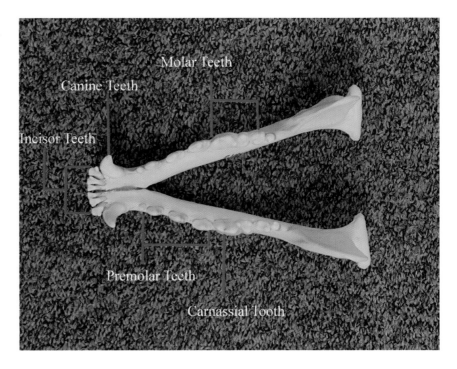

in order to create the characteristic appearance of their head. Gundogs, however, should ideally have a good mouth with a perfect scissor bite and be free of any of these defects.

A 'wry' mouth: A definite abnormality that can cause the dog potential discomfort and difficulty in eating. Here one mandible (lower jaw bone) is longer than the other, causing gross misalignment of not only the teeth, but also the jaws. The lower jaw will deviate to one side of the mouth, depending on which side the mandible is affected. If there is gross misalignment the defect may require surgical correction to provide the dog at least some degree of normal function.

Persistent canine teeth: In puppies the second (adult) set of canine teeth usually

appears behind the corresponding deciduous baby teeth. Occasionally the first 'deciduous' canine persists and is retained after the adult tooth has erupted and starts to grow to its predicted adult length. If this should prove the case, veterinary intervention should be sought and the persistent baby tooth removed before there is the risk that it might impede normal eruption and placement of the adult canine tooth.

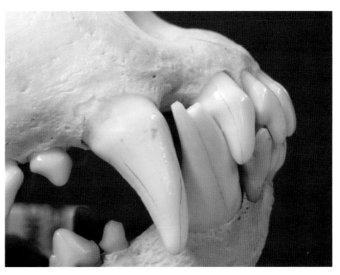

The 'scissor' bite, shown in this dog skull, is the normal arrangement where the incisor teeth in the top and bottom jaw meet and are in contact to overlap those in the bottom jaw.

31

Cryptorchidism

Sometimes called retained or undescended testes, cryptorchidism is the absence of one or both testicles in the scrotum of a male puppy by the time it reaches six months of age.

The testes are in the abdomen during foetal development and normally descend through the inguinal canal into the scrotum. The inguinal canal is a description for the region between openings in the wall of the abdomen, two each side, towards the bottom of the puppy's tummy. The openings are offset and the space between is described as the inguinal canal. Once the testes have descended the canal is occupied only by the blood supply to the testicles and the tube (called the vas deferens) whereby sperm pass out from the testicles; abdominal contents can't normally pass through the inguinal canal, and if they should, the condition is described as an inguinal hernia.

The testicles are normally completely descended into the scrotum by eight to ten weeks of age, though in some puppies it takes longer. Testicles can descend but later temporarily retract back into the inguinal canal, especially when a young dog is excited, very active or cold, but this is not cryptorchidism. Certainly by six months of age, however, both testicles should be fully dropped. Most breeders check male puppies for this condition before placing them with their new owners.

Sometimes, one or both testicles are retained in the abdomen and do not descend properly as a puppy matures. Retained testicles can occur in any male dog of any breed. There is a strong genetic component to this condition, and it is thought to be inherited as an autosomal recessive trait. Dogs with retained testicles have a greatly increased risk of developing testicular infection, torsion and cancer. If one or both testicles are retained by the time the puppy reaches six months of age, he is considered to be a cryptorchid and in most cases should be neutered.

Umbilical Hernia

An umbilical hernia is a condition in which abdominal contents protrude through the abdominal wall at the area of the umbilicus (the belly button). Umbilical hernias are most commonly a congenital malformation, so will be obvious at, or soon after birth. The umbilical opening contains blood vessels that pass through from the mother to the foetus as the umbilical cord. This opening then closes at birth in the normal dog, and a hernia only results if the opening fails to close.

The hernia appears as a soft abdominal mass at the area of the umbilical ring, and can usually be diagnosed by finding the swelling caused by the hernia on physical examination. Generally the contents of the hernia sac can be displaced back into the abdomen.

Depending on the size of the opening, abdominal structures, most commonly fat, can float into the opening. Generally this is of little significance, and small hernias are generally not a problem. However, if the opening is large enough, a loop of intestine can descend through the opening, become strangulated, and if left untreated, can then become a life-threatening problem. Signs of intestinal strangulation can include:

- Larger, painful hernia sac that may be warm to the touch

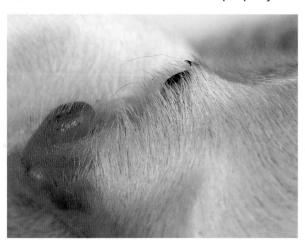

An umbilical hernia in a three-day-old puppy, seen as a swelling in the area where the umbilical cord was attached. In this case the hernia could be reduced and the abdominal contents, typically a small amount of fat, easily pushed back through the abdominal wall.

- Vomiting
- Abdominal discomfort or pain
- Anorexia or a lack of appetite
- Depression

For this reason, it is recommended that you take your dog to a vet to check any umbilical hernia; this allows him to determine the size of the hernia opening. A hernia that is of most concern is one that is similar in size to, or larger than an intestinal loop. The vet may then advise elective repair, which can often be done concurrently if a bitch is to be spayed or a dog castrated.

If a puppy has a small umbilical hernia, get into the habit of regularly pushing the contents back into the abdomen; your vet can show you how to do this if you are uncertain. The opening in the abdomen is essentially defective 'gristle', and will generally remain the same size as the dog grows progressively bigger to the point that, once mature, the opening is so relatively small as to allow little or nothing to pass through.

The exact cause of umbilical hernias is unknown, although most are thought to be inherited, and for this reason it is generally recommended that dogs with umbilical hernias are not used for breeding. Interestingly, some male dogs with umbilical herniation may also have a retained abdominal testicle.

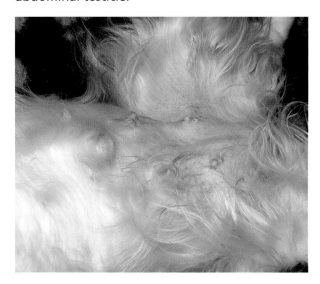

An umbilical hernia in a mature bitch.

HEREDITARY DISEASES

When acquiring a puppy it is extremely important to try to ensure that as far as can reasonably be expected, it will be free from hereditary (inherited) defects and diseases. Unfortunately it is not always that simple, because for many of these conditions, the mode of inheritance remains unknown and/or there is no means of testing breed stock to assure that they are unaffected and therefore unlikely to pass on the trait to their progeny. However, conscientious breeders will be aware of the occurrence of inherited conditions in their breed, and will either be able to assure you of the pedigree history of their stock, or preferably be testing prior to breeding to ascertain the health status of their dogs in these respects.

Wherever possible, ask to see evidence, ideally certification of any health testing that has been undertaken; don't simply take the breeder's word that they have carried out health tests. Most will be proud to show you the results, and even if some dogs may be asymptomatic carriers, they will discuss with you what precautions they take to avoid passing the condition on in their puppies.

Remember also that these diseases can differ significantly in their effects. Some may cause little or no discomfort, and if the puppy is likely to be no more than a 'carrier', it will be unlikely to show any signs. What we need to avoid is perpetuating the incidence of diseases and defects that are of greatest welfare concern – that is, those causing chronic pain and/or distress and discomfort, which are difficult to treat or improve.

In many cases these are diseases that can be found within the general dog population, and not just in pedigree gundogs; there are very few breed-specific diseases (although some are known to occur). Pedigree breeds, however, can be predisposed to a higher incidence of a hereditary condition as a result of selective breeding, and particularly if the gene pool is restricted – if the breed is numerically small and comprises many individuals that are closely related.

Pedigree gundog breeders are not, of course, typically selecting for hereditary defects or dis-

An eight-week-old Slovakian Rough-Haired Pointer puppy. One of a number of imported breeds introduced to the UK in recent years. Many of these numerically small breed societies are actively encouraging health testing to assure the long-term health status of their UK population(s).

eases: they will be selecting for some other desirable characteristic to which the disease or defect is in some way genetically linked. As a consequence, selecting for that one desirable characteristic may unfortunately, and in most cases unintentionally, lead to a higher incidence of the disease in that particular breed.

The more common and/or most significant hereditary conditions in the more commonly used gundog breeds, as well as other diseases having a particular breed predisposition are listed in the Appendix.

The lists are not necessarily inclusive of all conditions reported in the breed(s). To some extent hereditary diseases will be more easily recognized in the more populous breeds simply because there will be more dogs available that show the condition. It is conceivable that in the rarer breeds hereditary conditions may occur, but because they are recorded relatively infrequently, unless there are good breed health reporting and recording mechanisms, they might be more difficult to ascribe as having a particular breed predisposition.

It is important to reiterate that the number of conditions listed for a particular breed should not be interpreted as indicating that the breed is necessarily unhealthy. For most gundog breeds, the number of conditions listed reflects the dedication and commitment of the breeders to work with vets and other experts to identify and characterize health conditions in their breed with the aim of reducing the incidence or eradicating the defect.

2 MAINTAINING HEALTH AND REDUCING THE RISKS

The purpose of this chapter is to provide guidance on typical routine care, and to give a wider understanding of how best to care for your dog.

ROUTINE CARE AND TREATMENTS

The key to recognizing when your dog is ill is to understand what it is like when it is well. Often an owner will be able to detect subtle changes in their dog's behaviour or appetite, which indicates illness, and will see these well before anyone else can. Register with your local vet even if your dog is perfectly healthy, then you will know where to go in an emergency. Your vet can give you advice on routine health care and become a partner in caring for your dog. Regular visits to a vet for routine health checks and preventative health care such as vaccination allow you to build a relationship with your vet, who will get to know you and your dog. Early detection of clinical diseases will allow your vet to give more effective treatments.

Many working gundogs live as part of the family. Although the chance of you catching a disease from an animal is small, there are some diseases, called zoonoses, which people can get from animals. A healthy dog is unlikely to pass on any such disease.

ROUTINE EXAMINATION

Get into the habit of routinely checking your dog. Try to follow the schedule described below, at least initially. Although this may look complicated and long-winded to carry out at first, with practice and familiarity you will find it becomes second nature and takes only a few minutes to perform. Once you become used to regularly examining your dog, if necessary you can always modify the routine to better suit your individual needs and circumstances. Many people, for instance, would probably find it convenient to observe their dog moving and its behaviour whilst out training, and to examine it physically on some other occasion. The important thing is to be thorough and consistent. Make use of all your senses: abnormal sounds and smells can sometimes be the first indication that something is wrong.

- Note the general appearance and behaviour of the dog. It should adopt a normal posture when standing, and move freely with no signs of lameness. Notice if it shows any reluctance to move, if it is nervous or withdrawn, or if it shows any reluctance, resistance or resentment to being picked up or handled. It should show signs of normal social behaviour towards you, other people and other dogs
- Examine the dog's head, to include the external appearance of the eyes, ears, nose and muzzle. The appearance of each should be normal; there should be no evidence of abnormal discharge(s). Examine inside the mouth: inspect the teeth, especially for dental tartar accumulation, and the tongue, lips, and inside the cheeks
- Check the skin for signs of normal elasticity. There should be no evidence of hair loss, and no abnormal swelling(s). The dog should be in good bodily condition, well muscled, and should not be too fat or too thin for its age and weight
- Check the respiration: the rate, rhythm and depth of respiration should be normal. Check that there is no evidence of laboured breathing, or of a cough, or other abnormal respiratory noises.

- Gently palpate the abdomen. Look for evidence of abnormal swelling. The dog should not appear 'tucked up', and there should be no evidence of pain or discomfort when feeling around the abdomen. Check for umbilical or inguinal hernia, and the size and appearance of these if present. In the male there should be two testicles of similar size, fully descended in the scrotum. Check that there is no abnormal discharge from either the prepuce in a male dog or the vulva in a female. Check females for signs of oestrus.
- Check the legs, feet and tail. There should be no evidence of abnormal swellings, pain or fractures. Check that the nails are not overgrown, and trim them as necessary. Check the footpads: there should be no evidence of cracking or abrasions.

If your dog becomes ill and you need to take it to the vet, as well as making an examination, the vet will have to rely on the signs you report in order to make a diagnosis. Unlike our relationship with a doctor, a dog can't describe its symptoms. An animal can only display signs of illness, which vets have to determine and interpret in order to carry out an appropriate examination and make an accurate diagnosis. The more information an owner can provide, and the more accurate that information, the more helpful they can be in helping their vet identify the likely nature of the illness.

There are now proprietary veterinary ear-cleansing products available that have been specially formulated for the purpose.

EAR CLEANSING

A dog's regular maintenance routine should include a check of its ears. This is especially important in breeds such as Cocker and Springer Spaniels that tend to have heavily coated, pendulous ears, and in any dog that produces excessive ear wax and/or has a lot of hair in and around the ear canal.

If the dog's ears appear dirty, clean them with cotton-wool swabs moistened with either a proprietary veterinary ear-cleansing solution such as Epi-otic, or the human equivalent, or use olive oil. The lining of the inner, vertical ear canal is delicate, so if you have any doubts about carrying out this procedure, ask your vet or one of the nurses to show you how. This is especially important for dogs that produce excessive earwax, or have a lot of hair in their inner ear.

Never insert anything into a dog's ear, and don't attempt to clean further down than the region that you can clearly see. Never clean the ears so frequently or so vigorously that you cause irritation.

Occasionally a dog will grow excess hair down the ear canal, and many dog groomers will remove this hair in breeds such as spaniels. If you find your dog appears to have a lot of hair in its ear, discuss with your vet whether or not they consider routine removal is necessary.

Contact your vet if you find any of the following problems whilst cleaning your dog's ears:

- Any discharge from the ear, especially if it smells foul
- Any redness or swelling
- Any hair loss or crusty skin, especially around the margins of the ear flap

Dogs can become infested with ear mites, typically causing the ear to secrete a dark, greasy wax in which you might find tiny specks of material resembling coffee grounds. This can be especially problematic if you have a cat. Ear mites can cause less obvious problems in cats, but they can cross over to infect, and continue to re-infect, a dog, so have your vet check if there appears to be a problem.

NAIL CLIPPING

As long as a gundog is receiving proper routine exercise it should be wearing its nails down correctly, and you shouldn't need to have to trim its nails other than checking to make sure that the dew claws, if it has these, do not become overgrown. Include some lead walking over firm ground as part of routine exercise, as this should help wear down the nails to the correct length. If you hear the feet clicking as you walk the dog over hard surfaces then this is usually a sure sign that his nails may have become overgrown. When this occurs take your dog to the vet to have them trimmed, and should this procedure start to become more frequent, you can learn to trim the nails yourself.

Trimming a dog's nails is not particularly difficult, and is much easier if you do it regularly, and start when the dog is still a puppy. Puppies can have sharp claws, and trimming the tips is good practice; their nails are also quite soft, and it is generally easier to see and avoid cutting the 'quick'. The quick is the pink part of the toe, which is sensitive and contains blood vessels. Cutting the quick will cause the nail to bleed, and this seems to be what most people fear, which prevents them from trimming their dogs' nails.

If the nail grows too long it will lift the toe so that it doesn't meet the ground at the correct angle. This is likely to be uncomfortable, and tends to adversely influence the dog's movement. So it makes sense to check the nails regularly, and if necessary just trim off the tips. Make sure you use good quality nail trimmers that are designed to cut dog nails, and which are sharp and suitable for the size of dog. Two types are in common use: guillotine-type trimmers, and nail-trimming scissors. The former is suitable for all but the larger breeds and dogs with particularly hard or distorted nails. The nails of most gundogs can be trimmed with guillotine-type nail trimmers, although some people prefer the scissor type.

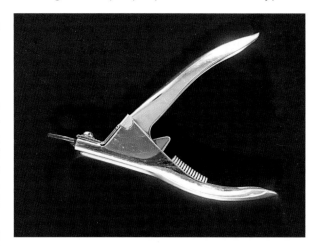

Guillotine-type nail clippers.

Close-up view of the clippers showing the guillotine blade.

Make the whole experience positive for your dog. Before you start, have some treats available. Reward your dog, don't try to trim more than is necessary, and don't assume you need to trim all the nails at once. If you are nervous or the dog is restless, reward him and come back later: choose a convenient opportunity when you have plenty of time, when the dog is likely to be calmer and most compliant. Try trimming nails after you return from training or following a good walk, especially if his feet are wet, because the nail will then be softer.

If you use guillotine nail trimmers, it will help you avoid inadvertently cutting the quick if you ensure the cutting blade is underneath when putting the nail through the hole, as shown in the accompanying photograph. Cut at a 45-degree angle, after visualizing the quick.

Similarly, if you are using the scissor type of trimmer, make sure you understand where the blades will cut, and ensure this is below the level

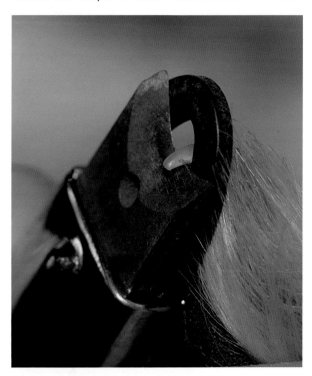

The tip of a toe nail being clipped. Always hold the clippers with the guillotine blade on top, so you can see how much nail will be removed when making the cut.

of the quick. You are less likely to cut the quick if you hold the handle of the trimmers flat against the pad and cut straight across the nail. The trimmed nail will then sit just above the ground.

If your dog has black nails, inspect the underside of the nail. You should see that, towards the tip, the nail becomes a triangular shape with two outer 'walls'. At this point there is no quick, and below this it is safe to trim. Otherwise use the technique of simply cutting straight across from the pad, rather than attempting to cut up at a 45-degree angle.

Older dogs tend to develop longer quicks and rather elongated nails, and the nails are often extremely hard. Trimming the nails after giving the dog a bath can help, as their nails will be softer. Cutting the nails so they are only just above the floor when your dog is standing can also help, particularly if an older dog has deformed nails.

If you can't clearly see the quick beneath the nail, just trim a little at a time. If you regularly take the tips off, you can often encourage the quick to recede over time. As long as your dog's nails are not touching the ground or causing the toes to splay, there is no need to worry about keeping them short.

If you accidentally cut the nails too short you can use a styptic pen, or potassium permanganate powder (beware, this stains!) to stop the bleeding. The dog will often be more nervous next time, so use lots of treats, plenty of reward, and take your time. If you have any concerns, ask your vet, one of the veterinary nurses, or a professional dog groomer to show you how they trim nails.

THE ANAL GLANDS

Dogs normally void a small amount of foul-smelling fluid from their anal glands each time they pass a firm stool. However, if the dog's stools are soft or small the sacs may not empty completely, and if this continues they can fill up and will become uncomfortable; if left untreated they may become impacted or even infected.

Most dogs will try and relieve this discomfort by licking or biting their rear end or dragging their bottom along the floor. Many owners mistake this behaviour as a sign of worms, but it is much more likely that the dog's anal glands need emptying. With a little practice and patience you can empty your dog's anal sacs yourself, as the procedure is relatively simple.

First, wearing a latex or household glove (gloves that are quite sensitive so you can feel what you are doing), gently feel each side of the anus for two swellings about the size of a large pea or small cherry. Have someone stand the dog for you, and have the dog at such a height that you can see what you are doing; with small dogs such as spaniels you will probably find it more convenient to have the dog on a table or bench.

With your index finger and thumb each side of the dog's anus, and with a wad of cotton wool or a piece of household tissue paper between finger and thumb, gently 'milk' the sacs using an upward/backward motion.

If nothing comes out, adjust your position slightly and adjust the angle of your 'milking', and try again. Don't squeeze. With a little persistence and patience you should feel the sacs deflate and start to empty. The fluid has an obnoxious 'fishy' smell, and can appear as anything from a clear or white smooth consistency to something resembling a brown granular substance. Try to ensure you collect the fluid in cotton wool or a piece of kitchen roll. Keep milking until no more fluid is expressed, then wipe the dog's bottom and reward it with a treat.

Don't press too hard, and if you don't succeed after a few tries, don't persist. It's better to stop and try again in a few days' time than to persist and risk bruising the area, and making the dog sore.

An alternative method, and one that vets often use if the anal glands are particularly impacted, is to insert a gloved finger gently into the rectum and express each gland separately, feeling each gland empty one at a time on each side of the rectum.

Some dogs have particular problems and require their anal glands to be emptied frequently. If this is the case, first check the consistency of the dog's faeces, and if it isn't generally passing large, firm stools, you may have to modify the diet accordingly. Try adding bran in the first instance. Add a couple of teaspoonfuls to the feed each day initially, and increase a little as necessary to 'bulk up' the stools. Reducing your dog's weight if it is overweight can also help.

Check the anal glands regularly, around once a month should suffice, and empty them if necessary.

SKIN AND COAT CARE

The concept of 'grooming' a working dog might seem alien to many gundog owners and handlers because the term is more normally associated with dogs that require regular bathing, brushing and combing to keep them looking their best. What we are really considering here is maintaining good healthy skin and hair coat.

A glossy coat is usually an indication that a dog is in good condition.

Although we rarely think about it, skin is a vital structure covering the body, and, rather like other vital organs, is essential in fulfilling a variety of important functions. It is a good indicator of the state of an animal's health, and can indicate the presence of internal disease. It prevents fluid loss from the body, and senses touch, pressure, vibration, heat, cold and pain. It prevents injury, protects against any invasion of micro-organisms and noxious chemicals, and helps to regulate temperature changes within the body. Skin is where a dog synthesizes vitamin D.

The subcutaneous tissues serve as a reservoir for fat, electrolytes, water, carbohydrates and proteins. Secretions from skin glands waterproof and lubricate the skin, and function as pheromones (substances that enable other dogs to recognize another individual of the same species, and respond accordingly).

The coat serves as a waterproof insulating layer between the skin and the external environment. It protects from cold in winter and from the heat of the sun in summer. It also serves as part of a dog's behavioural repertoire, such as when the 'hackles rise' on the back whenever a dog is threatened or frightened.

It is important therefore to ensure your dog's skin and hair coat are maintained in good condition, even though in many circumstances working gundogs, depending on the type of dog, its breed and lifestyle, require minimal intervention by their owner to maintain a healthy coat.

Examine the coat regularly, and especially after your dog has been working in thick covert and dense undergrowth. Although it may not be necessary to bathe working dogs regularly, do take some trouble when returning from a walk or from shooting to remove any excess mud and dirt from the coat, and to brush out any matted hair and attend to any tangles in longer-haired breeds.

Brushing (and combing as necessary) is probably the most important component of coat care as this will remove dead hair, stimulate blood flow in the skin, and help to revitalize your dog's coat. As a general rule, long-haired breeds should be brushed twice a week, and dogs prone to moulting should be brushed approximately once a week. Remember the purpose of brushing

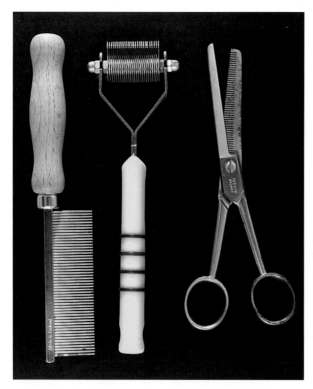

Basic grooming equipment: from left to right – a fine-toothed comb, a 'Mars' comb, and a pair of thinning scissors.

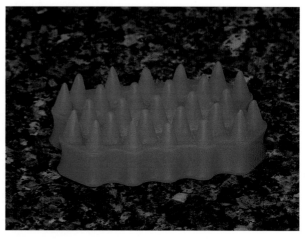

The 'ZoomGroom'. Even short-haired breeds will benefit from periodic brushing, and this product, made of soft rubbery plastic and comprising a series of conical projections rather than bristles, can be particularly appropriate.

a gundog is to remove superficial dirt and mud and dead coat, and to stimulate the skin.

Gundogs are quite content without a bath, particularly if they swim periodically. Do consider what they are swimming in, of course; pond water isn't necessarily clean or fresh, and it's particularly important to wash a dog's coat in fresh water after swimming in the sea or in a tidal estuary. Avoid bathing a dog too often because shampooing will tend to remove essential oils from the skin and coat. If you bathe your dog, wherever possible use a mild shampoo or baby bath. These mild detergents won't remove grime or grease, however, and in these circumstances use an appropriate veterinary shampoo that is specially formulated for the purpose. Ask the advice of your vet, or look online for products used by the professional dog groomers.

Periodically run a comb through your dog's coat, and otherwise inspect for parasites such as fleas, lice and ticks. Use a flea comb to check for flea infestations and to search for loose ticks, especially in longer-haired dogs.

Consider trimming the coat in dogs that have 'feathering' – long hair on their ears, behind the legs, in front of the chest and under the chest and belly – and decide if it's best to trim the coat or leave the hair long. Feathering is probably best trimmed in dogs that regularly get muddy, whereas it may be better to leave some feathering on dogs working in colder weather.

Excess hair can be conveniently removed using special coat-thinning scissors, which are available from good pet stores and suppliers of grooming equipment to the professionals. Using these scissors, make a series of sequential 'cuts' through the thicker parts of the coat, then immediately comb through the coat where it has just been scissored. You will find the comb removes only some of the hair that has just been cut, leaving the majority. Repeat as necessary until sufficient feathering has been removed.

Alternatively you can try using a 'Mars' comb on a thin excessive coat. This instrument comprises a series of blades, longer blunt-edged blades and intervening shorter cutting blades. Sequential combing gradually removes hair, thinning the coat accordingly. There are a variety of sizes, each suitable for particular breeds and coat types. A reputable stockist of professional dog grooming equipment should stock these combs, and can advise on which is best for your particular breed.

Thinning scissors have one conventional cutting blade and a toothed blade, like a comb.

A close-up view of the 'Mars' comb, showing the arrangement of the blades.

Blunt-ended scissor blades are particularly useful for trimming excess hair growing between the foot pads.

Finally, decide whether or not to remove excess hair from the feet and growing between the toes. This is probably best removed in dogs that are exercised and worked in thick mud, and particularly working over crops and ploughed fields. Mud tends to accumulate between the toes and unless removed can dry to form concretions, particularly between the pads where it becomes very difficult to remove subsequently and may cause the dog discomfort. Trimming the hair flush to the foot and level with the pads will help. If this needs to be done regularly, consider buying special scissors that are made for the purpose. These scissors are relatively short and have bulbous blunt ends that help to prevent cutting skin between the pads whilst trimming the dog's feet.

THE CONTROL OF PARASITES

Parasites are animals that live on or in dogs, and which thereby benefit at the dogs' expense. In evolutionary terms parasites are some of the most successful species, generally exploiting a finely balanced inter-relationship with their hosts, and having a complex life cycle that assists and promotes their survival. Although parasites may cause their canine host some harm, it is rarely in the long-term interest of the parasite to thereby threaten its own existence, and consequently owners may be unaware of parasitic infestation unless for some reason their attention is drawn to the problem.

Understanding the natural history of the parasite will be helpful when it comes to controlling infestations, because otherwise they can prove quite difficult to eliminate. The control of parasitic infestations in animals is also important because many, as we shall see, can also infect humans and cause what is known as zoonotic disease – diseases that can be passed from animals to humans.

Canine parasites can be conveniently divided into those that live inside the dog, normally in the intestines, and which are called endoparasites, and those that live on, or just within the surface of the skin or in the ears, called ectoparasites. Broadly speaking, endoparasites that infest dogs are various types of parasitic worm, and canine ectoparasites are fleas, lice, mites and ticks.

ENDOPARASITES

Roundworms

Dogs can harbour two types of large, ascarid roundworms, *Toxocara canis* and *Toxascaris leonina*; although there are some species differences, for simplicity both species will be considered together. Both are found in the intestine of dogs and are a major public health concern because ascarid roundworms are transmissible to humans, especially children who can become infected by ingesting substances such as dirt contaminated with faeces from infected dogs.

Although adult roundworms live in the dog's intestines, larvae can migrate from the intestine to survive, dormant for many years, in other tissues of the dog's body. This process is called 'larval migrans' and also occurs in humans; among the tissues that can potentially become invaded are the eyes, where encysted roundworm larvae may be indistinguishable from other otherwise serious ocular disease.

Dogs are infected prenatally (prior to birth), as suckling puppies, and later in life from ingesting infective roundworm eggs in the environment. Prenatal infection occurs in utero when, influenced by the bitch's pregnancy, immature roundworm larvae migrate from her body tissues, muscles and other internal organs, to her uterus and thence infect the developing puppies via their placentae (the point where the pup attaches to the wall of the uterus via its umbilical cord). Most puppies are born with roundworms, and early worming is an essential component of their control. Puppies can also become infected through the bitch's milk after larvae migrate to the lactating mammary glands.

Dogs can also be infected by ingesting roundworm eggs either directly from the environment, or indirectly by eating prey such as rodents that have picked up roundworm eggs whilst feeding; the eggs are given entry into the dog when the prey is ingested.

Once inside the dog the eggs hatch in the intestines. They then either develop directly into adult worms, or migrate as larvae through the gut and into other tissues. Adult worms in the gut are about 60–70cm long and whitish in appearance, like pieces of string. Larvae in other tissues will remain dormant unless induced to migrate onwards to the intestine, or in a bitch, to the uterus during pregnancy. If the larvae migrate to the lungs, they will be coughed up and immediately swallowed, to develop subsequently into adult worms in the intestine.

Many young dogs infected with reasonably high numbers of worms appear to develop a form of partial immunity at around four to six months of age, and undergo a sort of natural 'purge', passing a lot of worms and then seemingly surviving with a lower residual worm burden that causes little or no harm. This is an advantage to the parasites, which continue to pass eggs in their host's faeces. Should the intestinal population be depleted, for instance by worming treatments, then previously quiescent larvae will migrate to the intestine and replace those lost. In this way the parasite forms a type of symbiotic relationship with its host, which enhances its long-term survival.

It will therefore be obvious that roundworms have a complex life cycle to promote their survival, and one which complicates roundworm treatment. The following are the essential points to note:

- Roundworm larvae can migrate to survive in body tissues, for example the liver, lungs and skeletal muscle, and can remain there in a quiescent state
- Roundworm larvae resume active migration in pregnant bitches on about the forty-second day of pregnancy
- Dogs may pick up roundworms by ingesting infective eggs in the environment, or from eating other small animals that may have eaten roundworm eggs
- Roundworms live in the dog's intestines, but their larvae can migrate through the intestinal wall and survive for long periods in the dog's body tissues
- When larvae migrate through the lungs they may cause an infection of the small intestine via tracheal migration, being coughed up and then swallowed
- Roundworm larvae usually infect the foetal puppy via the umbilical vessels; initially they attack the pup's liver, then the lungs at birth
- Puppies can also become infected through the bitch's milk when larvae migrate to lactating mammary tissues

Bitches should be wormed before breeding, during the last week of gestation, and each time the pups are wormed. Once the initial infection is treated properly it is a good idea to occasionally check a stool sample for the presence of worms, or to consider prophylactically administering deworming medications if the situation seems to warrant it. It is hoped that at some point in the future a vaccine will become available for roundworm control, since current control measures seem to be only marginally effective. For the present, however, routine treatment of puppies and dogs, especially bitches, as well as environmental hygiene (picking up after your dog has passed faeces) are necessary and essential control measures.

Tapeworms

Tapeworms are typically much longer than round-worms. A whole adult tapeworm is rarely seen, as only segments of the adult worm body are passed, as egg-carrying cases, in a dog's stools. The adult tapeworm comprises a small head that attaches by hooks arranged around its mouth to the wall of the dog's intestine, and a long body consisting of numerous small individually discrete segments that are continuously formed at the head end of the parasite; these gradually mature as they get further down the body of the worm, and once fully mature and full of eggs, are constantly shed from the tail end of the tapeworm, to be passed in the dog's faeces.

The eggs can be seen in your dog's faeces or sticking to the hair around the dog's rear. These muscular segments of the worm are really egg cases, full of eggs and looking like a small, flattened grain of white rice that wiggle around spreading thousands of tapeworm eggs too small to be seen by the naked eye.

Dogs can harbour a variety of tapeworm species, notably *Taenia pisiformis*, *Dipylidium canium* and *Enchinococcus granulosus*. They are found in the intestine of dogs and are a major hygiene concern because they are transmissible to people. Tapeworms invariably use two hosts to complete their life cycle. Adult tapeworms in their definitive host, such as a dog, form eggs, which are shed to infect an intermediate host (a species that the definitive host will eat), where an infective form will develop awaiting consumption by the definitive host, after which it will develop into an adult tapeworm, thereby completing the cycle.

Dipylidium caninum, the common dog tapeworm, uses the flea as its intermediate host. The intermediate hosts of *Taenia hydatigena* are cattle, sheep and pigs, and consequently the feeding of raw offal can represent a risk of passing infection on to dogs; and finally the intermediate stage of *Echinococcus granulosus*, the tapeworm species of greatest public health concern, lives in sheep, and is most common in rural areas where dogs have the opportunity to feed on sheep carcases, especially on hills.

Public awareness of this condition is important in its control. Personal hygiene is important, especially when coming in contact with faeces from potentially infected pets. Children are particularly at risk. Mulch that potentially contains faeces from dogs, cats or foxes should not be used on gardens. Dogs should be discouraged from consuming the carcases of wild rabbits and hares, or any type of wild rodent, and offal should always be cooked, and not fed raw to dogs.

The life cycle of the dog–rabbit tapeworm (*Taenia pisiformis*) starts with the adult living in the small intestine of dogs and wild foxes, where they produce eggs that are shed in the faeces and subsequently contaminate the local environment. Rabbits become infected by ingesting these eggs, which then form hundreds or even thousands of 'hydatid cysts' in the tissues of the rabbit. When dogs or foxes eat these rabbits they become infected. These adults latch on to the wall of the intestines, and after about a month, start shedding eggs. These eggs are then immediately infective to other animals, including people, and can remain infective in the environment for several months.

Hookworms

Hookworms and whipworms (*see* below) are far less common in dogs in the UK than round-worms and tapeworms. There are four species of hookworm known to infect dogs: *Ancylostoma braziliense*, *Ancylostoma caninum*, *Ancylostoma tubaeforme* and *Uncinaria stenocephala*; of these, *Uncinaria stenocephala* and *Ancylostoma caninum* are the most common in the UK. Hookworms can be acquired in the mother's milk, from penetration of the skin by hookworm larvae in the environment, and from eating hookworm larvae.

Ancylostoma caninum hookworm infestation in dogs can lead to severe anaemia, especially in puppies. These hookworms attach to the intestine and feed on the dog's blood, and in areas where hookworms are prevalent, a skin disease called cutaneous larval migrans can also be associated with exposure to the larval worms. The following are the principal characteristics of hookworm infestation in dogs:

- It is primarily a disease of puppies. Adult dogs exposed as puppies develop immunity due to the presence of arrested larvae in their tissues
- It causes dermatitis, enteritis, bloody diarrhoea, anaemia due to blood loss, and pneumonia if the migrating larvae enter the puppy's lungs
- It can be life threatening for puppies, which may show signs as early as two to three weeks of age through to weaning, when there are eggs in the faeces, often apparent as a bloody stool

One of the problems with hookworms is that they can accidentally infect humans, causing cutaneous larva migrans. In humans, worm larvae migrating through the skin don't develop into adults, as they would in dogs, but just migrate around in the skin, causing sores and inflammation, until they die. This is good reason to keep dogs from defecating in playground areas, beaches and other places where people's skin is likely to come into contact with the ground.

Whipworms

Whipworms are relatively uncommon. They are primarily a problem in kennels, especially those having grass or dirt runs and generally poorer standards of hygiene. The worms, which get their name from their whip-like shape, live in the large intestines, the caecum and colon, where they attach to feed. These worms frequently cause no apparent problem, but occasionally they may cause abdominal colic or diarrhoea, which may often be tainted by blood and mucus. Eggs are laid in the intestines, then pass into the faeces and become infective within nine to ten days. When subsequently consumed by dogs the infective eggs hatch in the intestines and the larvae parasitize the small intestines until they mature further. The life cycle therefore includes a larval stage in the small intestine, an adult stage in the large intestine, and infective eggs that are passed in the faeces.

Dogs do not begin to pass whipworm eggs until about three months after being infected, and the eggs must then remain in the soil for about a month to mature before they can become infective. Female whipworms are long-lived, surviving for months or even years in the dog's intestines. Consequently infection builds up slowly, but once established tends to persist, especially in kennels, and especially where there are outside areas of grass or soil which can become heavily contaminated and difficult to disinfect and decontaminate. Kennels with concrete runs that can be disinfected and consequently decontaminated much more easily are far less likely to harbour whipworm infestations, and these parasites have become far less common as a result.

Lungworms

Lungworm infection in dogs, caused by the parasite *Angiostrongylus vasorum*, is becoming more prevalent in the UK. Dogs become infected through eating slugs and snails that harbour the larvae of the parasite. Whilst most dogs do not habitually eat slugs and snails, they may often do so accidentally either when the slug or snail crawls on to a bone or toy left in the garden, or from drinking from puddles and outdoor waterbowls.

Lungworm can infect dogs of all ages, however younger dogs seem to be more prone to picking up the parasite, and dogs having an active outdoor life, commonly visiting damp places, such as gundogs, can be more at risk. Formerly infections were most common in parts of Ireland, Wales and southern England. However, with climate change bringing generally warmer, wetter winters, recent outbreaks as far north as Scotland mean the parasite is now a nationwide threat.

Some dogs don't initially show visible signs of a lungworm, but there are then four principal signs associated with lungworm in dogs. Not all infected dogs will show all the signs, however, and many are also signs of other illnesses:

- Breathing problems: coughing and tiring easily
- Poor blood clotting: excessive bleeding from even minor wounds/cuts, nose bleeds, bleeding into the eye and anaemia (appearing very pale around the eyes and gums)

- General sickness: weight loss, poor appetite, vomiting, diarrhoea
- Behavioural changes: depression, lethargy, seizures (fits)

Your vet can treat for lungworm, and once diagnosed and treated, most dogs make a full recovery. The key to successful treatment is early treatment, so if you think your dog has eaten a slug or snail, or if it is showing any of the signs listed that are associated with lungworm, it is best to check with your vet, who if necessary can test for lungworm.

A few simple precautions can also help reduce the risk:

- Avoid using outdoor drinking water and food bowls, as these tend to attract slugs and snails
- Don't leave the dog's toys, chews, dummies and so on in places where they can attract snails
- Ask your vet about recommending a parasite control programme that includes the control of lungworm infection, especially if you live in one of the higher risk areas

Heartworms

Fortunately heartworms don't occur here in the UK, only very occasionally in imported dogs (and these normally have to be treated prior to importation). It is included here since it is relatively dangerous when it occurs, and can actually kill an infested dog. The life cycle includes a microfilaria stage, when microfilaria are found circulating in the infected dog's bloodstream. Microfilaria are passed on when the infected dog is bitten by a mosquito or similar bloodsucking parasite, which then passes on the infection to another dog. It can take as long as nine months for the infective microfilaria to become adults in the heart and lungs, and a threat to the dog.

Signs of heartworm disease include a dull coat, weight loss, difficulty breathing, fainting spells and an enlarged abdomen. Heartworms can clog the major blood vessels serving the heart, and ultimately the dog will suffer congestive heart failure.

Heartworms can be diagnosed by means of a blood test, and occur in the host dog in areas with a warm, wet climate where mosquitoes are prevalent; dogs are typically tested and treated on a routine basis. It is also possible to treat for heartworm disease once clinical signs are apparent.

Treatment and Control of Canine Endoparasites

Dogs should be wormed regularly, both to help keep them worm free, and to reduce the risk to public health from canine endoparasites. For obvious reasons, it becomes particularly important to worm your dog regularly if you have small children, or if it regularly comes in contact with other people's children.

Typically worm treatment remedies come in tablet form, however, increasing use is being made these days of alternative drug preparations that are absorbed through the skin. These formulations are very convenient as they require very little skill to administer, and generally only need to be applied once every four to six months. Such 'spot-on' preparations generally contain what is known as a 'broad spectrum' compound – drugs that are active against a variety of both internal and external parasites.

Drugs that are available in tablet form are generally best used when it comes to targeting particular parasites, and treatment tends to be cheaper. Providing you are confident to administer tablets, they enable you to develop a more strategic approach to controlling particular types of worm as well as the more common worm parasites.

Worm your dog four times a year against both roundworms and tapeworms. In addition if you wish to breed from your bitch, treat her for roundworms before she is mated and again about a week before she is due to whelp; this will help reduce the risk of her passing worms on to her developing puppies. Once the puppies are born, worm both the bitch and her puppies when they are three and six weeks of age, and then fortnightly thereafter until the puppies go to their new homes. Make sure that the wormer you use is suitable for use in young puppies; if in any doubt ask your vet to supply a suitable worming preparation, and take advice on how frequently it should be used.

ECTOPARASITES

Fleas

The flea is a small, wingless insect 2–4mm long with a hard and laterally flattened body that enables it to pass easily between the hairs of a dog's coat. It has long back legs that allow it to jump significant distances in comparison to its body size, and mouthparts that enable it to suck blood. There are several species of flea, including *Ctenocephalides canis*, the specific species of dog flea, but the one that most commonly affects dogs is *Ctenocephalides felis*, the cat flea. While this type of flea can also bite humans, it does not infest us, as people are not an ideal host.

Despite the fact that fleas are quite common, nobody wants to find fleas on their dogs, and most people seem reluctant to admit the problem. Knowing some basic facts about the risks and means of prevention and treatment for fleas you can better protect your dog from the threat. The life cycle of the flea comprises four stages:

- About forty eggs are laid each day on the host dog by each adult flea. These soon dry, drop off, typically into pet bedding, carpets and so on, and hatch in about two days
- Larvae emerge as tiny worm-like creatures that feed on flea faeces (basically dried animal blood) and other organic detritus in their environment. The larva goes through three moults before it is able to spin a cocoon and enter the pupal stage
- Pupae in their cocoon can remain dormant in the environment for many months, perhaps years, and will not emerge until they sense a host, which they do by detecting the proximity of factors such as warmth, vibration and carbon dioxide
- The adult flea emerges from its cocoon when a host is available, and immediately jumps on the host to begin a blood meal. A female flea will begin to lay eggs within twenty-four to forty-eight hours of her first blood meal. She defecates blood from her host, and this

falls off along with the eggs, re-starting the life cycle. Adult fleas live for about four to six weeks

Thus fleas can be seen as an environmental problem. As far as a flea is concerned, Utopia is a house with fitted carpets and central heating. Such an environment allows flea larvae to remain hidden and pupae to survive for months, even in the absence of a suitable host, and adult fleas are otherwise able to breed and multiply rapidly all through the year. It is estimated that the fleas living on a dog represent only 5 per cent of the species' biomass; the other 95 per cent is made up of their eggs, larvae and pupae living in the immediate environment. Therefore there is no point in just treating your dog and neglecting to treat its environment. You need to treat the dog's bedding, the carpets and soft furnishings, and anywhere in the house where the dog goes, and, similarly, any other animals in the household, especially cats. The problem can become very difficult to eradicate if there are feral cats in the vicinity.

There are also rabbit fleas, and dogs can become infested whist hunting around rabbit holes and the burrows of other species. The risk, however, appears to be relatively low in comparison to that of becoming infested by the much more common species of cat flea found on dogs in the UK. In addition to the obvious infestation problem, fleas also pose various health risks both to you and your dog:

- Flea allergic dermatitis is the real cause for dogs to itch and scratch excessively, when the dog becomes sensitized to flea saliva. Some animals are more sensitive than others, and it is not so much the flea biting that is the problem, but the fact that it might take only one or two fleas biting to lead to severe itching, irritation, and on occasions major skin infections in some individuals
- Tapeworm infestation with *Dipylidium caninum* (*see* above) can be contracted by dogs, or humans, after accidental ingestion of an infected flea. Flea larvae ingest the microscopic tapeworm eggs in their environment,

which subsequently causes adult fleas to be carriers

- If a sufficient number of fleas infests the host dog to suck blood, it is possible for the host animal to lose enough blood to cause it to become anaemic. Small puppies are especially at risk

If you suspect your dog has fleas, it probably does. They can actually be quite difficult to find, and it has been estimated that for every flea seen, there are most likely at least fifty you haven't detected. Fleas hop on and off their hosts, so you won't necessarily see fleas even if the dog is infested.

If you don't find fleas but see lots of tiny pieces of black debris on the dog's skin or on the comb, this is likely to be flea dirt. Flea dirt is flea faeces and consists mainly of dried animal blood. To confirm this, place some of the debris on white tissue paper and moisten it slightly; if you see a reddish-brown colour emerging from around the dark black debris, it is flea dirt.

Flea Treatment
Remember that three out of the four stages of the flea's life cycle are spent off the host. The eggs, larvae and pupae will be in your carpets, hardwood floors, on soft upholstery and in your pet's bedding. In order to treat infestations (and

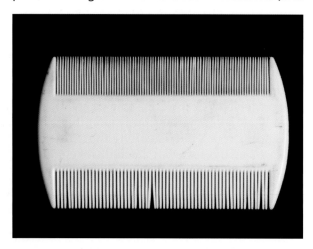

The best way to find fleas is to use a flea comb. Run the comb all over the dog's body, particularly along the back and around the base of the tail.

especially to prevent reinfestation) it is essential to treat the environment:

- Clean the house thoroughly. Thoroughly vacuum all carpets and floors, especially around the edges. Similarly vacuum all soft furnishings. Immediately empty the vacuum cleaner's dust bag directly into the household refuse bin, or discard the bag directly. If you sprinkle boric acid on carpets and upholstery and let it sit for an hour or more before vacuum cleaning, it will desiccate flea eggs, larvae and pupae, making it easier for the vacuum to pick them up
- Machine wash as much of the dog's bedding as you can in hot water, using bleach or a suitable safe insecticide when possible. Always rinse the machine thoroughly afterwards. If you just wash the bedding all you will get are clean fleas. Alternatively discard and incinerate all the bedding and replenish with fresh material
- For major infestations, special household sprays are available and obtainable from your veterinary surgeon, or consult your local environmental health department who may be willing to decontaminate the house for you
- Realize that your dogs and any other household pets, especially cats, allow fleas to continue their life cycle. So use your dog and any other pets as 'flea traps', treating them regularly with an effective flea-treatment product. Consult your vet because these days, more effective, longer-lasting and more conveniently applied treatments are coming into the market, and your vet can advise which product might be best to use in your particular circumstances

Lice
Lice are parasitic insects subdivided as biting and sucking lice. The distinction is purely a matter of the way they feed, and is otherwise relatively academic in terms of signs and treatment. Infection with lice is called pediculosis.

Transmission of infection requires relatively close dog-to-dog contact, although the eggs of lice, which are sticky and attach to hairs (where they are referred to as 'nits') can be collected into grooming equipment and thereby transmitted to other dogs unless the items are cleaned after grooming one dog and before starting another.

Large numbers of lice can cause intense irritation and associated self-inflicted trauma due to the dog scratching, biting and nibbling affected areas. Lice are dorsoventrally flattened insects about 2mm long, and typically light to dark brown in colour. Sucking lice are usually found head down, attached to the skin, whilst biting lice are generally more motile. The eggs are just visible to the naked eye and attached to hairs.

Lice are highly host specific, so lice from a dog won't survive on other species, whereas some other parasites such as fleas are more ubiquitous and can be found infesting a variety of other hosts.

Mites

Mites are technically arachnids, not insects, and all except *Trombicula autumnalis* (the harvest mite, whose larvae are parasitic) spend their entire life cycle on the one host. Mites may be subdivided into burrowing and surface mites; both cause dermatitis, which may or may not be itchy, depending on the type of mite. Infestation with mites is called 'mange', although the term is most commonly associated with the most pruritic form caused by sarcoptes species and hence referred to as 'scabies' or sarcoptic mange.

Sarcoptic Mange

Sarcoptic mange is caused by *Sarcoptes scabiei*. The parasite first affects the tips of the ears and the face, but ultimately large areas of the body can be infected in severe cases. Affected areas become hairless, thickened and inflamed. Infection in dogs can affect humans, although the lesions are small and generally self-limiting. Transmission requires close direct contact, and when owners are affected it is most often in areas where their dog lies up against them.

Demodectic Mange

Demodectic mange is caused by *Demodex* mites, small cigar-shaped parasites that burrow into the hair follicles. *Demodex* can be found in skin scrapings in clinically normal dogs without necessarily causing any problems whatsoever. The parasite is thought to be passed from bitch to puppies as they suckle. In some individuals, however, particularly young dogs of short-haired breeds, the number of mites increases dramatically, and this increased population causes dermatitis that is typically seen as non-itchy areas of hair loss. Often, areas around the eyes are first affected and the dog has a characteristic 'spectacle' appearance.

Some of these dogs may go on to develop a much more intense irritating dermatitis and eczema that is of much greater clinical significance. The problem is thought to arise when the mite for some reason breaks through the hair follicle, when the normal surface-dwelling parasite becomes exposed to tissue under the skin and causes an allergic reaction. These lesions then become secondarily infected with bacteria, pus forms, and they coalesce and erupt to result in further skin damage and irritation. Such lesions can become very debilitating, especially in a young dog. Before the advent of modern treatments, regrettably demodectic mange was previously a cause for euthanasia in severely affected cases.

'Harvest Mites'

Trombicula autumnalis are normally a problem in late summer and autumn, especially in areas of chalky soils and on grasslands, cornfields, heathland and scrubby woodland of southern England; they are less common on clay soils. The adults are non-parasitic and live in the soil, however the larvae, which are usually scarlet, red, orange or yellow in colour, are particularly problematic when they infest skin in the interdigital spaces between the footpads, where they cause intense irritation, driving the dog to lick and bite its feet.

Ear Mites

Otodectes cynotis is the parasitic mite that infests the ears of dogs and cats, and whilst frequently asymptomatic in cats, causing little or no problem, in dogs it stimulates the production of a dark brown waxy discharge. Sometimes if you look carefully, the tiny adult mites can be seen down the ear canal, walking on the surface of this debris as tiny white spots. Secondary bacterial infection will usually occur, and ear mites represent a major cause of external ear disease in the dog.

Ticks

Ticks are a natural hazard of working dogs, whether in field and wood or over moors and heaths. Ticks are problematic for a number of reasons, and the risk is somewhat dependent on the locality. There are definitely areas where ticks tend to be more of a nuisance than others, and especially if there are farm stock or deer, which typically act as the host for these parasites. A dog that puts its nose down a rabbit hole can sometimes return with its muzzle literally covered in small, immature ticks.

Ticks attach by means of modified mouthparts that they bury into the skin to suck the host's blood, on which they feed. The tick will gradually become engorged with blood, and its body will distend accordingly until it naturally detaches itself and drops off to digest its blood meal. The odd tick or two causes minimal harm to most dogs, and although most owners object to the sight of an engorged tick, given time it will simply drop off.

The greater problem from ticks is that they carry and transmit disease. The common indigenous species of tick in the UK, *Ixodes ricinus*, transmits Lyme disease, which affects humans as well as animals. Lyme disease causes an unpleasant, transient arthritis accompanied by a fever that over time can be recurrent and becomes very debilitating.

More recently, there are reports of introductions of more exotic tick species, notably *Dermalcentor reticulatus* and *Rhipicephalus sanguineus* (the brown dog tick). At the time of writing none has become established as indigenous populations, but dog owners need to be vigilant. If you find an unusual-looking tick on your dog, bring it to the attention of your local veterinary surgeon or public health authority.

Whilst many a country person will advise you of their favourite remedy that they swear is more effective than any other in removing the offending parasite, few take account of the risk of inadvertently transmitting blood-borne diseases. Appropriate methods of removing ticks are described in Chapter 3.

DIET AND NUTRITION

Feeding your dog an appropriate amount of a well-balanced diet is vital to its overall health and well-being. To understand how and what to feed your dog, it is helpful to understand what the nutritional requirements of the dog are, and how these requirements have evolved and further developed as the dog has adapted to domestication.

As a species, the dog is classified as being a member of the scientific order Carnivora, a large group of mammalian animals that share a similar arrangement of teeth. The dietary needs of different species of carnivore vary, and contrary to popular belief, although dogs are carnivores they don't necessarily need to be fed meat. Whilst some carnivores – the obligate or true carnivores such as the cat and ferret – do have an absolute requirement for meat in their diet, others can meet their nutrient requirements through a combination of meat and plants. If you consider the feeding habits of wild canines such as wolves, the pack will kill and consume the whole carcass, including the stomach and intestines, not simply the muscles and bones. Since herbivorous species

An engorged tick, in this case the common UK 'sheep tick', Ixodes ricinus. LAURIE CAMPBELL

constitute their common prey, wild carnivores must therefore consume a considerable amount of semi-digested plant material.

The teeth and the intestinal tract of the dog have become adapted to an omnivorous diet. This means that under normal circumstances dogs can meet their nutritional needs by eating a combination of plant and animal foods. For dogs, the source of protein and fat in the diet is less important than the quality and digestibility of these essential ingredients. Dogs can actually thrive well if they are fed a properly balanced vegetarian diet, whereas an all-meat diet would be unbalanced and would not meet all of a dog's nutritional requirements.

Evolving as carnivorous hunters, dogs have specialized digestive and gastrointestinal adaptations that allowed them to ingest a large meal followed by days of not eating. Along with other advantages, however, the subsequent process of domestication provided dogs with a more plentiful feed supply, and now it is recommended that most domestic dogs are fed once or twice per day. Indeed, small dogs will benefit from eating equally divided meals two to three times daily.

Note that whatever feeding schedule you choose, avoid allowing your dog to exercise vigorously after consuming a large meal, especially if it eats its food rapidly. This will help minimize problems with bloat or other serious digestive disorders.

ESSENTIAL NUTRIENTS

The basic nutrients required in a diet are water, proteins, fats and carbohydrates, and a well balanced diet must also include an appropriate quantity of vitamins, minerals, certain essential amino acids (which are derived from proteins), and specific essential fatty acids (derived from fats, especially unsaturated fats).

Water

Water is the most important nutrient consumed by animals. A source of fresh drinking water should always be available to your dog. A dog's body is primarily made up of water, and keeping hydrated is essential to maintain the body's vital functions – healthy blood pressure, heart and kidney function, and body temperature – and to transport nutrients and flush toxins from the body. Lactating bitches need to increase their water intake in order to produce milk to feed their puppies.

Proteins

The majority of body tissues and enzymes are made up of proteins, and proteins are essential for growth, maintenance, reproduction and tissue repair. The total protein requirement can vary depending on various factors such as age, breed and activity level; maintenance diets should normally contain between 13 to 19 per cent protein. Proteins are made up of amino acids and a dog requires ten essential amino acids in its diet: arginine, histidine, isoleucine, leucine, lysine, methionine, phenylalanine, threonine, tryptophan and valine. All are present in plants, and consequently it isn't necessary for dogs to eat meat; however, if only plant protein is given, the diet must be balanced to ensure that all these vital amino acids are in the plants being fed.

Fats

Fats are a dog's main source of energy from its food; they are also essential for fat-soluble substances to be transported and absorbed within the body. Although fats are essential at all stages of a dog's life, puppies require relatively more fat in their diet, and a higher dietary fat content is also necessary for bitches during pregnancy and whilst nursing. Dietary fat can be usefully decreased for senior dogs that are less active.

Carbohydrates

Carbohydrates are the other common source of energy for dogs, mainly in the form of sugar, starches and cellulose. Dogs are capable of making carbohydrates, and carbohydrates are a component of all types of food. Consequently there is no specific carbohydrate requirement in a dog's diet.

Vitamins

Vitamins are generally only required in small amounts, but they are essential to fuel many of the body's vital biochemical reactions. When feeding a complete balanced diet there is no need to provide vitamin supplements, unless instructed by a vet. Over-supplementing vitamins and minerals can cause significant harm, particularly in large, actively growing dogs and pregnant bitches.

Vitamin A: A fat-soluble vitamin with a number of important functions, such as aiding vision, and contributing to normal bone and foetal development. Dogs cannot synthesize vitamin A, but this essential nutrient is found in foods such as fish liver oils, animal liver, carrots and egg yolks.

B Vitamins: A group of water-soluble vitamins often associated with neurologic function and organ functions. Dogs need B vitamins as part of a balanced diet, and these can be supplied by including foods such as fish, offal, egg yolk and whole cereal grains in the dog's diet.

Vitamin C: A water-soluble vitamin that dogs can synthesize, and so it is not necessary to supply this nutrient in a dog's diet.

Vitamin D: A fat-soluble vitamin essential to regulate calcium metabolism. It can be synthesized by dogs as long as the body is exposed to ultraviolet light.

Vitamin E: A fat-soluble vitamin that acts as an antioxidant. The amount of vitamin E required in the diet varies depending on the amount of the mineral selenium present.

Vitamin K: A fat-soluble vitamin needed for blood clotting. It is not an essential nutrient as it can be synthesized by bacteria living in the dog's gastrointestinal tract.

Minerals

Minerals are essential nutrients that need to be provided in differing amounts depending on the respective mineral; for example, dogs require relatively larger amounts of calcium and phosphorus. However, it is important to understand that providing too much calcium and phosphorus can be detrimental, and therefore minerals must be part of a balanced diet.

Fibre

Fibre is needed to aid digestion, prevent constipation and help regulate blood sugar levels. It is not an essential nutrient, but is often added to commercial diets. High-fibre dog diets can, however, decrease the digestibility of some nutrients, and increase the volume of faeces passed.

All these dietary components are necessary to build and maintain the body's various tissues and enable all the body's various biological reactions to be carried out. The minimum dietary requirement has been established for many nutrients, but the amounts will vary somewhat depending on the dog's stage of life (puppy, adolescent, adult and senior) and if it is a bitch, whether she is pregnant.

Although nutritional guidelines have been developed as the general basis for the nutritional content of commercial pet foods, remember that these are only guidelines. A particular dog may need more or less depending on its individual needs, circumstances and health status. As a further complication in recent years, nutritionists and veterinary researchers have identified that there are definite breed variations regarding metabolism and nutrient requirements. Breeds of dog that were developed in specific locations may have adapted to specialized diets. Inbreeding and genetic differences between individuals can result in a further need for individualization of the dog's diet in order to optimize health. In addition to the breed differences and to individual needs, working dogs require different ratios of proteins and fats in their diets than sedentary household pets, and many experienced breeders and trainers will be aware of these individual idiosyncrasies.

TYPES OF FEED

Complete foods: The most popular choice for dog owners in the UK. Being 'complete' they contain all the nutrients required by a dog in the appropriate quantities to keep it fit and healthy.

This means they can, and generally should, be fed alone. Complete foods can be fed 'dry', when it is essential that you provide a readily accessible source of clean drinking water, or as a mash, normally mixed with hot water and allowed to cool before feeding.

Complementary foods: Wet or raw foods that do not contain the full range of essential nutrients, or which contain them in inappropriate proportions. For this reason other foods must be included in the diet. These other components can be home-prepared food, or mixer biscuits, a combination of both, or a complete food.

Many dog owners seem to increasingly favour feeding frozen raw foods (*see* below), which mixers can effectively complement to provide a satisfactory balance of nutrients.

Dry foods: The majority of British dogs are fed on dry complete foods, and these are very convenient, requiring no preparation prior to feeding and having no special storage requirements. Dry foods are manufactured using dried and ground ingredients and then cooked. Ingredients are typically listed on a dry weight basis.

Mixer biscuits are cereal based and sometimes flavoured with vegetables or herbs. They are nutritionally incomplete so need to be fed alongside a wet or raw food. They were formerly very popular in the UK, when many dogs were fed 'meat and biscuit' meals.

Wet foods: These foods are packed in tins, trays and pouches, and are less popular for feeding to working gundogs. Wet foods contain a large amount of water, and consequently the feeding amounts are much higher, making them more expensive and less convenient to feed. Wet foods can be complete or complementary.

RAW FEEDING

Raw feeding is regarded by many as the most natural way to feed a dog, and over the past few years has undergone something of a renaissance to become a very popular means of feeding gundogs in the UK. The term 'raw feeding' seems to be interpreted by some people, particularly those who criticize the practice, as equating to the feeding of uncooked chicken carcasses. That is not what is intended. Here I refer to the feeding of uncooked food items that are otherwise suitable for consumption. The feeding of raw chicken carcasses is not recommended for dogs, although many will claim otherwise. Chicken bones are brittle and can splinter, and so could damage and potentially penetrate the lining of the gastrointestinal tract; furthermore, unless properly sourced and suitably processed, chicken meat can be a cause of bacterial food poisoning.

Many people prepare their own feed for their dogs, typically using frozen ingredients, but a number of companies have developed prepared complete raw foods in the form of frozen blocks or nuggets, which provide all of the benefits of raw feeding with the convenience of a conventional dog food. There are both complete and complementary forms of raw foods; like wet foods, they inevitably contain a high proportion of water.

Some people advocate feeding bones and raw food; however, bones are neither essential nor generally recommended for feeding to domestic dogs. Those who favour feeding bones will often argue that it is more 'natural', and support their preference by citing how wild carnivores, wolves in particular, consume bone as part of their diet. If you observe wolves feeding, however, it suggests that what bone is consumed is no more than incidental to the ingestion of flesh from specific parts of the carcass.

Bones can cause two particular problems in dogs: they can cause potentially serious obstructions in various parts of the gastrointestinal tract, and they can lead to constipation by contributing to the formation of hard, dry, impacted faeces that are particularly difficult for dogs to pass. Sharp spicules of bone have also been known to penetrate the gut wall.

As far as dogs are concerned, the prime purpose of cooking is to render meat safe by destroying germs and parasites and to break down otherwise indigestible starches found in grain and vegetable matter. Providing these points are taken into consideration when selecting the constituents for raw feeding, there should be little cause for concern. Consequently, if you wish to raw feed:

Larger pieces of meat are gnawed from the bone.

- Don't feed potentially contaminated foodstuffs or fresh meat that would otherwise be unsuitable for human consumption
- Only feed freshly defrosted food, and never re-freeze raw food
- Feed only ripened fruit and vegetables
- Do not feed 'starchy' ingredients, such as potatoes, unless they are first cooked

HOW MUCH TO FEED

One of the best methods for determining how many calories to feed your dog is to determine what your dog's lean weight should be and feed according to that weight. Unfortunately, this requires constant monitoring (and weighing) and is not always practical. The standard formula used for calculating the energy requirements of

Wolves use their well developed incisor teeth to strip flesh from the bone; those bones are not ingested.

Having significantly stronger jaws than any dog, wolves can break down parts of the carcass, such as the ribs, into smaller chunks of flesh and bone that are immediately swallowed whole.

Wolves are able to literally 'wolf' down bite-size pieces of meat and bone; they do not chew bones in any way that resembles the habit of domestic dogs.

the average adult dog, kept indoors and receiving light daily exercise is:

30 × weight in kg + 70 = daily calorie needs

Regard this formula as merely a starting point, however, as many dogs will require fewer calories on a daily basis, while most dogs that are regularly worked will require more. Importantly, be aware that this daily calorie total includes not only your dog's meals, but also any snacks and treats.

You may find it more helpful to utilize one of a variety of body condition scoring systems that have been devised for dogs to determine any adjustment required in your dog's food intake or exercise programme. A number of schemes are accessible on-line, and a simple summarized example is given in the box [below]. The intention is to keep a working dog within the 'ideal' criteria, and to adjust any tendency towards its being categorized as 'thin' by adjusting its diet. Any tendency towards displaying the 'stout' criteria can be corrected either by providing more exercise or by feeding a lower calorie diet.

COMMERCIAL DOG FOODS

Feeding a commercial dog food has a number of advantages. Many are manufactured as 'complete feeds' formulated by expert nutritionists. Provided you understand your dog's nutritional

BODY CONDITION SCORING

1 = Very Thin
More than 20 per cent below the dog's ideal bodyweight
Ribs, spine, hip bones and all body prominences can be easily seen (in short-haired dogs)
No discernible body fat can be felt beneath the skin
Obvious loss of muscle bulk

2 = Thin
Between 10–20 per cent below the dog's ideal bodyweight
Ribs and spine can be easily felt, and may be visible with no palpable fat. The spine is visible. The hip bones are less prominent
Obvious waist and abdominal tuck
Very little fat can be felt under the skin

3 = Ideal
Ribs, spine and hip bones are easily felt
Visible waist and abdomen tuck
Very little fat can be felt under the skin

4 = Stout
General fleshy appearance
Ribs, spine and hip bones are difficult to feel
Waist barely visible with a broad back, abdominal tuck may be absent
Layer of fat on belly and at base of tail base

5 = Obese
Ribs, spine and hip bones difficult to feel under a thick layer of fat
Large fat deposits over chest, spine and tail base
No waist can be seen, and belly may droop significantly
Heavy fat deposits on lower back and base of tail

requirement for its age and lifestyle, and can match the correct type of commercial feed to satisfy those requirements, there is much to recommend them. They are convenient and provide a reliable, consistent diet usually of good quality that can be relied upon to provide for your dog's overall nutritional requirements. There are one or two important points to understand, however, particularly when reading the labelling on pet foods to help you select the most appropriate diet to feed your dog.

According to British law, all complete dog foods have to display the percentages of protein, fat, fibre and ash on the packaging. Some foods declare the contents of more nutrients, but this is completely voluntary. Be aware that some nutrients are listed as a 'minimum' percentage, while others are listed as a 'maximum' percentage, meaning that a particular batch of food may contain a higher or lower percentage of the ingredient than is actually shown on the label. The most important thing to look for on an ingredients list is clarity. Each ingredient should be named, and the most important ingredients (the three or four at the top of the list) should ideally be given with a percentage to tell you how much is present.

Sometimes terms such as 'meat and animal

A list of ingredients displayed on a bag of complete dog food.

GB/IRL/RSA/AUS - Complete feed for dogs
For adult medium breed dogs (from 11 to 25 kg)
From 12 months to 7 years old

COMPOSITION: maize, maize flour, wheat flour, dehydrated beef and pork protein*, dehydrated poultry protein, animal fats, wheat, hydrolysed animal proteins, minerals, beet pulp, fish oil, soya oil, yeasts, hydrolysed yeast (source of manno-oligo-saccharides). **ADDITIVES** (per kg): Nutritional additives: Vitamin A: 13100 IU, Vitamin D3: 800 IU, E1 (Iron): 55 mg, E2 (Iodine): 5.5 mg, E4 (Copper): 11 mg, E5 (Manganese): 72 mg, E6 (Zinc): 215 mg, E8 (Selenium): 0.14 mg - Preservatives - Antioxidants. **ANALYTICAL CONSTITUENTS:** Protein: 25% - Fat content: 14% - Crude ash: 6% - Crude fibres: 1.2% - Per kg: Manno-oligo-saccharides: 0.5 g - Omega 3 fatty acids: 5 g including EPA/DHA: 3.1 g. **FEEDING INSTRUCTIONS:** see chart. Batch number, factory registration number and best before date: see information on packaging. To be stored in a cool, dry place. For RSA: Guaranteed analysis g/kg: Crude protein (min) 230 - Moisture (max) 110 - Crude fat (min) 120 - Crude fibre (max) 22 - Crude ash (max) 66. Product registration number: - Act 36/1947.

*L.I.P.: protein selected for its very high assimilation.

derivatives' are used in dog food labelling; these ingredients can form any part of any animal and may comprise parts of the carcass not normally used for human consumption such as the head, feet, guts, hair and feathers. This is a perfectly legitimate practice, however it can be a means of disguising the inclusion of ingredients that some customers might otherwise regard as undesirable, and which might prejudice their choice. The use of these ingredients also enables the feed manufacturers to vary the source and type of animal by-product used; this can have a negative impact on dogs with dietary sensitivities.

As a general rule, try to feed known dietary ingredients provided by the manufacturer in the form of a fixed formula diet; that way you will know what you are feeding and can be fairly confident, if it is a reputable manufacturer, that your dog's dietary requirement is being appropriately satisfied. This is particularly important if your dog is prone to dietary intolerance, as identifying and eliminating problem ingredients is not possible unless you know exactly what you are feeding.

Always feed your dog the highest quality food you can afford. The differences between a premium food and budget food aren't necessarily obvious on the label; they are found in the quality and source of the ingredients. Two dog foods,

for example, may each contain a similar 27 per cent level of protein but can be vastly different when it comes to digestibility.

The label must also include feeding recommendations for dogs of different sizes. Use this simply as a guide, and be prepared to vary the amount as previously described, since working dogs that undertake a lot of strenuous exercise on a regular basis during the shooting season will obviously need more than at other times when they may be less active. Dogs fed appropriately for the work they do are able to work for longer, and at a greater speed, and to recover from exertion more quickly and suffer fewer injuries.

FITNESS AND EXERCISE

When it comes to determining an appropriate exercise regime in a gundog, there is no 'one size fits all' approach that can be recommended for optimum health and fitness. A lot depends on the breed and type of dog, the type of work it is intended to perform, and the amount and frequency of work that is to be undertaken. The intention here is to discuss some principles and variables that should be taken into consideration when deciding how best to exercise your dog, and what level of fitness, both mental and physical, is ultimately required.

Whilst working, gundogs are probably exercising at their optimum, but they must be fit to work, and we must maintain them at a level of fitness that enables them to sustain the level and frequency at which they are to be worked.

With few exceptions dogs have been developed to work. They have worked alongside us for thousands of years, and most dogs were bred for a particular purpose, such as hunting, herding or providing protection.

The manner in which a gundog is raised as a puppy and through adolescence is particularly important. It needs to build up its physical fitness gradually: too much, too early will be detrimental to bones and joints. It also needs appropriate stimulation, not simply training, so that it can learn to 'think for itself' and develop necessary problem-solving skills that will be used when it comes to hunting and retrieving.

Dogs' ancestors spent most of their time scavenging and hunting for food, caring for their offspring, defending territory and otherwise engaging in primarily physical, social interaction that maintains hierarchies and bonds the pack. They lead busy, complex lives, interacting socially and solving problems necessary for their survival. This is in marked contrast to the type of lifestyle led by their modern-day domestic counterparts. Time spent working and exercising helps redress that balance, and since we have control over what our dogs do whilst being exercised, it makes sense to do more than just put the lead on and take them for a walk, and to think about what best they might do during that time.

If dogs are deprived of things to do to channel their energy, they will find things to do for themselves, and the sorts of thing they do under such circumstances are frequently undesirable. Some of the common behavioural problems seen in dogs that don't get sufficient exercise include the following:

- Destructive chewing, digging and scratching
- Hyperactivity and excitability, night-time activities when they should be sleeping
- Unruliness, jumping up at people
- Excessive predatory and boisterous social play
- Attention-seeking behaviours such as barking and whining

If your dog exhibits any of these behaviours, the chances are that it's not getting the amount and correct type of exercise that it requires.

Don't underestimate the value of a good walk or jog with your dog, but do recognize that whilst jogging and running might be good exercise for us, dogs don't naturally engage in similar sustained exercise. Whilst working, hunting or retrieving, a dog will typically engage in short bursts of activity, interspersed with intermittent stops. During these stops the dog will do such things as sniff around the immediate environment, defecate and urinate, rest and generally 'take in the scenery'.

Give your dog(s), and yourself, the opportunity to rest between drives.

At least one good outing per day will help keep your dog physically fit and give it an opportunity to explore the wider world. However, vary the routine. Take different routes and visit new places whenever you can, so that your dog experiences novel sights and smells.

There are at least three core components to a dog's fitness. It needs:

- Strength: to develop muscle mass to protect bones and joints from exercise injury and keep it energetic throughout its life
- Cardiac fitness: to develop a strong heart to pump blood through the lungs and transfer that oxygenated blood to the muscles and vital organs. Some of the best cardiac exercises will be 'low impact' exercises that burn off calories and keep a dog fit and lean
- Core fitness: to develop the body's ability to respond to the energy demand of the muscles and heart. To be able to build up and then mobilize sufficient energy reserves, when needed, to sustain it through longer periods of more intense work

Be sure to modify exercise according to your dog's age and general state of health. Discuss this with your vet as part of any regular check up visits, and know how your dog responds to exercise. Take note and be prepared to intervene if he shows signs of tiring, or is stiff or lame after exercise. Early intervention is often the key to success in treating muscular and joint injuries.

Exercise that will improve strength might include running up hills, using the gradient to improve muscle strength, tone and condition. Winding your way back down the hill will help ease the load on your dog's joints.

TRANSPORTING YOUR DOG

Always ensure that your dog is safe, secure and comfortable whenever it travels. Never leave it in a vehicle on warm or hot days. If you ever need to leave the dog restrained in a parked vehicle, always ensure that it has access to drinking water and adequate ventilation.

Train your dog so that it readily enters the vehicle, becomes accustomed to travelling, and remains in the vehicle when required. Make sure that your dog is able to get out of the vehicle safely. Consider what might happen in the event of an accident. Are you confident that you could get your dog(s) out of the car safely if you are involved in an accident, and if it travels in the back of the vehicle, how likely is it to survive a rear-end impact?

Use some means of securing your dog in such a way that it is safe and cannot interfere in any way with your driving. It can be helpful to restrain it in a suitably robust and secure carrier. The dog should be able to see out of the crate or container, which should be large enough to allow it to stand comfortably, turn around easily and lie down in a natural position. Always make sure the vehicle, and importantly the carrier itself, is well ventilated and remains cool on long journeys.

Alternatively, you might wish to consider using a harness if your dog has to travel in the passenger compartment of the car. Measure the dog correctly and buy an appropriate size harness; follow the instructions carefully and fit the harness correctly before

Swimming is a very convenient form of 'low impact' exercise: weight is taken off the joints and the dog can exercise freely. Physiotherapy pools often have the facility for the dog to swim safely against a current of water, which is excellent for both building muscle and exercising the heart.

Folding crates are very useful. Indoors they provide somewhere for the dog to retreat, rest and sleep, then when folded up and taken out to the car, they can be used to confine the dog whilst travelling.

Custom-made dog transit boxes are cool, light and washable. This one provides good visibility and ventilation. Being washable means it is very hygienic, so that if necessary it can be adequately decontaminated and disinfected.

Some manufacturers produce dog gates to fit estate cars. Combined with a dog guard or grill behind the rear seats, the dog has adequate space, and is safe and secure in the back of the vehicle.

putting the dog in the car. The harness then attaches securely to the vehicle seat-belt system.

Don't feed your dog for two hours prior to a journey so it does not have to travel on a full stomach. On a long journey that would include the time the dog would normally be fed, inter-

rupt the journey at the appropriate time, provide a light meal, then allow the dog a little while to start digesting its food before continuing your journey.

Always take plenty of water with you, and ensure the dog has access to drinking water at intervals during a long journey. Provide suitable bedding that will prevent the dog slipping around whilst the vehicle is in motion.

Take regular breaks on longer journeys, and allow your dog time to 'stretch its legs' and go to the toilet. In such situations, always exercise your dog(s) on a lead whenever you are near a road or other vehicles.

SAFETY TRAINING

It is beyond the scope of this book to provide a training manual of how to train a dog to specific commands, and how those commands can be used to effectively work your dog to find, flush and retrieve game. Instead what is intended is a brief consideration of how training, and the use of some particular commands, can help assure your dog's safety and the safety of others, particularly when out on a shoot and working in the field.

Probably one of the most underestimated areas of risk to your dog on a shooting day is the area

Pick-up trucks and other similar larger vehicles can be equipped with custom-made dog transport boxes that include storage space below.

Dog trailers are used and recommended by many professional gundog owners and handlers. Reputed to have good suspension and to be extremely stable, their dogs travel in relative comfort. Well ventilated and secure, with ample storage space for water and accessories, a trailer is ideal where dogs have to be accommodated overnight whilst away from home.

Larger shoots provide dedicated transport for the beaters; some, like this one, even include built-in kennelling for the dogs.

On shoot days, keep your dog(s) in a vehicle where they will be safe when not working. Otherwise use a lead when you take a dog out of the vehicle for exercise or to 'relieve' itself. (Be considerate of the landowner, always pick up after your dog and take away any waste for disposal.)

A dog should be trained to enter a vehicle on command.

Train your dog to stay seated or to lie down in the vehicle until given a command to jump out. This is a very simple and effective means of keeping your dog safe and secure at all times until you are ready to go for a walk, set off for a day's sport, or go home.

where you park your car, especially when meeting prior to the shoot and packing up at the end of the day. These are busy times with a lot going on, when people can be easily distracted. There are likely to be vehicles moving about, drivers trying to negotiate other vehicles, people trying to park their cars.

If the shoot meets in a farmyard there may be other hazards. Your dog may be able to access barns and other storage areas, or places where there is likely to be rodent bait. Accidents can easily happen, and at times such as these your attention can easily be distracted.

You should train your dog to walk to heel, both on...

...and off the lead.

Walking to heel is a very basic form of obedience, but one that enables you to know exactly where your dog is, and if necessary, to easily further restrain it. Getting your dog to stay to 'heel' around other animals, particularly in the vicinity of cattle, sheep and horses, will keep it safe and out of harm's way, and will be a considerable reassurance for horse riders, enabling them to focus on controlling their mount.

Teach and reinforce the use of the stop whistle and the recall. Whenever danger threatens, these are your primary means of controlling your dog and/or bringing him back to a place of safety.

The recall: your vocal command should be reinforced with a suitable gesture.

The use of the 'stop' whistle.

Always praise your dog when it returns on command, and if necessary, be prepared to reward it immediately it comes to hand.

Train your dog to jump fences and other obstacles cleanly. Barbed wire fencing is probably the most commonly encountered hazard when working dogs on a shooting day, certainly on lowland shoots, and it is extremely useful if a dog can recognize and safely negotiate barbed wire.

A dog being trained to jump a fence.

This dog jumps a fence with ease; neither fore nor hind legs touch the fence, and there is little risk of it hitting either its chest or belly as it clears the obstacle.

Finally, it can be very useful to train your dog, if you can, to 'lie down' or to 'go over' (on its side) when you want it to lie down to be groomed, for instance. If your dog will lie down quietly out of the way in crowded places, whilst waiting to be seen at the vet's, for example, or if it should ever be injured and require treatment, is extremely helpful.

SAFETY WHILST WORKING

Many shoots require and will have a formal policy on health and safety, and will carry out regular risk assessments. These days there is undoubtedly a significantly higher awareness of the hazards and risks associated with shooting. The emphasis, however, is quite rightly on human health and safety, and landowners and shoot organizers will usually give less thought to the safety of any dogs engaged as part of the shoot.

But this is not always the case, and some gamekeepers provide suitable ways for their beaters' dogs to negotiate fences,

Above: *It can be useful to train your dog to jump your leg; extending your leg and putting it on or in front of the top strand of barbed wire enables the dog to clear the fence safely, even if it does use your leg as a stepping stage.*

Try to prevent your dog using the fence as a step, touching the fence as he goes over and using the fence to launch himself forwards as he jumps down.

Feed sacs wrapped around barbed-wire fencing and secured with baler twine.

stiles and other obstacles safely. They will also clear nettles from the vicinity of game crops prior to the start of the season, as well as where birds are most likely to drop on most drives.

Responsibility for the dog, and its safety on the shoot, lies with its owner or handler, so get into the habit of 'thinking ahead' for your dog, avoid obvious dangers, and reduce the risk of injury by anticipating hazards and understanding some of the risks.

Most people seem to agree that the greatest risk of injury to dogs when out shooting is from barbed wire. It is not so much the risk of injury from becoming impaled on barbed-wire fencing, as the risk of a dog encountering rusty barbed wire lying hidden in hedgerows, and particularly where old fencing has been replaced by new. It is not unusual to find a situation where the farmer has put up a new barbed-wire fence, but neither he nor the fencing contractor has seen fit to remove the old. As a consequence, the dog must negotiate not only the new barbed wire fence, but also decayed fence posts and rusty barbed wire, which together present a formidable hazard for any dog to tackle.

Always pay particular attention to fencing at the boundary of one farm and any neighbouring property. If the shoot takes place on a farm where there are livestock, have a regard for the type of enterprise. Sheep farmers will generally

On this shoot, an opening is provided next to a stile so that dogs can negotiate the fence

Broken and surplus barbed wire is often left lying around and becomes rapidly obscured in the undergrowth.

secure their fields with stock (net) fencing, whilst dairy farms and beef herds will more likely be kept from straying with barbed wire.

The fencing along the boundaries of these two distinctly different farming enterprises present as two obstacles that a dog, and often its handler, would need to negotiate separately.

Be aware of how slippery stiles and bridges across streams and ditches become in wet and frosty conditions. Many shoots secure chicken wire to the top surface of stiles and wooden bridges to give a better purchase, but in time this can rust and rot, and sharp pieces of wire can then easily cut into a dog's pad as it crosses the bridge.

Try to prevent your dog drinking from puddles or stagnant water courses. Bacteria can build up in stagnant water, particularly in the presence of decaying vegetation. Consider the type of land you are working on, and the likely source of any running or standing water. Similarly there is the potential risk of chemical pollution from vehicles in puddles along roadways.

ABOVE: *A stream or beck on mountain and moors is hardly likely to present any risk in comparison to the run-off from low-lying agricultural land where pesticides and fertilizers are most commonly used.*

LEFT: *Where you have to cross a stile, try to make sure your dog doesn't have to wriggle under the fence, and risk impaling itself on the lowest strand of barbed wire.*

69

Water collecting in puddles can become contaminated in a variety of ways.

If you are working a dog all day in the beating line, consider taking a bag just large enough to carry your dog's drinking water and a few first-aid items.

A further hazard is the risk of lungworm infection. Dogs pick up lungworm larvae from slugs and snails, which will naturally frequent damp places. If your dog is accustomed to drinking from puddles, always be sure to include lungworm treatment as part of a regular worming programme.

The best advice is always to carry a supply of fresh drinking water when working your dog. I use a lightweight drinking bottle of the type used by hikers and cyclists; along with a small collapsible plastic bowl that fits easily in any game or training bag. Offer your dog a drink between drives and you should find that he won't need to use a puddle to satisfy his thirst.

As mentioned previously, fertilizers, herbicides and other pesticides are commonly used and stored in quite considerable quantities on many farms. Always keep your dog well away from, and under control around the vicinity of farm buildings, not only for safety purposes but as a courtesy to the landowner – after all, few people appreciate some stranger's dog rooting around in their shed or garage at home! Farm buildings are also areas frequented by rodents, so there is both the risk of rodent-borne disease, such as leptospirosis, especially if the land around is wet and there may be puddles for the dog to drink from, as well as the probability that rodent bait insecticide has been put down.

HEALTH TESTING

The purpose of health testing is to attempt to identify and, where possible, control inherited disease both within the individual affected dog and, if the dog is to be used for breeding, within the breed population as a whole. (For the Control of Hereditary Disease in Gundogs, and the Inheritance of Genetic Disease and the Impact of Inbreeding, *see* Appendix.)

There are various forms of heath test, and the type of test used is largely dependent on the type and character of the disease to be identified. In this context it is important to understand and distinguish between the terms phenotype and genotype. A dog's phenotype relates to its outward appearance in all of its anatomical, physiological and behavioural characteristics. The phenotype may be influenced not only by the genetic make-up of the dog, but also by physical and environmental factors, such as the amount, type and frequency of exercise it receives, the type and quantity of food it is fed, and so on.

The genotype refers to the entire genetic constitution of an individual and is determined by the genes it inherits from the parents. The genotype is unaffected by any other intrinsic or external, environmental factors.

A typical rodenticidal bait box, usually a good indication that the building is likely to be infested with wild rodents.

Phenotypic Tests
Traditionally vets have had to rely on examining the phenotype to determine the presence and severity of inherited diseases. These are clinical tests that seek to identify and in some cases classify, specific characteristic signs of the disease that can be observed in affected individuals. Using these tests, a variety of formal testing schemes has been devised and applied that have helped breeders reduce the incidence and/or severity of the disease in the breed population, and owners to understand how best to try to ameliorate the signs of the disease should their dog be affected. Examples of those used in gundogs include the BVA/KC Hip Scoring Scheme, The BVA/KC Elbow Grading Scheme and the BVA/KC/ISDS (International Sheep Dog Society) Eye Scheme (see Appendix, Phenotypic Tests).

Information regarding the tests that are available for particular gundog breeds can be found on-line via the Kennel Club's Breed Information Centre, or by contacting the relevant breed club, or your veterinary surgeon and/or your dog's breeder.

The Benefits of Health Testing
The results of health testing are valuable to owners and breeders alike. Knowing that your dog has an inherited disorder, you can make informed decisions as to how much exercise to give it, what to feed it, whether it is suitable for breeding, and if so what type of dog to mate it to – and of course whether or not it is likely to require veterinary drug treatment or surgical intervention to alleviate the signs of the disease. You

71

may even decide that the dog is not fit for the work you intended and therefore better brought up as a pet. Health testing can potentially save time, money and disappointment in the event of you training your dog, only to realize eventually that it is not as capable as you had anticipated.

Using health test results, breeders can similarly make informed choices: on whether or not to use the dog for breeding, and on the type of dog to take it to for mating. Significant progress is now being made in developing a variety of tools, which, used intelligently, can help breeders to increase the likelihood of producing healthy puppies. (*See* Appendix, The Benefits of Health Testing.)

Health testing and the application of informed breeding strategies provides a means of controlling hereditary diseases and maintaining a healthier gene pool.

3 FIRST AID IN THE FIELD

Accidents are likely to happen no matter how careful you are when working dogs, so it is helpful to be prepared, and to be in the right frame of mind to best deal with the situation so you are less likely to panic and, importantly, can properly care for your dog. Consider the likely scenarios: the salient points of this chapter will outline most of the common injuries. Know how to administer basic first aid; this chapter will explain and illustrate most of the techniques, and then should something untoward happen you are likely to have an understanding of how best to respond.

BE PREPARED

FIRST-AID KIT

Put together a small first-aid kit, have it available, and know how to use it. A basic kit is illustrated here where everything packs away into a plastic sandwich box that can be conveniently carried either in the car, the beaters' wagon or on the game cart.

It's a good idea to seal the lid with tape; not only will this help to keep the contents clean, but it will also help to deter people from using these items for other than their intended purpose. At

the very least try to have a small selection of bandages available: plain cotton bandages to dress wounds, and adhesive bandage or 'Vetrap' (a proprietary veterinary product that sticks to itself and which can easily be removed) to cover and protect dressings, along with cotton wool and gauze pads, some antiseptic wound powder, a skin cleanser and a pot of glucose (either in the form of powder or as a syrup).

Carry either a pair of scissors, and/or a multi-tool, depending on whether your multi-tool incorporates a scissor tool – and if you include a few sticking plasters you will have a first-aid kit that can be used for humans and dogs alike. You will need good light to examine injuries properly, so a small torch can be useful, especially if, for instance, you suspect your dog has picked up something in its foot and you are trying to find a thorn or small pieces of glass.

SAFETY FIRST

Always have due regard for your own safety and that of others; take care, and again, don't panic. Assess the situation and think ahead. Don't allow a simple accident on the shooting field – or anywhere else, for that matter – to escalate so as to put yourself, your dog or others at risk of further harm or injury. An injured dog may be fearful or in pain, and its natural instincts take over. It will certainly be under the influence of adrenalin so

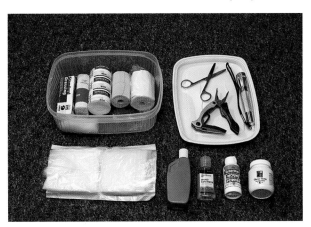

The author's basic first-aid field kit comprising (clockwise) a selection of cotton, crêpe and soft bandages, two rolls of Elastoplast dressings, a pair of blunt-ended scissors, a pen torch, a multitool (knife and pliers), some glucose syrup, wound dressing powder, hand cleansers, and sterile gauze swabs.

it's in 'flight or fight' mode, and in such circumstances even the most placid of dogs can bite if it's in pain and frightened of what's going on around it. Consequently it is advisable to muzzle the dog unless you are convinced it is safe to handle.

The accompanying diagram shows how to apply a comfortable muzzle. This type of muzzle is very simple to tie quickly in an emergency, and can be conveniently manufactured using, for instance, a traditional corded gundog lead or a length of bandage. It won't hurt or inconvenience the dog, and you should find that even the act of gently holding the dog and tying the muzzle, and talking to it in calm, soothing language as you do, will have the effect of reassuring the animal. It then recognizes who you are, that you are there to help, and that what you do won't pose any further threat.

Once you have suitably restrained the dog,

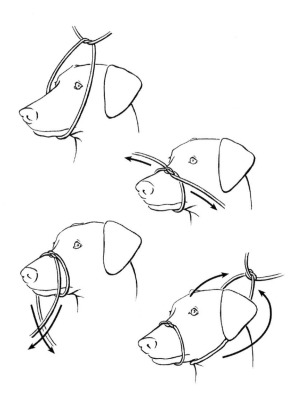

How to apply a muzzle using a gundog lead or a suitable strip of bandage.

make sure you are in a safe place to examine it and to administer any necessary first aid. You need to be in the best position in terms of your own safety and where your dog is best treated. If this is not the case, is the dog sufficiently mobile, or do you need help to move it? Ensure that someone else knows there's a problem so they can assist, or if necessary can summon further help.

Always retreat as necessary to a suitable place to administer first aid. This may be where there is sufficient light to find the cause and treat an injury, or even somewhere out of the rain so you can apply a bandage. If you have to move the dog, make sure you pick it up keeping your back straight and bending your legs; it's all too easy to hurt yourself. Remember the safe weight to lift at work is around 12kg, and a full-grown Labrador Retriever weighs significantly more, so if necessary find a friend to help you lift and carry the dog.

First Impressions can be Deceptive

Probably the most common types of injury that gundogs sustain on shooting days are cuts or lacerations, most frequently cut pads and lacerated tails, along with cuts to their ears (typically the tip). All these injuries involve some form of bleeding, and blood on a dog's coat can make the injury appear very much worse than it actually is. Remember that acute, life-threatening injuries are actually quite uncommon, but that a wounded dog may be in shock or likely to go into shock, and that treating the effects of shock will be as important as focusing purely on treating the wound. So don't panic, and take time to assess the situation properly.

ASSESSING AN INJURY

First, stay calm and don't panic. Try to maintain a sense of perspective; this may not be easy when you witness your dog actually sustaining an injury and realize that it may be in pain, but just remind yourself that critical emergency, life or death situations are relatively uncommon. Particularly in more serious circumstances, however, try to avoid 'rushing in' in an immediate attempt

THE PRIMARY OBJECTIVES OF FIRST AID

Applying first aid to an injured dog generally involves the following:

- **Restraining the dog** so that it doesn't run away or try to bite somebody if it is in pain. Put it on a lead, put on a comfortable muzzle if necessary, and unless entirely inappropriate, let it get itself into a position where it feels comfortable
- **Comfort and reassure the dog** by speaking in a calm, soothing voice
- **Ensure that the dog is able to breathe freely:** if it has collapsed, and in particular if it is unconscious, extend its neck, then pull out its tongue and fold it under the lower jaw
- **Control bleeding**, either by using a pressure bandage, or, if blood is spurting from the wound, by applying pressure locally with your finger until it stops; alternatively, if this doesn't work, use a tourniquet, though be sure that it is released temporarily every ten to fifteen minutes to restore blood circulation
- **Keep the dog lightly covered and warm:** if the dog is on cold ground, place something underneath it to retain its body heat. If it needs to be transported to a veterinary surgery for treatment, make sure it is kept comfortable, covered and warm

to deal with the obvious injury. The first questions to ask yourself should be as follows:

- How does the dog otherwise appear?
- What is the dog's general demeanour?
- Does it appear to be frightened (and therefore more likely to 'take off' or bite you or someone else if it's in pain)?
- Carefully check the dog over: does it have any further injuries?
- In particular, just take a moment to watch its breathing. Notice whether or not it is breathing rapidly and taking shallow breaths, or if its breathing appears more laboured: the former could be a sign of shock, the latter perhaps a sign of a more serious internal injury
- Are there any obvious signs of shock?

If you are used to regularly examining your dog, you should be able to quickly and easily detect any change in the colour of the skin inside the mouth, and in the feel of the lips and gums. If the skin is pale in colour, check whether the circulation is good or not: press on the gum, then withdraw your finger – that area will be pale, but it should rapidly refill with blood, restoring the normal pink colour. If these mucous membranes around the mouth look pale, or feel cold and 'clammy', and there is evidence of poor (peripheral) circulation, then the dog is likely to be in shock or perhaps bleeding internally, and you will therefore need to treat it accordingly.

Notice if there are any nervous signs, or any obvious likelihood that there could be nerve or brain damage, because this will determine if, when, and how you move the dog. If the dog has collapsed, is it twitching or convulsing? If so, it will be better not to move it immediately, and to wait to see if it recovers. The dog should at least be able to withdraw each leg if you pinch a toe, and blink as you move your finger towards the eye or (very gently) touch each eyelid. Normally the pupils in each eye contract if you shine a bright light into the eye. If a dog has a broken leg and no pinch withdrawal reflex, then there is the possibility of incidental nerve damage (which need not necessarily be permanent), and if this is the case you will need to take greater care in transporting the dog to the veterinary surgery. Similarly the immediate absence of ocular (eye) reflexes could indicate the dog has sustained a head injury, and depending on how soon these reflexes return, whether or not it is likely to have any lasting effect.

This brief examination will take a matter of seconds, but will tell you immediately whether or not your dog's condition is potentially more serious, and then you can decide if immediate first aid or more urgent veterinary attention is required.

LAMENESS

If the dog is lame, look carefully at the way it's walking: which leg is it favouring, and is it able to weight bear, or is it holding up a paw? Then think where the cause of its lameness might lie. You can then start to examine the most appropriate area to see where it hurts, and what might be the cause. A dog will generally avoid putting a painful foot to the ground. A dog bearing some weight on a limb but 'favouring' that leg as it walks is more likely to have suffered a shoulder or elbow injury, or in a hind limb, a hip or stifle injury. Remember these are generalities, to help locate the problem, not hard and fast rules.

To examine a paw, always make sure you have good light, especially if you think the dog has something like a thorn or sliver of glass in the paw. Try to locate any 'seat of pain' by gently squeezing each pad in turn and gauging the dog's reaction. If a dog immediately withdraws its foot, then you can assume you have located the affected pad and can begin a more thorough search.

Sprains and strains are more difficult; it's often the case that we assume the dog has sustained a sprain or strained a muscle when all other possibilities have been eliminated. Try to flex and extend each joint in turn. You can usually feel the dog 'flinch' and/or 'stiffen up' when you move the joint that's most painful – but of course, it's difficult to flex one joint without moving another associated joint, because most are linked and move together by muscles and tendons, and you have to bear in mind that some dogs, and certainly some breeds like Labradors and Golden Retrievers, can be extremely stoical.

CUTS AND LACERATIONS

These are probably the most common types of injury that we have to deal with in the field, typically presenting as a dog that either returns with blood on its coat or is seen to be limping or holding up one foot.

Blood on a dog's coat will often make the injury appear much worse than it actually is, especially if it has injured its tail or cut its ear – in this case, after wagging its tail or shaking its head, blood splattering from even a small wound can make it look as if it is covered in blood. However, if it is, first of all, don't panic. Calm the dog using soft, soothing commands in a reassuring voice; muzzle it if necessary, and if possible get someone to hold and gently restrain it whilst you try to determine the nature of its injury.

ASSESSING THE WOUND

Carefully examine the affected area by gently parting the hair where the blood appears to be coming from until you find the wound. Wetting the coat will usually make it easier to part the hair and see the skin. If the wound is bleeding, assess by how much. Dab clean absorbent material, a gauze pad from the first aid kit if possible, on the wound to absorb the blood, then remove it and see how quickly the wound refills.

How readily a wound stops bleeding will depend largely on whether the injury involves either an artery or, more commonly, seepage from a vein or veins. Arteries are the vessels that carry oxygenated blood from the heart to the organs and tissues around the body. Veins are the vessels that convey blood back to the heart. Consequently, arterial blood is bright red and is seen to 'pump' or spurt from the wound, as it will be under greater pressure from the heart. Venous blood is darker, and because it is under lower pressure, tends to ooze from the wound. Unless a major artery is involved, bleeding will usually stop relatively quickly once the blood starts to clot; generally, however, blood from a severed artery needs more immediate, direct attention to encourage it to clot. Unless there is severe haemorrhage, puncture wounds are best left to bleed until your vet can decide how best to treat the injury.

STOPPING BLEEDING

Try to stop any arterial bleeding by applying pressure: literally put your finger where the blood appears to be coming from, and hold it there. If the bleeding stops, continue to apply that local pressure; if it doesn't, adjust the position of your finger until it does. After several minutes release the pressure slightly; if there is no further bleeding, or substantially less, all is well and you can continue to bandage the wound.

If digital pressure is unsuccessful, you might try again, or use a firmly applied 'pressure' bandage. If the bleeding looks to be severe, apply a tourniquet (see below) and seek urgent veterinary attention. Once the bleeding is under control you can apply a bandage. If you find it difficult to control the bleeding a 'pressure' bandage can be applied; when it is later removed the wound should be much dryer, and can be cleaned up and a clean dressing applied.

Wounds from barbed wire can be quite extensive, and tend to be more severe because the wire often tears as well as penetrates, causing skin damage and the potential risk of infection. However, with good shoot management, appropriate training and intelligent handling, the risk of injuries from barbed wire can be significantly reduced.

TREATING OPEN WOUNDS

As far as treatment is concerned, open wounds can be broadly characterized as abrasions, incised wounds, lacerated wounds and puncture wounds; recognizing and assessing each type of injury is necessary in order to determine the most appropriate form of first aid treatment required.

Abrasions

Abrasions are superficial grazes that don't penetrate the full thickness of the skin, and consequently there can be little bleeding. However, depending on the cause, these wounds can be quite extensive and tend to be painful. They often result from accidents where the affected skin is dragged along the ground, so a dog that lands awkwardly and stumbles on stony ground or on to a road surface will often suffer abrasions. Abraded wounds are often contaminated and there can be the risk of infection, so they are best cleaned and covered with an antiseptic wound dressing, and then either left open if there is little risk of further injury or infection, or else covered with a protective bandage.

Incised Wounds

Incised wounds are cuts to the skin following contact with a sharp object, such as a shard of glass, a flint, or a sharp metallic object. Barbed-wire tears can also be incised wounds. The skin edges are clean cut and usually gape. The skin is penetrated to its full thickness, and the wound usually bleeds freely from severed blood vessels. Superficial wounds are best bandaged in the first instance, and small incised wounds will often require no more than treatment with antiseptic wound powder and suitable bandaging until they can be left open to heal naturally.

Larger incisions will require bandaging until you can get the dog to a vet, who will decide whether or not to suture the wound. If the wound is deep, then depending on the site of the wound there may be the risk of further damage to underlying structures such as nerves and tendons. Any deep incised wound should be bandaged to help stop bleeding and to keep the area clean until the dog can receive appropriate veterinary treatment.

Lacerations

Lacerations are the most common type of injury. The wounds are irregular in shape with jagged edges. The edges tend to gape because the skin has been torn apart, and in certain circumstances some skin may have been lost. The severity of these wounds depends on how deeply the wound has penetrated; it is not uncommon to see muscle exposed, and occasionally, particularly if the wound is the result of a road accident, it may be deep enough to affect tendons, ligaments and the more superficial bones, for instance those of the foot. Surprising as it may seem, there is often relatively little bleeding because the ragged tearing of the injury causes an elastic recoil in any affected blood vessels, and this invokes a natural healing process to limit blood loss. If the wound is contaminated from ingrained dirt then there will be the risk of infection.

Dogs can impale themselves whilst jumping fallen trees and broken branches, causing potentially serious injuries. When picking up, always consider how your dog will return from retrieving game, and wherever possible try to position yourself so your dog avoids such hazards.

Abrasions and other superficial wounds heal by a process called 'granulation', where the wound heals naturally as new skin grows in from the sides and bottom of the injury. Some scarring will be inevitable, but such scars usually shrink in time and hair will grow over so little permanent damage is visible.

Larger abrasions, particularly those resulting from road accidents, will usually require surgery. First aid treatment should be directed towards cleaning up the wound in the first instance, then drying the area before applying antiseptic wound powder and a protective dressing. Flush away any obvious contaminating dirt and detritus using plenty of clean water or ideally saline; try to avoid using water from streams and ponds unless absolutely necessary. Dab the wound dry, then apply an antiseptic, either as a powder or ointment, and a clean dressing that will protect

the area and prevent the dog licking the injury until it can be left open to heal naturally.

Puncture Wounds

Puncture wounds result from penetrating blows from sharp objects and bites from other animals (wounded ground game and squirrels can inflict quite nasty bites), but will also include wounds from stakes, thorns and fish hooks. Airgun pellets and shot will cause puncture wounds. The actual skin wound is usually small but leads into a long, narrow track of damaged tissue that penetrates deep into the underlying tissue. Puncture wounds commonly become infected because bacteria will be carried deep into the wound along with the offending item. The skin wound often heals quite rapidly, leaving this infection trapped in the underlying tissues, where an abscess can form.

Puncture wounds invariably require veterinary treatment, but in many cases simple preliminary measures can reduce the subsequent risks. As has been previously described, puncture wounds are best left open to bleed; this encourages and enables the body's inherent defence mechanisms to access the area, dissipate any toxins and start to overcome infection. Depending on the cause of the injury, puncture wounds can be extremely painful, so take care not to get bitten, and be on the lookout for any signs of shock, especially if the dog has been shot (the signs of shock and its immediate treatment are described in the section on road traffic accidents).

TORN TOE NAILS

Occasionally a dog may go extremely lame, and be unwilling to put the foot to the ground: upon examination it will be seen to have broken a claw. These injuries can be extremely painful, so take care not to get bitten.

Put on a muzzle – even the most placid dog is likely to react when you try to examine and treat these injuries. If the torn claw is obviously detached and hanging off, grasp the detached portion firmly with pliers, and with a quick, sharp tug, pull it off. Apply antiseptic powder or ointment, gently, to the exposed toe. The dog should then be substantially more comfortable and you can bandage the foot, as described in the section 'Bandaging' below.

TENDON INJURIES

The tendons we are particularly concerned about with respect to cuts and lacerations are the white bands of fibrous material that connect muscles to bones, and particularly those that act on joints. These tendons serve to transfer muscle action to a more remote site and/or focus its force. As you can appreciate, if such tendons are injured, and particularly if they are cut through, the consequences can be much more serious than the skin wound itself might at first indicate.

Injuries to be most aware of with respect to tendon injury are those above the dog's forefoot, and especially behind the carpus (the dog's wrist), and in similar locations on the hind leg:

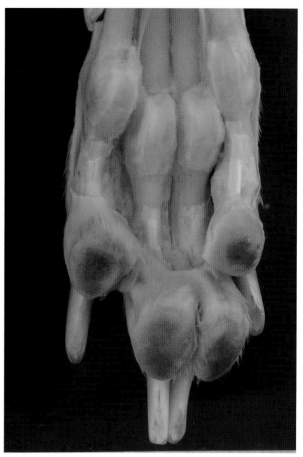

The superficial tendons beneath the foot. Deep wounds affecting the soft fleshy part of the foot above the pads risk severing these tendons.

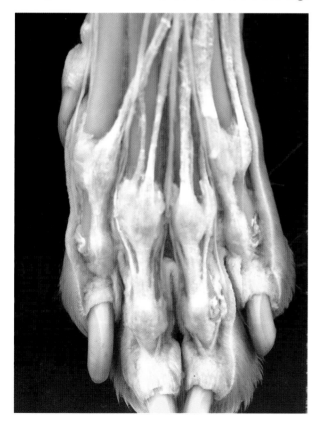

An anatomical specimen illustrating the superficial tendons that lie on top of the toes.

behind the hind foot, and above and behind the tarsus (the hock). Because these tendons transfer forces from muscles much higher up the leg, and because in many instances they focus the power of those muscles, cuts and injuries can cause irrevocable damage and can cause the dog to be lame for the rest of its life.

Gross damage, where the tendon is severed, is normally fairly obvious because, as well as sustaining a wound, the dog is seen to over-extend the foot, wrist or hock, whichever is affected by the action of the respective injured tendon. In extreme cases the dog won't be able to flex the foot, and consequently will walk on its wrist or hock rather than its toes.

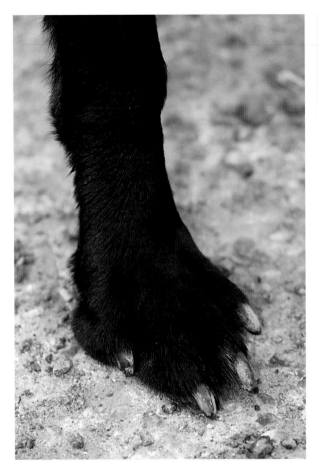

An overextended carpus. This dog has sustained an injury to the deep flexor tendons beneath the forefoot, causing the toes to drop, level with the ground, when weight bearing.

The same dog illustrating the effect of a tendon injury, comparing the affected right foot, nearest the camera, with the unaffected left leg.

Whilst gross injuries may be immediately obvious, more frustrating for a dog's owner are the relatively small skin wounds that betray the fact that underlying tendons have been partially severed. Due to the mechanical forces involved, the injury causes the tendon to stretch as those fibres that are still intact take the full direct power of the muscles pulling above. The result will be similar to gross injuries, but the signs are not immediately obvious. The skin wound will heal, but the dog becomes progressively lamer until it cannot take full weight on the leg, during which time the damage will have become increasingly obvious.

Gross lacerations, where the tendon has been severed, require immediate surgery to attempt repair of the affected tendon. The more insidious onset of lameness can be more difficult to treat. Recent injuries can be supported with a splint or plaster to flex the foot and extend the wrist or hock (depending on whether it is the fore or hind leg affected) whilst the injury heals. Longer lasting injuries may require investigative surgery to try to identify where the tendons have been damaged, and to attempt a successful repair.

The sooner surgery is performed following injury, and how effectively the dog can be rested – often this will be for many weeks/months following surgery – the better the prognosis (the ultimate outcome). It will also depend to some extent on how heavy the dog is, and consequently how much force is normally exerted on the tendons even when just standing.

It is best to have any injury in these particular areas assessed by a vet, and to continue to check the dog for a week or so afterwards to assure yourself that there is no underlying tendon damage if your dog sustains a wound in an area involving a superficial tendon.

EYE INJURIES

Check your dog's eyes regularly, as they can be prone to injury, particularly when the dog is worked in dense covert, and exercised in the summer and early autumn through long grass or heather, and in dry, dusty conditions. Examine the conjunctiva (the 'white' of the eye and the lining inside the eyelids): if the conjunctiva of one eye is reddened, the problem is likely to be confined to that one eye. Blood can collect under the conjunctiva – for instance, if the dog receives an injury to the eye. If the conjunctiva is reddened in both eyes, the problem may be more 'systemic', perhaps an infectious conjunctivitis, an allergic response, or even a sign of some other disease. In such circumstances it is wiser to seek veterinary attention than to try and identify the cause yourself.

Look for the presence of any excessive discharge or any pus in the conjunctival sac – the area exposed when you pull back the eyelid. Check that the cornea (the front of the eyeball) is clear and not cloudy.

Ocular foreign bodies: An excessive watery discharge in one eye may indicate that the dog has something in its eye, particularly if it appears to be irritating. Stop the dog scratching or pawing its eye. Pull back the eyelid and look for any obvious cause. If you find foreign material in the conjunctival sac and it can be easily removed by washing the eye with clean, fresh water or a proprietary eye wash, then do so. However, never attempt to do more than wash out the eye, or flick some superficial item out of the eye with a small piece of cotton wool soaked in water, oth-

erwise you may risk causing further damage to the eye. Take the dog to a vet, who can carry out a more thorough examination, and if necessary, apply a local anaesthetic to the eye before attempting to remove any foreign body.

Wounds to the Eyelids

Wounds to the eyelids require a special mention. Examine around the eyelids for small wounds. Skin wounds around the eyes usually heal quite quickly and are best left untreated, though if you wish to keep working the dog, then it is useful to apply a little Vaseline or clear petroleum jelly just to protect the wound and keep it from becoming further contaminated. A cut that affects the eyelid, however, may require suturing, particularly if it is a gaping wound, and especially if it is the lower lid. This is because such a wound can act as a gutter for tears to flow through, and this constant trickle prevents the edges from closing and healing properly.

A reasonable course of action to take would be to protect the wound from further contamination by smearing a little petroleum jelly or Vaseline on it immediately after it has occurred, and then have it checked by your vet at the earliest opportunity. A vet can assess whether or not the wound warrants stitching, he will examine the eye itself to ensure there is no sign of further injury, and typically will prescribe an antibiotic eye ointment to treat or prevent infection.

WOUNDS TO THE EARS

Wounds to any part of the ear, especially the tip, will bleed profusely, so rather than waste time locating the wound immediately, it is sometimes easier to simply apply a bandage, then clean up the dog and locate the wound later, once the bleeding stops and the dog has calmed down.

BANDAGING

For the purpose of first aid the function of a bandage is to stop initial bleeding, or control bleeding until professional help is available, and to prevent the wound from becoming further contaminated. Bandaging is a relatively simple procedure that many people seem to get wrong, sometimes with unfortunate effects if the bandage is applied too tightly and the blood supply to the area is constricted. Only apply a bandage if absolutely essential, and do not leave your bandage in situ for longer than two to three hours.

A Cocker Spaniel continues working with its foot bandaged. In this instance the bandage has been covered with waterproof tape. Ideally the dressing would continue further up the leg, making it more secure and helping to prevent the bandage from slipping off.

BANDAGING A FOOT

Even though it may be only a small wound affecting one pad that needs attention, always apply a bandage that goes further up the leg, don't just bandage the foot – this will help prevent the bandage slipping off. If you are treating a wound further up the leg it is often useful to include the foot.

- Never apply a bandage too tightly, and always apply padding under a bandage. Wrap cotton wool or a soft crêpe bandage up the leg first, and then cover this padding with your bandage
- If a bandage is too tight or if it slips down the leg, blood circulation can be impeded. Tissues starved of vital blood will become damaged, and at worst the foot may have to be amputated

The manner in which a foot may be bandaged is described in the steps below and illustrated in the following series of photographs:

- Start the dressing by trapping the end of a soft cotton bandage between the dog's leg and a finger held underneath the dog's leg. Bring the bandage down underneath the foot, over the foot and then up the leg, where you trap it under your thumb

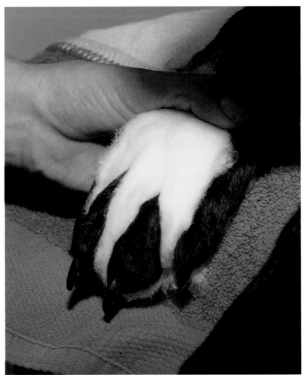

Start by placing small pieces of cotton wool between each of the pads (this can be omitted in an emergency if the dressing is only to be temporary).

- Keeping your finger and thumb in position, take the bandage back down, under the foot and up under the leg to where you started
- Make a half twist in the bandage, and then wrap the bandage around the leg; you can then release your finger and thumb
- Holding the leg at the top of the bandage, continue wrapping the soft bandage down towards the foot, in firm (but not tight) overlapping turns, and then back up again to where you started

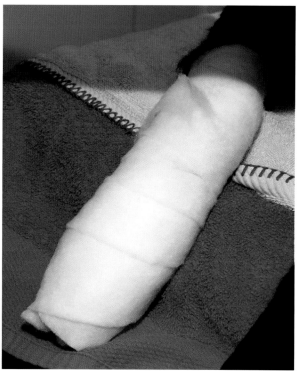

The initial soft cotton layer is completed.

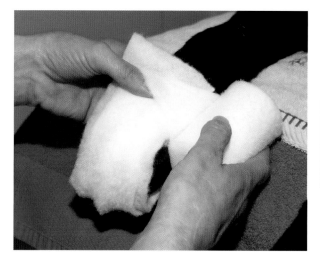

Making a half twist before wrapping the bandage around the leg.

- Next cover the soft cotton layer with an open weave bandage. If necessary secure the top of the bandage with a strip of sticking plaster

The first turns of the soft cotton bandage complete before starting to continue further up the leg.

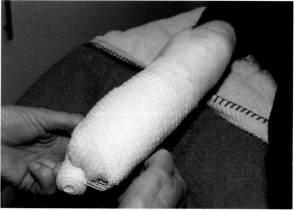

A cotton weave bandage is next applied over the soft cotton layer.

- Finally protect the bandage with either Vetrap or an Elastoplast bandage. Apply this similarly but as a single layer. First wrap this over (not around) the foot. Then apply overlapping turns of bandage up, over and beyond the cotton bandage

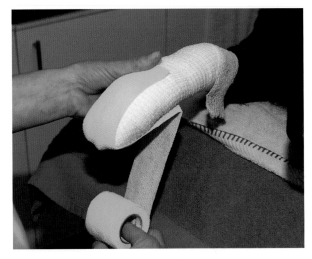

The bandage is covered with Vetrap or similar self-adhesive bandage. This secures and helps further protect the bandage. If it gets dirty, this layer can be removed and replaced with a fresh layer of Vetrap or similar material.

The completed dressing.

BANDAGING A TAIL

Bandaging a dog's tail is essentially similar to bandaging the foot (see illustration). However, it is often the tip of the tail that is injured, and it is difficult to bandage just the end of a dog's tail because as soon as the dog wags its tail, it simply dislodges your bandage!

- If the tip is bleeding, apply a cotton bandage or gauze pad to cover the wound, and then use Elastoplast, which will adhere to the hair, to bandage the tail
- In longer coated dogs, you can trap tail feathering within the overlapping turns of your bandage; this will help to prevent it slipping down off the tail

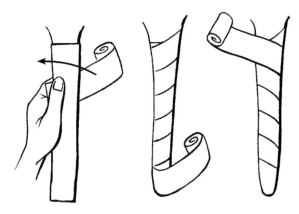

How to bandage a tail.

You may have to keep the tail bandaged until the wounds start to heal, which may take about five to seven days (sometimes longer), otherwise the exposed wounds are likely to be knocked and start bleeding again.

Try not to work the dog in covert until the tail is completely healed. Many undocked dogs that repeatedly 'injure their tail' are usually injuring partly healed scar tissue that is more prone to damage and will subsequently take longer than skin to heal properly.

A typical lacerated tail injury.

'TORN' DEW CLAWS

Normally small tears around the dew claw go unnoticed, and the only hint that something may be wrong is that the dog keeps licking the area. Severe tears in the dew claw are much more noticeable and can bleed quite a lot. Apply direct (digital) pressure to stop most of the bleeding. Usually treating a torn dew claw is simply a matter of taping it down until it heals.

- Put cotton-wool padding between the dew claw and the leg, change the bandage often (after the first twenty-four hours, then every two to three days), and apply antiseptic powder each time
- If the wound becomes infected (usually a wound that is slow to heal and inflamed, or when there is any sign of pus in or from the wound), always seek veterinary advice
- Don't apply the bandage too tightly or it will impair blood supply to the foot. If the foot swells, remove the bandage immediately and reapply a looser, plain cotton bandage

Don't be surprised if the dog limps quite badly after damaging a dew claw. These injuries are quite painful, but if you are concerned seek veterinary attention because your vet may wish to prescribe a pain killer or advise an alternative line of treatment.

BANDAGING AN EAR

Ear wounds tend to bleed profusely and often appear worse than they really are because the dog inevitably shakes its head and blood splashes the surrounding coat. Bandaging the ear on top of the head, as shown in the diagram [below], will encourage the wound to stop bleeding.

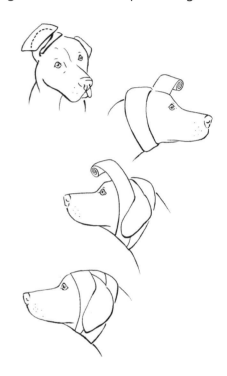

How to bandage an ear.

- Apply some antiseptic powder to the wound before you apply the dressings
- Apply a gauze pad to the top of and beneath the ear flap; this will cushion the ear whilst it is strapped up, and helps to absorb any blood until the wound stops bleeding
- Use a soft, pliable, cotton crêpe bandage whenever possible, which will tend to 'mould' itself to the contours of the head and neck more easily than a stiffer, plain cotton bandage
- Start by wrapping the bandage diagonally across the head, so that it goes down, and comes back up on each side of the head in front of and behind the left and the right ear in a figure-of-eight fashion

- Finally, apply an Elastoplast dressing that will stick to the hair in front of and behind the previously applied bandage

Don't apply the bandage too tightly: make sure you can pass two fingers easily under the bandage, but do make sure the bandage can't unwrap. Remove the bandage after twelve to twenty-four hours when any bleeding should have stopped, and you can continue to clean up the dog. If the ear starts to bleed again, reapply a bandage and seek veterinary attention, as the wound may require suturing (stitching).

If subsequently the ear starts to swell, there may be blood collecting in what is known as an 'aural haematoma' and your dog should be seen by a vet.

REMOVING A BANDAGE

Vetrap bandage adheres to itself and can easily be unwrapped; other types of bandage, such as Elastoplast, may have to be cut off. Always use scissors with at least one 'blunt', round-ended blade, and hold the scissors as shown in the illustration: use your forefinger to 'control' the scissors by placing it on the joint of the blades, and open and close the blades using your thumb and another finger.

- First slide the scissors, blades closed, under the bandage. Open the blades as far as you can, and withdraw the scissors. This creates a 'tunnel' between the bandage and the underlying skin. Never try to cut off a bandage without first making the 'tunnel' so you are certain where the scissor blades are cutting
- Then slide the blunt blade into the 'tunnel' you have created and cut the bandage
- Repeat as necessary until the bandage can be gently removed

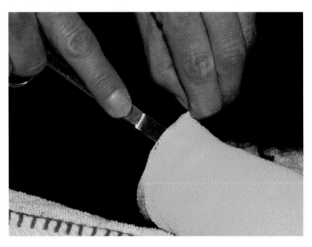

When removing a bandage, first insert the scissors with the blades closed.

The correct way to hold surgical scissors.

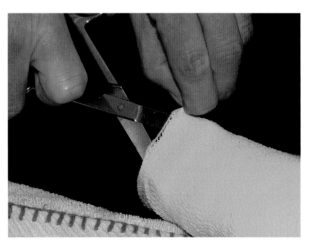

Opening the blades creates a clear space between the dressing and the skin.

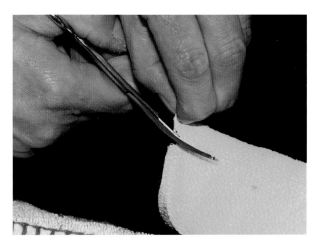

A blunt-ended blade can then be inserted to start cutting the bandage.

How to apply a tourniquet.

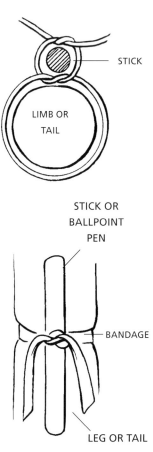

APPLYING A TOURNIQUET

A tourniquet stops bleeding by constricting the arteries supplying blood to a wound on a leg or tail. As a tourniquet restricts blood supply to the affected region of the body it must only be used where there is severe bleeding that cannot be stopped by any other means.

- In an emergency the tail or leg can be held tightly by hand, but usually an elastic band or a length of strong bandage is used. String or rope is not a good material to use as it digs in and can cause damage and subsequent irritation
- Wrap the material around the leg or tail just above the wound – that is, nearest the body – and then around a stick, ball-point pen or anything similar that you can then use to wind, and hence tighten, the tourniquet
- Tighten the tourniquet by turning the stick
- Once the bleeding stops or is substantially less, maintain the tourniquet and apply a firm 'pressure' bandage to the wound: only then slacken off the tourniquet. Sometimes a small roll of bandage placed over the point of bleeding and then covering with the bandage can provide local pressure to help stop further bleeding under the bandage

If it is necessary to apply and maintain the tourniquet whilst the dog is taken to a veterinary surgery, be sure to slacken the tourniquet periodically at ten- to fifteen-minute intervals to allow blood to circulate before reapplying pressure.

PENETRATING INJURIES AND OBJECTS

Objects that cause penetrating injuries, and other deep puncture wounds, will invariably require veterinary attention as there is, at the very least, a risk of infection. Barbed wire can tear as well as penetrate skin, causing quite severe wounds.

- First aid measures will aim towards containing (but not necessarily immediately stopping) any bleeding and making the dog as comfortable as possible whilst it is taken to the veterinary surgery

87

- If the object is still in situ, don't try to remove it. Sticks and small branches can penetrate quite deeply and might be lying in the vicinity of a major blood vessel or vital internal organ. If you attempt to remove the object, there is risk of causing more damage, major haemorrhage or internal injuries. The other concern is that a part may break off in the attempt to remove it, leaving the remainder deep in the wound where it is more difficult to locate later
- If the skin is torn, wash the wound, using saline if possible; for emergency purposes mix a little household salt and water. Fold any flap of skin back into position, apply gauze swabs soaked in saline to the wound, and secure with a light bandage to contain any bleeding

Some penetrating wounds may result in the skin being torn away from the underlying body tissue whilst the skin itself remains relatively intact. This type of injury is most commonly seen following dog fights, particularly the scruff of the neck where the dog has been shaken by its attacker, when all that can be seen afterwards are a few small puncture wounds. The space thus created under the skin will tend to fill with pus if the wound is infected, which often happens following bite wounds.

Similarly the wound will be slow to heal if the space fills with blood or fluid from the traumatized tissues. The wound has to heal from the bottom up, with the space under the skin filling with granulation tissue. This can't happen if the wound is filled with pus, blood or serum, however the wound will heal rapidly once it is drained and the infection controlled, since all that is then left are the small superficial puncture wounds. You may not feel you need to take the dog to a vet immediately, but do check the wound afterwards, and if you can feel fluid under the skin then it is best to have it checked in case it has to be drained.

If a wounded leg or tail bleeds profusely and it is difficult to stop the bleeding using any of the methods previously described, then you will need to apply a tourniquet to quench the bleeding whilst the dog is taken to a vet for further attention. Blood loss from open wounds on other parts of the body can't be treated with a tourniquet, and in such cases all you can do is apply and maintain pressure to the wound.

GRASS SEEDS AND BURRS

Dense-coated dogs, particularly spaniels with their pendulous feathered ears, are prone to getting foreign material in their ears, causing irritation and chronic infection. Both grass seeds and burrs are a problem when working your dog early in the season or when exercising it in long grass and hedgerows during late summer and early autumn. Burrs will cause the hair to matt up, and grass awns have a habit of migrating either into the skin or into the ear. Prevention is always better than cure, albeit not always totally effective. Clipping the hair from under the ear helps, as does regular cleansing, and your vet or

A working English Springer Spaniel, after emerging from dense covert.

Grass awns.

veterinary nurse will usually be willing to show you how best to do this.

Grass awns (the spiky seeds found especially in long grass during the summer months) can easily slide down the ear canal, and because they have long, backward-projecting 'hairs' attached to the seed case, they are not easy to remove. Furthermore grass seeds are sharply pointed and can penetrate skin, the lining of the ear canal, and even the ear drum. They often cause intense irritation, so the dog will suddenly start shaking its head in distress, and once they descend into the ear canal they become difficult to extract without using suitable equipment. If the ear is left untreated, chronic infection can become established. It is therefore advisable to seek veterinary attention, particularly if your dog becomes distressed by the intense irritation these particles can sometimes cause.

Remember that grass awns don't just penetrate a dog's ears – they can just as readily penetrate between the toes, and they can also irritate the eyes and become lodged behind the 'third eyelid', where they can damage the cornea (the transparent front of the eyeball).

Always remove burrs as soon as you see them, and later comb out the hair both over and under the ears to make sure there are no bits that you have missed that can later find their way into the dog's ear canal. These matted burrs become very difficult to tease out, and often the only way to remove them is to carefully cut off the clumps of matted hair.

Picking burrs from a spaniel's ear.

STINGS AND BITES

NETTLES AND INSECT BITES

Nettle stings and insect bites can cause significant irritation, though to what extent does depend on the sensitivity and subsequent response of individual dogs. Irritation and sensitivity tends to be greatest where the dog's skin is less protected by hair, therefore on the muzzle, abdomen and between the legs. If a dog becomes severely distressed, use one of the many proprietary human skin creams that contain an 'antihistamine' – for example 'Antisan' cream, which contains mepyramine. This is most effective when applied as soon as possible to the affected area, so if you have a sensitive dog and you are working in an area where nettles are common, or there are likely to be insects about, it may be wise to carry a tube of antihistamine cream.

Here, stinging nettles grow in dense clumps, but are routinely cleared from the corners of this covert at the beginning of the season.

In a mild autumn new growth can spring up rapidly, and the ground soon becomes covered with small nettle plants.

'Nettle foot': this spaniel is frequently stopping to lick its feet after running through nettles. Low-growing young plants seem to cause particularly intense irritation.

TICKS

When you attempt to remove ticks, always try to avoid squeezing the body, because this can cause the tick to regurgitate and increases the risk of transmitting Lyme disease. It is better to use specially developed tools, which, properly applied, can remove the tick intact. The head and mouthparts of a tick are covered in backward-projecting hairs that help secure it in the host's skin. These tools twist the tick, which tends to release these hairs, making the tick easier to remove. Alternatively use the 'tick pen', a small 'lasso' that is slipped over the body of the tick, drawn down close to the skin and tightened, and the head and body of the tick can then be withdrawn from the skin.

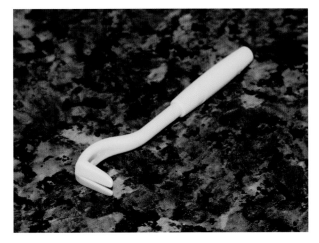

A typical type of instrument used to remove ticks. The forks are slipped between the body of the tick and the skin, and the instrument is twisted to withdraw the tick.

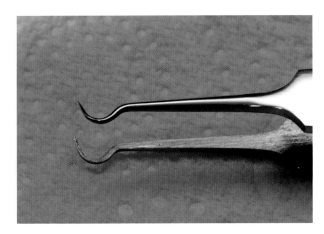

Alternatively the tick can be grasped between its head and body using these special tweezers. Again, the insect should first be twisted, to help loosen the mouth parts, before being removed.

SNAKE BITES

We have just one species of venomous snake in the UK, the European adder (*Vipera berus*), although there are two other non-venomous species that are frequently mistaken for adders by concerned owners. The slow worm (*Anguis fragilis*) is a limbless reptile more closely related to a lizard than any snake, and can be confused with the adder, although its colouring, silvery-gold with black longitudinal markings, is quite distinctively different.

Adders have a relatively localized distribution. They are timid and secretive, and rarely strike unless provoked; most adder bites are a defensive response, when the dog disturbs the snake out of curiosity, or simply unintentionally steps on it, especially in the spring and summer when the snakes are more active – they can sometimes be spotted basking in the sun.

Adult adders are around 50–60cm long, and can be identified by the black/brown zigzag pattern along their back and the V-shaped marking on the back of the head. They are commonly found on dry sandy heaths, sand dunes, rocky hillsides, moorland, and woodland edges, particularly in the south of Britain.

Adders can be distinguished from the common grass snake (*Natix natix*) by size and colour: the grass snake is larger, around 90cm in length, and is metallic green, studded with black markings. It generally prefers damp habitats, and normally lives near water (it can swim); however, it can also be found in hedgerows, on heaths and in other drier areas.

*The European adder (*Vipera berus*). Note the characteristic black/brown zigzag pattern along its back, and the V-shaped marking on the back of the head.* LAURIE CAMPBELL

Smooth snakes (*Coronella austriaca*) are relatively uncommon, and are found only in southern England; they live near water at the edges of woods and on heaths. Smooth snakes are a similar size to adders, although some individuals can be larger. These snakes have smooth, glossy scales, giving the snake its name, and are usually brown, reddish-brown or grey in colour, with a series of small dark spots or blotches extending down the length of the back and tail; some more heavily patterned individuals may be mistaken for an adder.

In summary, the main features distinguishing venomous and non-venomous snakes in the UK are these:

- The adder has a distinctive zig-zag pattern of dark markings along its back, and a V-shaped marking on the head
- The smooth snake is far less common with soft, smooth scales, and although of similar size and colour, it lacks the adder's distinctive markings
- The grass snake is larger in size and prefers a damp habitat

Adder bites result in local swelling that is often dark in colour, and can become severe. You may be able to see two small puncture wounds in the centre of the swelling. Bites most commonly occur on a dog's legs or face. Your dog will show signs of pain, and may appear nervous. Other signs include pale gums and lips, bruising, salivation/dribbling, vomiting, diarrhoea, restlessness, and then drowsiness and lethargy. Eventually animals may collapse, have blood-clotting problems, tremors or convulsions. Bites on or around the face can lead to swelling of the face and muzzle, which may result in breathing difficulties.

The appropriate action to take if a dog sustains a snake strike is as follows:

- Calm your dog and try to keep it as still as possible; this will help minimize the venom spreading further around the body
- Carry your dog (rather than allowing it to walk)

- Bathe the wound in cold water to help control the swelling
- Seek veterinary attention quickly. Try to get to the closest practice, as they will have more experience in dealing with adder bites, being in an area inhabited by adders, and will be more likely to stock anti-venom

Typically the vet will provide pain relief, will treat any swelling and shock, and if appropriate, will administer anti-venom.

ROAD VEHICLE ACCIDENTS

There is always a chance of an accident when shoot vehicles are about, or you are working your dog in the beating line or picking up near a road. Be aware that many dogs will choose to lie under a parked vehicle or trailer, so be particularly vigilant before moving off, especially after lunch when someone's dog may remain sound asleep under a vehicle, unaware of the fact that it is about to move. Such incidents are extremely distressing for all concerned, and unfortunately, they can happen all too easily.

Being involved in, or witnessing a road accident involving a dog is very frightening and upsetting, but if you can stay calm and remember the following basic points, you may well save a dog's life or prevent it from further serious injury.

- **Stay calm:** Not only for your own sake but for the sake of your dog. The actions you take in the first few minutes can make all the difference
- **Prevent the situation deteriorating:** By ensuring that you, the dog, and other people are safe. Have someone stop any traffic, and have it remain stationary until the dog is safely restrained. Ideally have another person go further up the road to warn oncoming traffic of the potential hazard
- **Use a temporary muzzle, if necessary:** Be aware that even the most placid dog will snap and try to bite out of fear and pain in these situations. If a muzzled dog looks as if it is about to vomit, remove the muzzle as quickly as possible to prevent it from choking

- **Get the dog out of harm's way:** This is the first priority at the accident scene. Protect any bleeding wounds with a clean cloth. Move the dog to the side of the road without risking further injury by dragging it as gently as possible off the road using the skin on the back of the neck; alternatively slide it gently on to a coat or towel, employing this like a stretcher
- **Avoid stressing the dog:** Any movement should be in a slow, calm, deliberate manner. Be gentle, and speak in a calm, soothing voice to the dog or when speaking to anyone in the vicinity
- **Notify a veterinary surgeon** of what has occurred, and that the animal will be on its way to them. Some veterinary surgeries can deploy a veterinary ambulance
- **Apply the ABC of first aid:** Check that the dog's airway is clear, that it is breathing, and that it has circulation – meaning a pulse or heartbeat. If there is no pulse or breathing, commence CPR – this is the equivalent of mouth-to-mouth resuscitation, but in a dog's case it is mouth to nose. You make a seal around the dog's snout, closing the mouth and gently blow in the nostrils. Use one breath to every five chest compressions
- **Stop any bleeding:** Place clean cloths over the wounds where there are copious amounts of blood. Stop major bleeding by applying pressure with any clean fabric available. If you have a first aid kit, you can bandage the area
- **Stabilize broken bones:** If there is bone protruding from the wound, pack a clean cloth around the protruding bone and apply light pressure to the area to hold the cloth in place. If the dog is on its feet but seems to have a broken leg – if the leg appears misshapen, or the dog refuses to put weight on it, or it is hanging limp – immobilize the limb if you can by encouraging the dog to lie quietly on a stretcher whilst it is moved to a vehicle and taken to the vet. Don't attempt to move or splint broken bones: you are likely to do more damage and the movement will cause the dog pain
- **Treat for shock:** The dog will probably appear weak and disoriented, its gums will be pale and its paws will feel cold to the touch, and its breathing may be rapid and shallow. At this point, try to keep the dog calm, still and warm. Put a coat or blanket under and over the dog to keep it warm and to prevent any further heat loss. On no account give it fluids because it will need surgery
- **Transfer the dog to a vet:** Getting the dog to veterinary care as quickly as possible will ensure it has the best chance of survival

The key is to move the animal as little as possible. Try to find something rigid that can be used like a stretcher. Use a board, or make a stretcher out of a blanket or something similar; most people with dogs will have items in their car that can be utilized for the purpose. Keep the animal warm, and be aware that internal and spinal injuries are not always self-evident.

SHOOTING INCIDENTS

If a dog is shot, treat the situation in the same way that you would for a road accident. Unless the dog has sustained a fatal wound to a vital organ, shock and blood loss will be the greatest concern, so treat the victim accordingly, phone ahead so the vet can prepare to receive the patient, and then transport it to the surgery.

FRACTURES

A fracture is a break in the continuity of bone – that is, a broken bone. Fragments are the pieces of bone that result from a fracture. Be aware that fractured bones don't always fragment, especially in young dogs that can suffer 'greenstick' fractures, where one side of the bone is broken whilst the other is simply bent. A greenstick fracture is extremely painful, and should never be overlooked as a possibility if a young dog remains very lame after suffering a seemingly simple accident.

Most fractures are fairly obvious and easily recognized. The limb is deformed and there is likely to be swelling at the fracture site. The dog will be lame – sometimes the limb is dysfunctional and the dog reluctant to move. If you feel (palpate) the swelling, you will often appreciate 'crepitus' – a dry, crackling sensation that is characteristic of the fragments of bone grating against each other. Crepitus is a sensation that is difficult to describe, but once felt will subsequently be instantly recognizable.

The pain associated with a fracture originates primarily from the outer fibrous tissue that surrounds the bone, called the periosteum. This tissue has a rich nerve supply, and if it is forcibly separated from the underlying bone, the pain will be intense. This explains why greenstick fractures are so painful, and why it is necessary to try to immobilize fractures when moving a dog for further treatment.

There may, of course, also be pain originating from other surrounding structures that, depending on the type of fracture, may or may not have been involved in the injury.

The different types of fracture are described as follows:

Simple: The bone is cleanly broken into two pieces

Compound: There is a wound between the skin and the fracture site

Complicated: Other important organs and tissues around the site are broken, such as nerves, blood vessels, the spinal cord or the lungs

Multiple: The bone is fractured in two or more places with an appreciable distance between the fracture sites

Comminuted: There are many fragments at the fracture site

First-aid treatment for a fracture is to minimize the movement of the fracture fragments. This will alleviate pain and prevent the situation deteriorating. Under no circumstances should you attempt to reset the limb or reduce the fracture.

If a vertebral fracture is suspected the dog must only be moved with extreme care. Keep the whole of the spine supported at all times, and avoid any twisting movements. This means the dog should not be turned over unless absolutely essential, and then only with the support and assistance of several people.

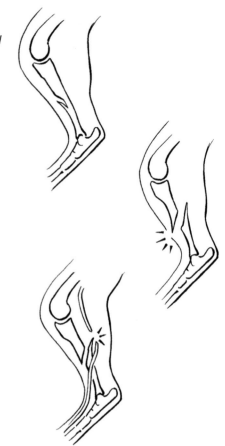

Simple, compound and complicated fractures

Once the fracture is immobilized, sharp fragments cannot cut into surrounding tissues and larger pieces of bone cannot jar into one another, causing the dog pain. The following is to be recommended:

- Handle the broken bone as little as possible
- Control haemorrhage for a compound fracture
- Support the fracture

Haemorrhage of a compound fracture is best controlled by applying a dressing. Avoid using digital pressure, or only apply pressure with care so as to avoid displacing fragments and causing further complications. Keep the dog still, warm and comfortable until professional help arrives, or, once it has calmed down, it will allow the leg to be splinted without struggling.

APPLYING A ROBERT JONES BANDAGE

- Cut two strips of 1in wide adhesive plaster, long enough to cover the foot below and including the 'wrist' (or below and including the hock in the hind limb), plus a couple of inches. Apply these strips longitudinally in front of, and behind, the wrist/hock, respectively and as appropriate
- Cover the entire length of the leg using a roll of cotton wool like a roller bandage
- Bandage the cotton wool firmly in place; ideally use white, open-weave bandage because this doesn't contract once applied, and there is less risk of restricting the blood supply to any part of the limb
- Fold the ends of the longitudinal strips that were previously applied upwards, over the bandage. This prevents the dressing slipping down the leg
- Bandage these strips in place using adhesive roller bandage applied over the open-weave bandage
- The toes are left open for observation: should they start to swell, the dressing will have been applied too tightly and should be removed and reapplied

Only support can really be provided for broken limbs. One of the most useful dressings for fractures of the elbow or stifle joints, or any bones below these joints, is the Robert Jones dressing. It consists of layers of cotton wool that are then bound tightly with rolls of bandage so that the cotton wool becomes compressed and almost rigid. Consequently it is effectively a soft dressing that conforms to the contours of the limb. It is difficult to apply too tightly, controls soft tissue swelling, and is well tolerated by most patients. Cotton wool is not always readily available in an emergency, so you may need to improvise using a suitable soft material that will cushion the injury and provide sufficient rigidity when compressed.

Another means of dressing a fracture is to simply bandage the affected part of the body firmly to an unaffected part of the body. In this way the shoulder, for instance, can be bandaged to the ribcage, or broken bones in the foot can be supported by the adjacent unbroken bones, by simply bandaging the foot. Such support will also significantly decrease the amount of swelling around the fracture. This makes any subsequent reduction necessary to set the fracture much easier for your vet, as well as minimizing the amount of pain experienced by the dog.

COLLAPSE

EXERCISE COLLAPSE

Occasionally a dog may either become rather wobbly and/or collapse during or immediately after strenuous exercise. Typically this affects the more excitable type of dog, for example a spaniel 'given its head' in the beating line, but a hard-worked retriever may also suffer these signs. The dog may either appear to be panting heavily, looking a little wobbly and 'spaced out', or it may simply appear to be getting progressively weaker, until it literally falls over. Be aware that if this occurs in a young retriever, especially one that collapses soon after being first worked early in its first season, or if it starts to show signs when strenuously exercised during training sessions, the problem, in the long term, may be more serious.

If a dog should collapse under these circumstances it is most likely to have become hypoglycaemic. This means its blood sugar levels have dropped, and it has literally used up its available energy and hasn't the time or the opportunity to call upon and mobilize its body's reserves. The dog needs to be treated accordingly: it needs an immediate source of sugar to boost its blood glucose levels, and then rest, or at least very gentle exercise for the rest of the day, so it has the opportunity to mobilize its energy reserves.

- First ensure the dog is able to breathe easily: maintain the airway by extending its head, and if necessary pulling out the tongue
- Give the dog some glucose or something similarly 'sugary'; ideally sprinkle glucose powder, or smear syrup or honey, on the lips, gums and under the tongue
- Keep the dog warm, particularly if it has collapsed and is lying on its side. Put something waterproof if possible under it if it is lying on cold ground: this is important to keep it from losing heat, as well as covering it over with something like a warm coat
- Once the dog has recovered, see if it will eat something sweet and sugary. If it is thirsty, let it drink – ideally this would be glucose mixed in water; otherwise try sugary tea, if it will take it

The first time a dog suffers this condition give it no further exercise until it has been checked over by a vet; be aware that some retriever breeds suffer a genetic, hereditary disease called 'exercise-induced collapse' (EIC). Thereafter most dogs can continue to be used, but you will need to take precautions in future to prevent your dog's blood-sugar levels dropping too low. Never work such dogs on an empty stomach: provide a light meal first thing in the morning, and carry some form of glucose with you in case of emergencies. Otherwise provide sweet titbits occasionally but throughout the working day, and make sure you give the dog a drink periodically so it can satisfy its thirst. Don't rely on it drinking from puddles (which is never to be recommended in case the water is contaminated).

HEAT STROKE

Dogs don't have sweat glands like humans, except for a few on their foot pads and on their noses, and again unlike humans, cannot lose body heat via the process of creating sweat and then losing it through evaporation from their bodies. When they become warm, they pant, exhaling overheated air and breathing in fresh, cool air in order to maintain and if necessary lower their internal core body temperature. Access to cooler fresh air is essential, and when a dog is confined to a small space in conditions of high temperature and humidity, it will begin to acquire heat more quickly than it is able to dissipate it by panting. Consequently its core body temperature rises, and if this continues to increase beyond 106°F (41°C), internal organ damage can occur. The causes of heat stroke include:

- Being left in a car in hot weather
- Exercising strenuously in hot, humid weather
- Being confined without shade and fresh water in hot weather, especially on concrete or asphalt surfaces

Once the core body temperature starts to rise, the progressive signs of heat stroke include the following:

- Heavy panting, difficulty breathing, and increased heart rate
- A bright red appearance to the tongue, lips and gums
- Drooling thick saliva, and often vomiting
- The rectal temperature rises to between 104° and 106°F (40° to 41.1°C)
- The dog becomes progressively unsteady on its feet, and may pass bloody diarrhoea
- Shock sets in, with the lips and mucous membranes turning pale and grey
- Finally collapse, seizures, coma and death rapidly ensue

Whilst dog owners are warned not to leave their dogs in cars in hot weather, few realize how easily heatstroke can occur, and remain uninformed of the other circumstances under which dogs can just as easily similarly suffer. Furthermore they are all too frequently warned of the danger, but not informed of what to do should the circumstance arise!

A dog that has collapsed through heat stroke requires immediate emergency treatment, and even if you only suspect that a dog is suffering from heat stroke, remove it from the hot environment and take it indoors to a cool room, preferably one with a tiled floor, or outdoors into fresh air and shade. Emergency measures to cool the dog must begin at once; these are as follows:

- If you can, take the dog's rectal temperature. Mild cases may be resolved by simply moving the dog into a cool environment, wetting the coat, and providing cool drinking water
- If the rectal temperature is above 103–104°F, begin rapid cooling by immersing the dog in a bath, or something similar, of cold water (not iced water), or spray the dog with a hose. If you can, place the wet dog in front of an electric fan
- Cool packs applied to the groin area may be helpful, as well as wiping the paws with cold water
- Monitor the rectal temperature every ten minutes, and continue the cooling process until it falls below 103°F (39°C)
- At this point, stop the cooling process and dry the dog
- Take the dog to a vet as soon as possible. Ring the surgery at the earliest opportunity, explain the situation, what first-aid treatment you are providing, and how the dog may be responding so that the surgery can advise further necessary treatment, and is prepared to receive the dog on arrival

With appropriate prompt attention, a dog's rising core body temperature can be lowered and restored relatively quickly, causing little, if any, lasting harm. Knowing how to deal with heatstroke when the emergency occurs in locations and under situations where veterinary assistance isn't immediately available, can potentially be life-saving.

POISONING

Virtually any substance can cause adverse effects if consumed in sufficient quantities, so we tend to classify as poisons those substances that, on ingestion, inhalation, absorption or injection through the skin in relatively small amounts, may cause structural damage of the body's tissues or

SOME SIGNS OF POISONING

Vomiting
Diarrhoea
Lethargy
Staggering
Lack of appetite
Bleeding
Mouth irritation, salivation, foaming of the mouth, gagging and drooling
Skin irritation and rash
Difficulty breathing, or panting
Muscle tremors or rigidity
Seizures
Effects on the heart – a rapid or a slow pulse
Coma and death

functional changes in organ systems. Although dogs can be poisoned in various ways, eating or drinking toxic materials is the most common. Dogs tend to be curious by nature, and will sniff and taste anything interesting, and their indiscriminate eating habits often lead to poisoning.

The other point to be aware of is that whilst there are many signs of poisoning (see panel above), few are specific, and the signs observed can be due to various causes and other diseases. Nevertheless some poisons do have characteristic signs.

POISONOUS SUBSTANCES

The poisonous agents most likely to be encountered by dogs in a rural environment are listed in the table below, along with an indication of the potential risk of exposure, the signs most commonly reported, and the time taken for those signs of poisoning to appear. The list is not exhaustive, since a more comprehensive coverage of canine toxic substances would be beyond the intended scope of this book – nevertheless this should serve as a quick guide as to what is poisonous, what should be avoided, and the signs to look out for if these more common agents are encountered.

Poisonous Agents and their Effects

Agent	Risk	Onset	Common Signs
Allium species (leek, garlic, spring onion), wild garlic, etc	AMBER	24 hours to several days	Inappetence, vomiting, abdominal discomfort and diarrhoea, anaemia
Bluebells	AMBER	Within a few hours	Vomiting and diarrhoea (may be bloody), abdominal discomfort, lethargy, depression, altered heart rate (either fast or slow)
Blue-green algae	RED	15–60 minutes	Variable: includes vomiting (including blood), tender abdomen, pale mucous membranes, weakness, ataxia, collapse, muscle tremors, convulsions, irregular heart rate, cyanosis and coma
Cannabis, marijuana	AMBER	Within 4 hours	Ataxia, weakness, diluted pupils, vomiting, drowsiness, incontinence, behavioural changes, hyperaesthesia
Carbamate insecticides	AMBER	Within 3 hours	Salivation, ataxia, diarrhoea, constricted pupils, muscle tremors, weakness, urinary incontinence, hyperaesthesia
Carbon monoxide	RED	Dependent on concentration and duration	Non-specific and variable: vomiting, depression, tremors, drowsiness, lethargy, anorexia, increased heart and respiratory rate, ataxia, mucous membranes bright red, or grey/cyanotic
Chocolate	AMBER	4–24 hours	Vomiting, abdominal tenderness, salivation, increased thirst and increased urinary output, excitability, increased heart rate, ataxia
Autumn crocus/meadow saffron	AMBER	Within 48 hours	Gastrointestinal irritation, lowered body temperature, weakness, dehydration, recumbency and collapse, shock secondary to gastric signs
Cotoneaster species	AMBER	4–6 hours	Salivation, vomiting, diarrhoea (including blood), lethargy, ataxia
Crocus species	AMBER	2–4 hours	Anorexia, vomiting, diarrhoea, abdominal pain
Diquat herbicides	AMBER	24 hours or longer	Ingestion: diarrhoea, vomiting, salivation, increased thirst, inappetence and abdominal discomfort in severe cases Skin: severe irritation, painful chemical burns
Ethanol, industrial methylated spirits, solvents and as a fuel	AMBER	1–2 hours	Vomiting, diarrhoea, excitability, agitation then depression, ataxia, vocalization and drowsiness

Agent	Risk	Onset	Common Signs
Ethylene glycol, antifreeze	RED	30 minutes–12 hours	*Stage 1:* 30 minutes–12 hours: Central nervous system signs of ataxia, weakness and convulsions *Stage 2:* 12–24 hours: Increased heart rate and respiratory signs. Then there may be signs of recovery, followed by convulsions and coma *Stage 3:* 24–72 hours: Renal signs of increased thirst and urinary output, leading to renal failure
Fertilizer	GREEN	2–10 hours	Vomiting, diarrhoea, abdominal tenderness, increased thirst, lethargy
Fungi	AMBER	Depends on species and syndrome. Gastrointestinal signs usually within 25–120 minutes	Dependent on species. Commonly, combinations of vomiting, diarrhoea, salivation, abdominal tenderness, ataxia twitching, convulsions, constricted or dilated pupils, depression, anxiety. Generally if signs develop within 6 hours outlook is favourable
Glyphosate herbicides	AMBER	30 minutes–12 hours	Initially gastric irritation (salivation, vomiting, diarrhoea), excitability, increased heart rate followed by ataxia, depression and decreased heart rate
Hyacinth	GREEN	Within a few hours	Vomiting, retching, diarrhoea and abdominal discomfort
Holly	GREEN	2–3 hours	Vomiting, diarrhoea, salivation, inappetence, depression
Horse chestnut (conkers)	AMBER	Usually within 6 hours	Vomiting, diarrhoea, salivation, abdominal tenderness, increased thirst, anorexia, dehydration
Iron (moss killer)	RED	Early signs within 6 hours, then 24 hours	Severe vomiting, diarrhoea, gastrointestinal haemorrhage and dehydration Later: shock, coma, bleeding, liver and kidney failure
Common ivy	AMBER	Within a few hours	Salivation, vomiting, diarrhoea and abdominal pain
Laburnum	AMBER	Within 2 hours	Salivation, persistent vomiting and diarrhoea, also lethargy. Death can result from respiratory paralysis
Lead	AMBER	Variable	Variable dependent on dose, duration, amount, and time over which consumed. Gastrointestinal and nervous effects. Anorexia, vomiting, salivation, abdominal pain, diarrhoea or constipation, weakness, lethargy, tremors, retching and convulsions

Agent	Risk	Onset	Common Signs
Metaldehyde (slug bait)	RED	Within 30 minutes	Hyperaesthesia, muscle spasm or rigidity, tremors, twitching, convulsions
Mistletoe	GREEN	Within a few hours	Vomiting, diarrhoea, salivation and weakness, blood in vomit and stools, anorexia, lethargy and acute renal failure
Narcissus and daffodils	AMBER	15 minutes–2 hours	Vomiting, diarrhoea, abdominal tenderness, anorexia, salivation, lethargy and pale mucous membranes
Organophosphate insecticides	AMBER	12–24 hours	Salivation, ataxia, diarrhoea, constricted pupils, muscle twitches, weakness, shaking, convulsions and coma
Phenoxy acid derivative herbicides	AMBER	Within a few hours	Gastrointestinal irritation, increased thirst, depression, ataxia and weakness
Puff balls	AMBER	Variable. Rapid to several days	Non toxic if eaten, but spores can cause respiratory signs if inhaled. Lethargy, cough, sneezing and increased body temperature and respiratory rate
Oak (leaves and buds) and acorns	AMBER	1–24 hours	Retching, vomiting with blood, shaking, skin rash, gastrointestinal obstruction, kidney and liver damage
Green potatoes	AMBER		Salivation, vomiting, diarrhoea, inappetence, lethargy and ataxia, dehydration, collapse
Rhododendron	AMBER	20 minutes–2 hours	Salivation, vomiting, diarrhoea, inappetence, abdominal tenderness, trembling, staggering, lethargy, weakness and exhaustion
Rowan (mountain ash)	GREEN	Usually within 8 hours, may be delayed for 24 hours	Vomiting, diarrhoea and salivation
Sodium hypochlorite (bleach)	AMBER	6 hours or delayed to 24 hours	Salivation, vomiting, diarrhoea, inappetence, ulceration of mouth and tongue, increased thirst, vomiting blood, collapse, respiratory distress, convulsions, mild skin irritation (dependent on concentration) if splashed on skin
Toad venom	AMBER	Within a few minutes	Salivation, frothing and foaming at the mouth, vomiting, vocalization, anxiety, ataxia and shaking
Yew	AMBER	Within 6 hours	Vomiting, diarrhoea, salivation, dilated pupils, lethargy, trembling, ataxia
Zinc	AMBER	Variable	Gastrointestinal signs, then anaemia with anorexia and depression

Particular mushrooms and toadstools can be poisonous, but because there are thousands of species of larger fungi in the UK, and identification is difficult without specialist knowledge, these will be described collectively as 'fungi', since only a small number are poisonous. Note that puff balls, although fungi, are not toxic if eaten, but their spores are poisonous if inhaled, and so these are listed separately.

The relative risk of exposure is indicated in the table as a visual 'traffic light' reference for those cases where a quick response may be needed, and is based on the system used by the Veterinary Poisons Information Service. This service is only available to offer specialist advice and support to UK veterinary surgeons dealing with cases of confirmed or suspected poisoning. Consequently the best course of action if poisoning is suspected is to take your dog to a veterinary surgeon, along with any information you may have that indicates the nature of the substance to which the animal either has been, or is likely to have been exposed.

Toxins can also be delivered in the form of insect stings and snake bites. These are described separately in Chapter 4, since most people would probably consider these as discrete incidents rather than as a form of poisoning per se.

In the author's experience the most commonly encountered cases of poisoning that require specific treatment in veterinary practice are due to the effects of rodent bait; antifreeze, de-icer and screen wash; slug pellets; lead; pesticides and fertilizers; plants; and prescription medicines and drugs of abuse.

Rodent Bait

Rodent bait most commonly contains 'anticoagulants', substances that prevent or hinder blood clotting, for example warfarin. These substances act by preventing blood from clotting, and thereby lead to bleeding, both internal as well as superficially; this is often seen as tiny blood spots on the lips and gums. The effects are not immediate, and usually progress slowly, depending on the amount consumed. The signs include lethargy, exercise intolerance, pale lips and gums, bleeding (both internal and external), and ultimately shock due to blood loss.

If you see that the dog has consumed rodent bait or rat poison try to make it vomit by giving it salt or mustard, and seek veterinary attention.

Antifreeze, De-icer and Screen Wash

Antifreeze, de-icer and screen wash are acutely toxic to dogs: the signs appear within thirty minutes to one hour of exposure, and include vomiting, staggering, weakness and mild seizures. Within twenty-four hours the dog may suffer a rapid heart rate (pulse) and rapid shallow breathing. There may be transient recovery periods, but these signs are often followed by coma. If the dog is not treated, then there is a risk that the condition will deteriorate and result in renal failure. Any attempt at treatment needs to be immediate by getting the dog to vomit, but always seek urgent veterinary attention, taking a sample or the container with you to the surgery or veterinary hospital.

Slug Pellets

Slug pellets containing metaldehyde are extremely poisonous in dogs, causing twitching, tremors, muscle spasm, panting, and distressed breathing within thirty minutes of consuming the bait. The lips, gums and tongue may be seen to be going blue (a sign known as 'cyanosis'). The best course of action is to take the dog to a vet immediately, along with a sample of the bait, or the container if available.

Lead

Lead is a fairly ubiquitous metal, and the common causes of poisoning are lead shot, older fishing weights, lead flashing on buildings, and as a constituent of old paint and paintwork. The signs of lead poisoning are extremely variable depending on the amount, the time over which the dog may have been consuming the lead-containing agent, and the age and condition of the dog. The common signs include a loss of appetite (inappetence), vomiting, drooling saliva, abdominal pain, diarrhoea or constipation, tremors, weakness, lethargy, twitching and convulsions. Again, the best course of action if you suspect your dog has been exposed to lead is to take it to a vet, who will be able to conduct appropriate tests upon which to base an accurate diagnosis, and will be able to treat the dog accordingly.

Pesticides and Fertilizers

There is a wide range of pesticides and fertilizers available that vary in their effect. Although many are relatively non toxic and there are clear instructions on their safe use, it is always advisable to seek veterinary opinion regarding the risk, especially if your dog is known to have been directly exposed to pesticides over any period of time, even if it is not showing any immediate signs of poisoning.

Fertilizers are not particularly toxic, but can cause unpleasant effects due to their rather irritant nature, so the dog may vomit, or have diarrhoea or abdominal tenderness, drink more than usual, and be listless and generally 'off colour'.

Organophosphate insecticides can also include petroleum distillate solvents, so it will be helpful if your vet can see the container or any other list of ingredients. Signs of OP poisoning are predominantly neurological, including drooling, weakness, lack of co-ordination, diarrhoea, constricted pupils, muscle tremors, twitching, shaking, restlessness and urinary incontinence.

If your dog becomes covered in any of these substances, try to stop it licking itself and wash off the material, preferably by bathing the dog in lukewarm water using a mild detergent.

Plants

It will be obvious from looking at the list of commonly encountered poisonous substances that many plants can potentially pose a health risk to dogs; however, few are particularly toxic, and the likelihood of a dog suffering any particular ill effects proves remarkably rare. The list includes holly, hyacinths, ivy, crocuses, horse chestnuts, field garlic, onion (and other related allium species), potatoes, rowan/mountain ash, and of course fungi (field mushrooms and toadstools). Common signs include vomiting, diarrhoea, a lack of appetite, and abdominal cramps depending on the plant.

If you see your dog eating plants, particularly field mushrooms and toadstools, and are concerned, the best advice is to take it, along with a sample of the plant, to your vet, who is likely to treat the dog symptomatically – according to the signs shown – or will contact the Veterinary Poisons Information Service for further advice.

Prescription Medicines and Drugs of Abuse

Prescription medicines and drugs of abuse should be mentioned here because dogs can habitually consume their owners' medication or other similar substances found around the house. The signs shown will obviously depend on the drug, and in the author's experience some particular medications and recreational drugs seem to be more commonly ingested: dogs that have consumed oral contraceptive tablets or cannabis (marijuana) are not uncommon. If you see your dog eating medicines or drugs, try to make it vomit by giving it salt or mustard, and then take it to your vet, together with any of the substance that remains, and any relevant labelled or packaging.

IF YOU SUSPECT YOUR DOG HAS BEEN POISONED

- Be aware that signs of poisoning may not be immediate, and in some cases may take several days before they become apparent
- If you know your dog has consumed, or otherwise been exposed to, something harmful, collect a sample and/or take the container or any labelling with you to show the vet. Try to determine how much of the substance your dog has ingested. Wear gloves to collect a sample, and place any vomit or diarrhoea in a plastic bag
- If your dog is showing life-threatening symptoms such as seizures, loss of consciousness or difficulty breathing, gather up the items mentioned and get the dog to a vet as quickly as possible. Have someone call the surgery or hospital to tell them a poison case will be arriving soon

4 INJURIES AND MISCELLANEOUS CONDITIONS

ORTHOPAEDIC CONDITIONS

Locomotory problems and lameness are most commonly caused by diseases and injuries that affect bones, joints and muscles and cause interference with normal movement. Those affecting bones and joints are classified as orthopaedic conditions, and the most common and/or serious are described in more detail below. A discussion of degenerative inflammatory joint disease (osteoarthritis) follows in Chapter 5.

ANTERIOR CRUCIATE LIGAMENT RUPTURE

Rupture of the anterior cruciate ligament is probably one of the most, if not the most common cause of sudden onset hind-leg lameness in dogs.

The stifle, or knee joint, is relatively complicated, comprising the lower articular surface of the femur or thigh bone, and corresponding articular surfaces of the two shin bones, primarily the larger tibia and, to a much lesser extent, the smaller fibula. There are also three small 'sesamoid' bones associated with the joint: two at the back of the tibia and fibula, and a larger, better known sesamoid bone, the patella or knee cap, in front of the stifle and running up and down in a groove in the anterior femoral articular surface. All these bones are held together, and the joint stabilized, by a series of ligaments. Importantly these include lateral ligaments each side of the joint that prevent the joint from flexing inwards and outwards, and two cruciate ligaments that cross (hence the name 'cruciate') in the middle of the joint.

Cruciate ligaments are bands of tough fibrous tissue that attach the femur (thigh bone) to the tibia (shin bone), preventing the tibia from moving forwards relative to the femur. It also helps to prevent the stifle joint from over-extending or rotating. These various structures are each illustrated in the accompanying photographs.

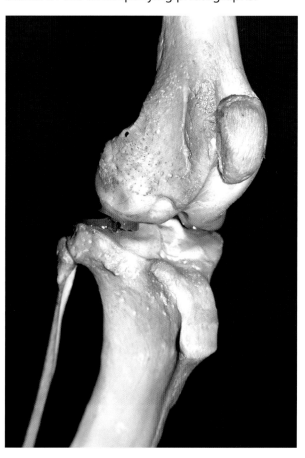

Anatomical specimen illustrating the bones of the normal canine stifle joint. Looking here at an oblique angle towards the tail, the patella (knee cap) can be seen resting in a groove of the femur (thigh bone), and the femur articulating with the tibia and fibula (shin bones).

103

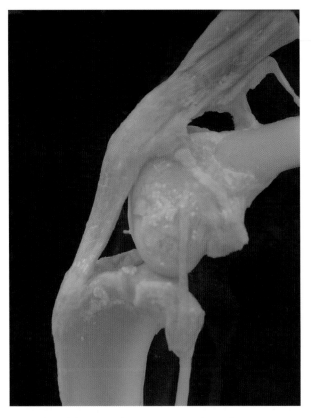

Lateral (side) view of an anatomical specimen illustrating the primary ligaments of the normal canine stifle joint. The stifle joint is reliant for stability on soft tissue ligaments that, in life, hold the various bones together.

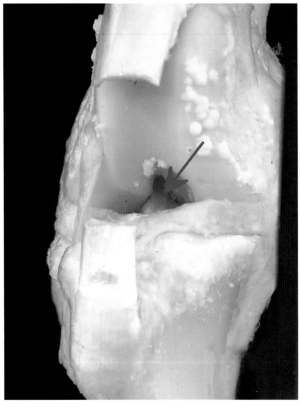

Anatomical specimen of the normal canine stifle joint. In this case the patella (knee cap) has been removed to show the anterior cruciate ligament (arrowed) running between the back of the upper femur to insert at the front of the lower tibial articular surface.

Lying between the articular surfaces of the femur and the tibia are pads of cartilage called menisci. These act like cushions, and it is quite common for the menisci to be damaged along with the anterior cruciate ligament: this is believed to account for much of the pain that accompanies these injuries.

Causes of Anterior Cruciate Ligament Rupture

The anterior cruciate ligament is commonly torn when a dog twists on its hind leg, which puts too much tension on the ligament and it snaps. This can happen if a dog slips, especially when turning at speed. The ligament can also rupture if, when jumping a fence, its hind leg gets trapped

in the top strand of wire, for example, and it can be torn in a road accident if the dog is hit by a car.

Most commonly, however, the ligament is believed to deteriorate and weaken over time, rather like a rope fraying. Ultimately the weakened ligament gives way, but already there will be other, secondary changes in other associated structures in the unstable joint. Consequently some degree of inflammation and osteoarthritis will already have become established by the time the cruciate ligament finally ruptures.

This is important to appreciate and understand, since surgical repair, no matter how successful, can only replicate and restore the function of the ligament. It cannot reverse these early arthritic changes, which, being irreversible, will gradually become apparent over time and will likely result in some form of chronic lameness.

Signs and Diagnosis

With anterior cruciate rupture the dog usually goes lame suddenly, and is unable to bear any weight on one hind limb. Typically this will occur in a young, boisterous, athletic dog that injures its leg jumping or turning suddenly whilst being strenuously exercised, or it may happen to an older dog that suddenly goes lame on one hind leg after a seemingly minor action such as jumping out of its bed or the car. Larger breeds will normally suffer the first instance of injury, but more commonly dogs, and particularly overweight dogs, will suffer the second instance. The affected leg is often carried, and the dog hops along on three legs. Left alone the dog tends to improve over the course of the next two to three weeks, but the joint is often noticeably swollen as arthritis starts to set in.

To diagnose anterior cruciate ligament rupture, the vet will stabilize the femur by holding it firmly, and will then attempt to move the lower tibia/fibular; if it slides forwards (known as the 'anterior drawer' sign) the anterior cruciate ligament is ruptured. Very often the dog resents a painful joint being manipulated and tenses up. Tense muscles will tend to stabilize the joint and hence mask the anterior drawer sign, so it is not unusual for the vet to have to anaesthetize or deeply sedate the dog in order to make a diagnosis. This also facilitates X-ray examination to access the degree of any osteoarthritis that may have become established in the joint.

Treatment

There are essentially two treatment options: either conservative treatment, or one of a variety of surgical procedures that are intended either to replace the torn ligament and/or stabilize the stifle joint to restore function.

Conservative Treatment

Conservative treatment involves complete rest and supportive drug treatments to reduce inflammation and pain. With time the joint will stabi-

lize, and the dog will often be pain free and able to walk with relatively good joint function. This works quite well in small dogs, but the larger the breed, and especially if the dog has a tendency to be overweight, the greater the stress on the remaining joint tissues, and the greater the risk of early onset osteoarthritis as a secondary consequence of the initial cruciate ligament injury. Conservative treatment will obviously mean the dog cannot be worked throughout the healing process, and if work is resumed too early, the greater the likelihood of the dog having to retire earlier due to osteoarthritic complications.

Whilst some dogs will respond remarkably well to conservative treatments, if a young dog is to return to work after suffering traumatic anterior cruciate ligament injury, surgical treatment is usually the most appropriate option. In most cases the only alternative is to treat the injury conservatively and retire the dog.

Surgical Procedures

There are a variety of alternative surgical procedures; some are claimed to work better than others, but there is little good comparative scientific evidence to rank any one procedure as superior. A successful outcome is more likely to be dependent on the timing of surgery, and the experience and expertise of individual veterinary surgeons in the use of a particular technique. Usually a surgeon will be recommending the procedure that he finds most successful, and it is wise to heed this advice rather than delay in attempting to find someone offering any alternative 'best' procedure.

The three most commonly used surgical techniques are tibial plateau levelling osteotomy (TPLO) and tibial tuberosity advancement (TTA), and, if indicated as contributing to the injury, meniscal (cartilage) surgery. These three techniques have largely superseded ligament replacement procedures, which were previously used quite extensively to treat anterior cruciate ligament injuries.

Tibial plateau levelling osteotomy (TPLO): This procedure involves altering the angle of the top of the shin bone (the tibial plateau) by cutting the bone, rotating it, and stabilizing it in a new position, normally with a stainless-steel plate and screws. The technique seems to work best for young dogs with a ruptured cranial cruciate ligament that have persistent lameness and stifle joint instability. Exercise following TPLO surgery must be very restricted for the first few weeks until tissues and bone have had a chance to heal. Jumping and climbing must be avoided. Thereafter exercise may be increased and controlled gradually. Hydrotherapy may be recommended to help restore full function.

Tibial tuberosity advancement (TTA): This procedure also involves cutting the top of the thigh bone, but then moving it forwards, and stabilizing it in the new position, again with a plate and screws. Dogs with persistent lameness and stifle joint instability following cruciate rupture often benefit from this technique. Again, exercise following TTA surgery must be very restricted, and hydrotherapy may be recommended.

Meniscal cartilage surgery: Cartilage injury, as many people know, can be very painful, and is a significant cause of lameness in dogs that have damaged the cartilage when the anterior cruciate ligament ruptured. The damaged portion of cartilage needs to be surgically removed. Recovery after meniscal surgery is usually relatively quick, providing exercise is restricted for a few weeks and then gradually increased.

Cruciate Ligament Replacement
Replacement was, and for some vets is still, the conventional treatment for dogs with anterior cruciate rupture, certainly here in the UK. The technique was first pioneered by a Finnish veterinary surgeon, Paatsama, back in 1952. It involved drilling two bone tunnels, one through the bottom of the thigh bone (femur) to enter the top of the stifle joint at the point of origin of the anterior ligament, and another up through the top of the thigh bone (tibia) to enter the stifle joint where the ligament inserts. He then threaded and secured a piece of tissue through these two tunnels to replace the ruptured cruci-

ate ligament. Later, Professor Leslie Vaughan at the Royal Veterinary College modified the technique, substituting skin as the graft material, and achieved a significant level of success.

This technique has subsequently stood the test of time, and many UK vets still prefer to use this rather than any other surgical option. The procedure seems to work best if the surgery takes place as soon as possible after the injury occurs. Aftercare following replacement is very important: exercise has to be restricted, and hydrotherapy can be very helpful.

Prognosis
The outlook or prognosis following anterior cruciate ligament rupture is quite variable. Certainly small dogs can be managed successfully with conservative treatment, particularly by exercise restriction and reducing weight. However, there is no doubt that larger working dogs benefit from surgery, which will normally restore function and enable the dog to return to work much more quickly, albeit in some cases not always to the same level of performance. Surgery is probably most effective the earlier the intervention occurs after rupture of the ligament, the more compliant the owner is in providing the recommended aftercare, and the more tolerant the dog is to having exercise restricted, especially once it starts weight bearing on the affected leg. However, it is worth remembering that dogs with anterior cruciate ligament rupture are likely to develop some degree of osteoarthritis. In many cases, despite the success of surgery, this can still ultimately result in some form of permanent lameness.

HIP DYSPLASIA

Hip dysplasia is a relatively common inherited condition of the canine hip joint. It is a disease of bone development – the term 'dysplasia' means abnormal development – affecting the bones that together form the ball and socket joint in the hip. Dogs are not the only mammals that suffer hip dysplasia, and therefore it is not surprising that it affects many breeds, and not just gundogs. The heavier and more active breeds tend to be most clinically affected, however, so its significance in gundogs attracts more attention.

The anatomy of the normal hip joint is shown in the accompanying photographs, and the appearance of normal hips and those showing signs of hip dysplasia can be compared in the accompanying radiographs. As can be seen, the joint is composed of a ball that forms part of the head of the femur, or thigh bone, that articulates in a socket that is formed by bones making up the pelvis. Normally the ball fits firmly in the socket, but abnormal growth of either or both components will cause excess movement and hence more wear on the delicate articular surfaces.

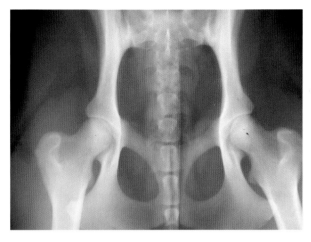

X-ray photograph of a normal canine hip joint. DR GARY CLAYTON-JONES

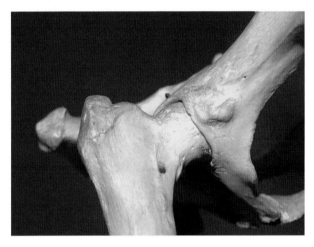

Dog skeleton illustrating the hip. Looking here at a slightly oblique angle towards the tail, it can be clearly seen how, in the normal joint, the ball of the femoral head (thigh bone) fits relatively tightly into the acetabulum (the socket of the hip bone), and how between the head of the femur (thigh bone) and the femoral shaft there is normally a well defined 'neck'. In a dysplastic hip, changes can take place that affect both these structures.

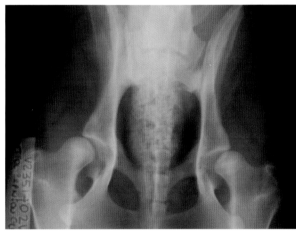

X-ray photograph of a dog with hip dysplasia. Note in particular how the femoral heads are less rounded and luxated (so they lie partly out of the sockets), and that the femoral necks are less well defined. DR GARY CLAYTON-JONES

The primary bone changes become apparent as the dog grows, particularly during the rapid growth phase in adolescence, and cause abnormal wear and tear on the joint. This in turn can lead to secondary changes such as osteoarthritis and degenerative bone disease, and the joints become mechanically defective. At this stage clinical signs associated with hip dysplasia may be seen that can include the following:

- Exercise intolerance
- A swaying gait – the rear end moves back and forth and the dog appears to 'swing' its hips
- 'Bunny hopping', especially as the dog ascends an incline or goes upstairs
- Stiffness and pain in the hips

- Difficulty in getting up after sitting or lying down
- Reluctance to jump
- Hind-limb lameness that is worse after exercise
- The back legs held closer together compared to the front legs – that is, a 'narrow stance'

As hip dysplasia progresses the following signs may appear:

- Muscle wastage around the hind quarters
- Arthritis, especially in later onset, and a general reluctance to having the hind legs manipulated

It has to be emphasized, however, that not all dogs with hip dysplasia will necessarily suffer severe clinical signs; it very much depends on how badly the joints are affected, and the type of dog and its lifestyle. Many dogs in certain breeds seem to be able to tolerate mild to moderate radiographic signs of hip dysplasia reasonably well, and may never become lame. Nevertheless affected dogs are seldom able to tolerate prolonged exercise, and are rarely capable of working regularly during the season. Furthermore, because the disease is inherited, these clinically sound dogs can still pass on the disease to their progeny.

However, hip dysplasia is a disease that can be effectively treated, and these days vets are able to offer a variety of treatment options, which, whilst not necessarily able to restore full function to make the dog suitable for prolonged hard work, can provide affected dogs good joint movement, an acceptable quality of life, and freedom from pain.

Treatment
Hip dysplasia can be treated conservatively, or by a variety of surgical procedures; the choice of treatment is largely dependent on the age, weight and type of dog, and the severity of joint movement.

Conservative Treatments
Conservative treatments will include weight control, nutrition, balanced exercise, physiotherapy, analgesics – drugs that relieve pain – and anti-inflammatory drugs.

Weight control: Is important, particularly if a dog is overweight. Excess weight puts more strain on the joints, and reducing weight will decrease the pressure applied to painful hip joints, and reduce the amount of inflammation around the joint.

Nutrition: Both the type and quality of the diet can help alleviate the progression and signs of hip dysplasia. Vets will advise against feeding high calorie, high protein and high 'energy' diets, especially to puppies and young adolescent dogs. These diets, by promoting rapid weight gain, will increase the likelihood of the disease developing because the dog's bones and musculature grow too rapidly. Dietary supplements can also help, particularly glucosamine and chondroitin sulphate, and there are now proprietary treatment diets available that will often contain such substances.

Balanced exercise: This includes avoiding high-impact activities, such as jumping to catch balls and frizzbees, which put additional strain on the dog's hindquarters, and similar repetitive activities that strain the joints or are unnatural to a dog's movement.

Anti-inflammatory drugs: Particularly non-steroidal anti-inflammatory drugs (NSAIDs), which these days have far fewer side effects and can be well tolerated. Be aware, however, that your vet may try various different NSAIDs until he or she finds the type that is best suited to the dog.

Surgical Procedures
Several surgical procedures are available for hip dysplasia, and the choice will usually depend on the age, weight and condition of the dog, and the severity of any secondary joint changes. The most common procedures that are currently applied include juvenile pubic symphysiodesis surgery (JPS), triple pelvic osteotomy (TPO), total hip replacement (THR), and excision arthroplasty.

Juvenile pubic symphysiodesis surgery (JPS): Normally performed on dogs younger than six months old. The procedure involves fusing part of the pelvis together, with the objective of improving the stability of the hip joint, thereby reducing the laxity in the joint and hence the secondary wear and tear.

Triple pelvic osteotomy (TPO): Comprises a surgical reconstruction of the hip joint, usually performed in dogs under a year of age. It is normally indicated for dogs with poor coverage of the femoral head. Again, the intention is to reduce laxity in the joint and prevent subluxation, which often leads to severe arthritis. As long as there are no signs of degenerative joint disease, TPO is usually chosen for dogs with subluxated, but otherwise good hips, where it provides reliable surgical treatment.

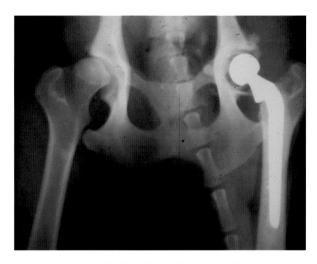

X-ray photograph of a dog with a total hip replacement. Note how the other joint is showing obvious signs of hip dysplasia. DR GARY CLAYTON-JONES

Total hip replacement (THR): Considered the current 'gold standard', where both the ball and socket are replaced with appropriate prostheses. Usually the replacement socket is made of a special form of plastic and the ball of a high grade metal alloy. Special bone cement is used to hold these implants in position, although there are systems now available that are made in such a way that new bone grows in to secure the prosthesis. Essentially THR provides a dog with an artificial hip. Dogs that meet the selection criteria are found to be more comfortable, and most have an improved quality of life.

Excision arthroplasty: Typically performed when hip replacement surgery is cost-prohibitive. The operation is to remove the ball of the hip joint in its entirety, leaving the leg attached by the muscles of the hip, which then form the joint. The procedure works best in lighter dogs with well developed hip musculature.

ELBOW DYSPLASIA

Elbow dysplasia is a collective term used to describe a number of specific conditions, each of which affects the correct formation of the elbow joint; the term itself means simply 'abnormal development of the elbow joint'. These primary conditions will induce secondary, consequential changes in the joint, which if sufficiently severe will result in osteoarthritis of the joint, pain and lameness. In general, medium to large breeds are considered most vulnerable to the disease, and notably among gundogs the Labrador and Golden Retriever.

The most common causes of elbow dysplasia are Osteochondritis dissecans (OD or OCD) (*see* the following section for a description of OCD), a fragmented or un-united coronoid process, and an un-united anconeal process.

Fragmented or un-united coronoid process: A detachment of the piece of bone forming the front of the joint and normally part of the ulna; one of the two bones that together form the forearm.

Un-united anconeal process: A small piece of bone that forms the very back of the joint becomes detached from the tibia, near the region that we call the 'funny bone' in humans. This form of the disease is the easiest to recognize on X-ray, but is rare among gundogs.

The following diagram and radiographs illustrate the joint and these detachments.

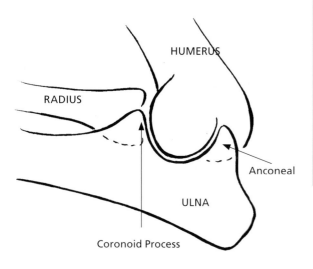

The canine elbow joint indicating the position of the anconeal and coronoid processes.

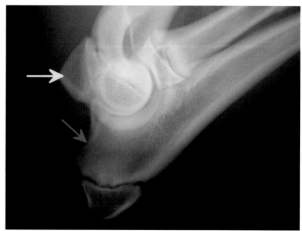

X-ray photograph showing Osteochondritis dissecans (OD) of the elbow joint, with significant secondary osteoarthritis (arrowed).
DR GARY CLAYTON-JONES

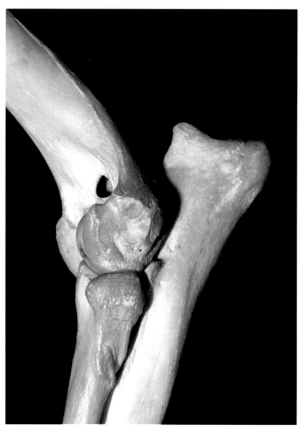

X-ray photograph illustrating an un-united anconeal process (white arrow). The red arrow shows where the anconeal process should normally attach.
DR GARY CLAYTON-JONES

LEFT: *Anatomical specimen illustrating how the bones of the normal canine elbow joint articulate. Looking here from the side, the bottom of the femur articulates primarily with the ulna, and also with the smaller radius that here lies hidden behind the larger ulna.*

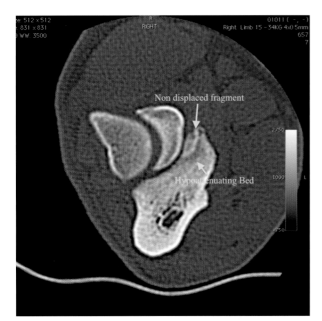

A CT (computed tomography) scan illustrating a fractured or un-united coronoid process. The CT image cuts a virtual cross-section, enabling small changes, such as those illustrated, to be visualized, which would be difficult to see on X-ray.
DR GARY CLAYTON-JONES

The cause of each condition is genetic, inherited from one or both of the parents, and each can present in varying degrees of severity. Elbow dysplasia is neither caused by one defective gene nor by a simple mode of inheritance: instead it is 'polygenetic', due to a variety of defective diseases, and can be exacerbated by a variety of contributory factors such as diet and exercise. As a consequence, not every dog that has elbow dysplasia is necessarily going to show clinical signs to the same extent, and indeed some may never go lame.

The problem is that even sound individuals can still pass on the disease to their offspring, which may be extremely lame in one or both front legs with severe arthritis of the elbow(s). Fortunately, these conditions can be detected on X-ray, and a grading scheme has been devised to recognize unaffected dogs and the severity of the condition in affected dogs. The scheme, described in

Chapter 2 and detailed in the Appendix, enables breeders to select appropriate dogs to breed from, and to avoid breeding from symptomless dogs that could pass on the condition to their offspring. The scheme is run jointly by the British Veterinary Association and the Kennel Club, which publishes results of all dogs submitted for examination. If you intend purchasing a puppy from any of the commonly affected breeds, then you should ask if the parents have been screened, and to see a copy of the results.

If you intend acquiring a working dog from parents that have not been elbow graded, always try flexing the elbows when you examine it. If you cannot flex the elbow fully, the joint is likely to be dysplastic.

OSTEOCHONDRITIS DISSECANS

Osteochondritis dissecans (OCD) is a disease of cartilage that affects various joints of young large and giant breeds of dog, including a number of the gundog breeds. OCD of the elbow joint is one of the causes of elbow dysplasia.

Where any two bones meet and there is movement, the ends of the bones are covered in a smooth covering of cartilage that cushions and protects the underlying bone. If the surface of that cartilage is disrupted, any movement in the joint becomes painful. In OCD the disruption is believed to be caused by growth, possibly part of the surface is not nourished properly, and the disrupted cartilage either lifts as a flap or becomes detached and floats loose in the joint. Loose, detached pieces of cartilage are known as 'joint mice', from their appearance on X-ray.

OCD can affect the shoulder, elbow, knee or hock joints, and signs of OCD most commonly occur when the dog is between four and ten months of age. Males, probably because of their larger body size, tend to be more commonly affected than females. The dog will become lame in the affected limb; some dogs show a mild limp, while others can't bear any weight on the leg. When it affects the shoulder, the forelimb stride may be foreshortened as the dog is reluctant to flex and extend the joint. If both legs are affected the dog may be reluctant to move.

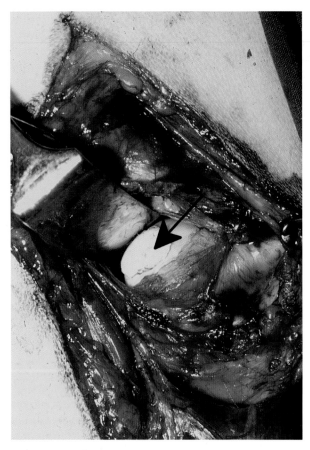

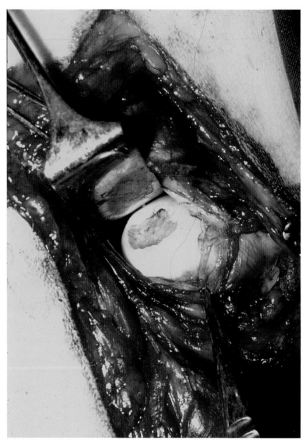

An operation to remove a flap of cartilage. The flap (arrowed) can be clearly seen in the centre of the photograph, comprising a circular detachment on the head of the humerus. DR GARY CLAYTON-JONES

Here the flap has been removed, leaving the affected area on the head of the humerus exposed. The defect will subsequently heal over and be covered with healthy cartilage. DR GARY CLAYTON-JONES

OCD is diagnosed on the basis of the history related by the owner, on physical examination, and by X-ray. Dogs don't normally resent the shoulder being fully extended and flexed, but those with OCD will be reluctant to have the joint manipulated, and will often cry out with pain when the joint is fully extended. When the affected joint is X-rayed either a change in bone underlying the damaged cartilage can be seen, or a free-floating piece of cartilage, known as a 'joint mouse', may be seen.

Treatment
Treatment comprises either conservative or surgical treatment. Conservative treatment – com-plete rest complemented by anti-inflammatory drugs and painkillers – is indicated in mild and early cases, or where the cause cannot be confirmed. Surgery is indicated for severe lameness, and where large lesions are visible on X-ray. The affected joint is opened, and either the area of defective cartilage or the flap of cartilage or a joint mouse removed as appropriate.

OCD is prevented by being careful to breed from animals with no known history or signs of OCD. Young, rapidly growing individuals of the susceptible breeds should not be subjected to strenuous exercise until fully mature – once their bones have stopped growing and the joint cartilage is fully formed. OCD of the elbow is best prevented by X-raying all breeding stock and submitting radiographs of the elbow joints for grading. Only dogs graded as 0 (normal) or 1 (mild) should be used for breeding; those graded as 2 (moderate) or 3 (severe) should not be bred from.

CERVICAL DISC DISEASE

Intervertebral discs are shock-absorbing pads that fill the space between each vertebra from the neck to the tail with the exception of the first two in the neck, which have articular surfaces enabling the skull to move up, down and sideways. Each disc comprises a thick outer fibrous element and a central core of gelatinous material called the nucleus pulposus. Intervertebral disc disease occurs when the outer fibrous layer degenerates or ruptures, allowing the inner gelatinous material to escape, under pressure and almost always upwards, into the space occupied by the spinal cord. This puts pressure on the spinal cord and associated spinal nerve roots, accounting for the accompanying clinical signs.

Whilst the vertebrae in the chest and back, the thoracolumbar region, are most frequently involved in the so-called chondroplastic breeds – those with relatively long backs and short legs, such as the Dachshund and Bassett Hound – in gundogs it is more usual for those in the neck, the cervical vertebrae, to be affected. In particular spaniels and occasionally Labrador Retrievers suffer cervical disc disease, and middle-aged dogs seem to be most at risk. The reason for such a predisposition is unknown, but spaniels are 'busy' dogs, rushing around, running from side to side and sniffing everywhere, and all this activity means a lot of neck movement, which is quite likely a cause for the intervertebral disc to break down, tear and eventually rupture.

The principal sign of cervical disc disease is neck pain, with the dog yelping or crying out if touched or when turning or lowering the head, or displaying more subtle signs such as reluctance to jump or climb, or walking around with a lowered head carriage. The disease tends to be progressive, so it is not unusual for the signs to be seen intermittently.

The disease is typically diagnosed on X-ray, where a narrowing of the affected intervertebral space is usually obvious. Other, more advanced imaging techniques such as MRI (magnetic resonance imaging), enable the actual prolapsed disc material to be visualized, and increasing use of these techniques is being made these days in the diagnosis of intervertebral disc disease.

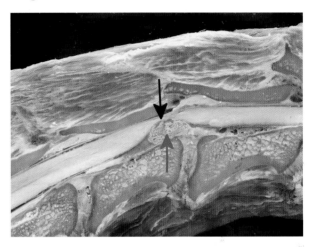

Anatomical specimen showing intervertebral disc disease. In this cross-section of an affected neck, the red arrow points to where gelatinous material from inside one of the intervertebral discs has escaped upwards, into space otherwise occupied by the spinal cord. This puts pressure on the spinal cord (black arrow).

Treatment

Treatment in the early stages is likely to be conservative, when your vet may prescribe drugs such as NSAIDs (non-steroidal anti-inflammatory drugs) to relieve the pain and pressure on the spine, along with 'rest' – which whilst difficult in the case of a lively spaniel, will essentially mean the avoidance of any exercise or activity that might place undue strain on the neck and forelimbs.

Ultimately if the disease progresses and conservative therapy is unable to control the associated signs, your vet may advise surgical treatment. This typically comprises removing the prolapsed material, or preventing any further residual disc material from escaping, by scooping out the material from the affected and close-ly adjacent intervertebral spaces (a technique referred to as 'fenestration'). It is also possible to relieve pressure or pain by removing a section of bone from the bottom of the spine (the 'ventral slot' technique).

Whichever form of treatment is advised, the overall outlook, or prognosis, for cervical disc disease in gundogs is usually good.

INFRASPINATUS CONTRACTURE

Infraspinatus tendon contracture is an injury often sustained by active working dogs, such as spaniels and Labrador Retrievers, and is the result of damage to the infraspinatus muscle and its tendon. The muscle helps support the shoulder

joint, and allows for flexion and external rotation of the shoulder. Initially there is a sudden onset of lameness as a result of trauma or during exercise. The lameness and pain associated with the injury usually subsides in ten to fourteen days, but as the damaged muscle and tendon heal the normal tissue is replaced by fibrous scar tissue. Eventually the muscle loses its normal function, and the presence of scar tissue limits the ability of

ABOVE: *Infraspinatus tendon contracture, showing how the affected joint cannot be fully flexed.* DR GARY CLAYTON-JONES

LEFT: *Infraspinatus tendon contracture; the dog is holding its leg in the manner characteristic of the condition.* DR GARY CLAYTON-JONES

the shoulder joint to move through its full range of normal movement.

A characteristic gait abnormality develops approximately three to four weeks after the original injury. The dog is unable to rotate the shoulder internally, but shows no signs of pain; when it walks, it rotates the affected leg outwards. The contracted tendon also causes the dog to have a characteristic stance, in which the elbow and foot are held away from the body. The affected leg is slightly shorter than the normal leg, and the dog cannot fully extend the shoulder.

Because the muscle is no longer functional, it undergoes atrophy (reduces in size), and so the shoulder bone becomes more prominent and conspicuous; this will be particularly obvious when feeling around the shoulder. Although affected dogs are lame at first, once the initial injury heals, the contracture is not painful.

Treatment

There is no medical management for infraspinatus tendon contracture; the only treatment is surgery to carry out a procedure known as tenotomy. This involves making an incision over the shoulder region to expose the contracted tendon, which is severed as it crosses over the shoulder joint.

MUSCULAR SPRAINS AND STRAINS

Muscular sprains and strains are to be regarded as the incidental, 'wear and tear' problems most commonly encountered in strenuously worked dogs, and dogs not necessarily in optimum condition but nevertheless expected to do an occasional full day's work. Typically the dog will return lame if it has sprained a muscle, or it will return sound but will be seen to be lame later. A strained or sprained muscle is normally the most obvious explanation if no other form of orthopaedic injury is obvious.

Treatment

Treatment comprises rest, but should the condition persist, again in the absence of no other explanation, then supplementary support with anti-inflammatory drugs, especially NSAIDs (non-steroidal anti-inflammatory drugs), can be advantageous in speeding recovery. Obviously dogs suffering any form of muscular problem should be given incremental gentle exercise to ensure they return to optimum fitness before being expected to undertake a continuous full day's strenuous exercise in the shooting field.

AUTOIMMUNE OR EOSINOPHILIC MYOSITIS

Autoimmune myositis is an expression of autoimmune disease among gundogs. The affected muscles, typically the muscles of mastication of

Infraspinatus tendon contracture: the appearance of normal and affected limbs when extended – the affected limb is on the left. DR GARY CLAYTON-JONES

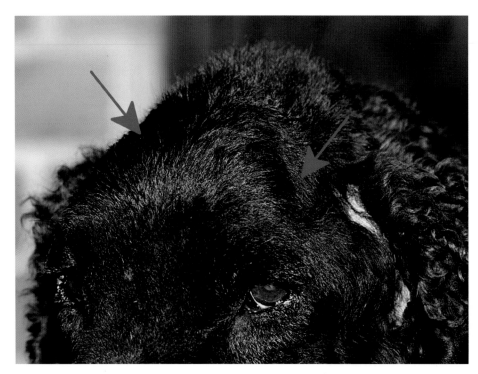

Autoimmune myositis, here in the chronic (degenerative muscle-wasting) form. The affected muscles over the top of the head have degenerated and 'wasted' (arrowed), and as a consequence the bones above the eye and the side of the cranium have become more prominent.

the head, are initially inflamed and become swollen, but subsequently tend to degenerate and waste away.

Autoimmunity is a situation where the body fails to recognize its own protein materials (in this instance muscle protein) as 'self', and cannot distinguish them from 'foreign' proteins (to which it would normally mount an immune response to isolate and reject the protein, for example as it would in response to infection). The consequence is that the body tends to reject some of its own protein, causing disease. Autoimmune diseases can be an indication of detrimental inbreeding. Other examples of autoimmune disease are the inflammatory skin diseases lupus and inflammatory thyroiditis, resulting in thyroid deficiency.

The disease is recognized in both the acute (inflammatory) and chronic (degenerative muscle wasting) form. The acute phase is recognized by drooling (when the jaws may be clenched or sag open) and difficulty eating; the eyes may appear to bulge slightly, or the third eyelid may be more prominent. There may be some pain when opening the jaws or when trying to yawn

or swallow. The disease may affect muscles in the limbs, causing lameness. There is frequently an elevated body temperature.

Not all animals exhibit each of these signs: in some, only the temporal muscles on top of the head may be affected, while in others the reverse may be the case. Relapses are not uncommon. The clinical signs are often accompanied by characteristic findings in blood samples, where there is an increase in the number of circulating eosinophils (a particular type of inflammatory cell) from which the disease was initially named.

Treatment

Most cases respond to high doses of steroids, which are reduced gradually as the signs subside, but many dogs are left with some muscle wastage or weakness.

CENTRONUCLEAR MYOPATHY (CNM)

CNM in Labrador Retrievers is a hereditary myopathy characterized by muscle weakness and exercise intolerance. It is also known as juvenile myopathy and hereditary myopathy of the Labrador Retriever (HMLR). The disease is debilitating and ultimately fatal. CNM is found in both working and show Labradors in the United States, Canada and the United Kingdom, as well as Germany, France, Sweden, and many other countries.

The distinguishing features of CNM-affected puppies are swallowing difficulties, an inability to walk normally, and a tendency to tire quickly. CNM is distinct from dystrophic myopathy and degenerative myelopathy (DM), two inherited diseases also found in Labradors, and is also very different from exercise-induced collapse (EIC). At birth, affected puppies are indistinguishable from their littermates, but from two weeks of age progressively fail to gain weight by comparison. By two to five months of age, affected puppies start developing an awkward gait and display decreased exercise tolerance, associated with a generalized muscle weakness.

In CNM dogs, the muscular tone of the œsophagus is weakened, and this predisposes to food accumulating in the oesophagus prior to entering the stomach, causing the pup to have difficulties swallowing. Small pieces of food may also get into the lungs, causing respiratory complications. Providing raised bowls so the dog does not have to reach down for food and water can enable them to eat more efficiently, with less chance of food and water getting into the lungs.

The disorder shows an autosomal recessive mode of inheritance: this means that two copies of the defective gene (one inherited from each parent) have to be present for a dog to be affected by the disease. Individuals with one copy of the defective gene and one copy of the normal gene – called carriers – show no symptoms but can pass the defective gene on to their offspring.

Signs of the disease can be exacerbated by cold conditions, so it is important to make sure that the affected dog is always warm, never cold, and that the dog's stress levels are kept to a minimum. Avoid kennelling affected dogs outside, except in warm climates, and do not allow them to swim in excessively cold water; indeed, take care whenever these dogs are swimming because of their tendency to tire easily.

LIMBER TAIL SYNDROME

Limber tail syndrome (LTS) is a curious condition, most frequently reported in working gundogs, and particularly Labrador Retrievers, although other breeds can be affected. It is widely described as 'limber tail', especially in the USA, and as 'cold tail', 'water tail', 'dead tail', and probably a whole variety of other descriptive terms. Until relatively recently, the condition has not been reported extensively in veterinary literature, so many vets,

In working gundogs limber tail syndrome is often reported following swimming, especially in cold water, particularly at the start of the season in dogs that have not been regularly exercised through the summer months. Swimming isn't the only cause, and some dogs will show signs after a period of hard work retrieving game.

unless they have actually seen this presented in their surgery, may not be familiar with the condition. Typically the dog presents with a 'paralyzed' tail, where the tail is either held firmly between the legs, or part of the tail hangs limp. There is usually some pain or discomfort at the base of the tail, the dog is reluctant to wag its tail, and many will be very uncomfortable and distressed.

As part of more recent studies in the UK, LTS was reported in approximately 0.5–0.7 per cent of the Labrador Retrievers whose owners took part. Furthermore, assuming that swimming may be considered a form of vigorous exercise, then the vast majority of cases experienced some form of vigorous exercise prior to developing LTS, and approximately half of those dogs had been both cold and wet. A small number of dogs were reported as developing LTS after wagging their tail 'vigorously'.

The precise cause is unknown, although many vets seem to agree that it is most likely a sign of muscular damage, most likely caused by muscular fatigue. This would make sense, as the tail is a powerful organ used a lot whilst working, and particularly for swimming where breeds such as Labradors will use the tail as a 'rudder' to help propel them through water. Bearing in mind the resistance that water must effect as the dog moves its tail from side to side as it drives through the water with a retrieve, and you can easily appreciate how this might cause the muscles to become fatigued. Some genetic influence on the risk of developing LTS is implicit from the fact that in one UK study, the cases were significantly more related than might otherwise be expected from a random population.

Treatment

Treatment is rest, and recovery will be spontaneous, albeit over a period of several hours or days. Many vets will aid recovery by administering a non-steroidal inflammatory drug, such as 'Rimadyl', or will give the dog corticosteroids to reduce inflammation, particularly if the tail is very painful and the dog resents it being touched. Don't be surprised if your vet considers taking X-rays, as the presenting signs could

indicate a fracture, and the possibility of caudal nerve damage may also need to be eliminated as an alternative differential diagnosis.

NEUROLOGICAL CONDITIONS

SEIZURES, FITS AND EPILEPSY

There are many causes of canine seizures, and for some dogs seizures are no more than isolated incidents. The terms 'fit', 'convulsion' and 'seizure' are to all intents and purposes synonymous, but epilepsy and seizure are not. Epilepsy is only one of a number of various causes of seizure. Furthermore 'epilepsy' is the term used for the disease in humans, and there are distinct differences between the human and canine forms of epilepsy. For this reason the term 'idiopathic epilepsy' is now used as the umbrella term for the condition in animals. The causes of seizure include the following:

- Toxins – for example antifreeze, toxic plants, chocolate (theobromine) and lead
- Trauma – head injury can cause scarring in the brain and lead to the onset of seizures
- Meningitis – inflammation of the tissue surrounding the brain (the meninges)
- Encephalitis – inflammation of the brain
- Canine distemper – a viral disease that we commonly vaccinate against still occurs and can infect the nervous system. Such affected dogs can suffer seizures long after recovering from the initial signs of canine distemper
- Tumours – a brain tumour can directly or indirectly cause seizures
- Hypoglycaemia – low blood glucose (sugar) levels, if severe, can lead to seizure
- Liver disease – seizures can be a complication of the disease in some dogs
- Idiopathic epilepsy – periodic recurrent seizures are usually a result of epilepsy, although in the majority of cases the exact cause is unknown. In some breeds of dog there is an inherited risk of developing idiopathic epilepsy, meaning the puppies of epileptic parents (male or female) have an increased risk of developing the disorder

Idiopathic epilepsy has been recorded in a number of gundog breeds including:

Labrador Retrievers
Golden Retrievers
English Springer Spaniels
Cocker Spaniels
Irish Water Spaniels
Welsh Springer Spaniels
German Short-Haired Pointers
Hungarian Vizslas
English Pointers

Idiopathic epilepsy is sometimes referred to as 'recurrent seizure disorder' due to the fact that dogs suffering the disease experience frequent, periodic seizures. Idiopathic epilepsy is only one of a number of potential causes of seizure in dogs, and dogs of those breeds predisposed to hereditary idiopathic epilepsy are just as prone to other causes of seizure as any other type of dog. Just because your dog suffers a seizure and is one of the listed breeds does not necessarily mean it has inherited idiopathic epilepsy, and attempts should always be made to establish a proper diagnosis.

A seizure might best be described as being the result of brain cells suddenly firing in a random, uncoordinated manner. The dog will have no control during the period it suffers a seizure, and will be unconscious. Consequently there is only rarely any pain or discomfort directly associated with a seizure. The animal is essentially 'out of it' the whole time it is convulsing, and whilst the episode may be extremely distressing for the owner to witness, it is important to understand that the dog most likely knows little or nothing of what is happening.

There are different types of seizure. Those most commonly and easily recognized in dogs are generalized seizures, but less easily recognized, more localized forms of seizure called partial seizures also exist. Partial seizures might affect a limb or the facial muscles, causing a 'twitching' of the affected part. Complex partial seizures are otherwise called psychomotor disorders, and these are quite different and more difficult to recognize. They cause behavioural disturbances rather than convulsions, and signs include agitated barking, staring into space, snapping at invisible objects, and obsessive licking and chewing.

Most people will associate the term 'seizure' with a dog suffering a convulsion or fit. Such generalized seizures are easily recognized because they affect the whole of the body. There will be rapid contraction and relaxation of muscles and you may find the expressions 'tonic-clonic seizure' or 'grand mal' used elsewhere to describe this type of generalized seizure. The sudden tonic contraction will normally lead to collapse, and usually vocalization. The dog will typically salivate, sometimes quite profusely, and owners usually recognize running movements as part of the seizure.

This state of unconscious generalized uncoordinated muscular activity normally lasts no more than a matter of several seconds, perhaps a minute or so, and then the dog relaxes, becomes conscious of its surroundings and will return to normal; in many circumstances whilst the owner might be distressed, the dog will recover, wondering what all the fuss is about.

The best thing to do if a dog has a fit is to try to leave it alone to come out of the fit quietly and ensure there is no risk of it injuring itself. Make sure, for instance, that it can't knock anything over or risk falling in a ditch. Move people away, especially children, in case it inadvertently snaps if they try to intervene. The only occasion to be concerned is if the dog suffers either 'cluster seizures' – multiple seizures over a twenty-four-hour period, or what's called 'status epilepticus', a persistent seizure lasting longer than five minutes. In such circumstances there is the risk of more permanent brain damage occurring, and veterinary assistance should be sought immediately.

Successful treatment of seizures is dependent on identifying the cause – hence the need for appropriate veterinary advice and intervention. Many owners will find it helpful to record a 'seizure diary', detailing events such as the time and duration of seizures, any pertinent observations relating to the seizure itself, the circumstances that preceded the event, environmental conditions, and so on. This will help the vet establish a diagnosis and access the effect of treatment. There are already a number of apps that can be downloaded from the internet if you find this would be useful.

Treatment

The treatment of idiopathic epilepsy will aim to reduce the duration and frequency of seizures. Unfortunately many drugs used to treat epilepsy in humans are either ineffective or more toxic in dogs. Vets will normally prescribe either the sedative drug phenobarbitone, in one or other of a number of various formulations, or potassium bromide, an anticonvulsant. Sometimes these treatments are combined, usually when the seizures are severe, or either drug is ineffective when used alone.

There are unfortunately side effects associated with anti-epileptic drugs (AEDs), including increased thirst and hence urination, and an increased appetite, and these, in association with increased sleeping, leads to obesity, restlessness, impaired muscular coordination, vomiting and diarrhoea. These side effects tend to be worse during the first two or four weeks of treatment and then decline, but in other dogs they can be permanent. Some vets are now challenging seizure freedom as the absolute goal of anti-epileptic drug treatment, although this is usually the owner's preference. They argue, quite rightly, that vets and owners should not lose sight of the potential harms of treatment, and should always keep this fine balance in mind, and in favour of the dog's quality of life.

HYPOMYELINATION, 'SHAKING PUPPY SYNDROME'

'Shaking puppy syndrome' can affect a young dog's central or peripheral nervous system. Tremors start soon after birth at around twelve to fourteen days of age and affect the entire body. An affected puppy also shows problems with coordination and balance. Puppies tend to shake more when eating, and excitement generally makes the shaking worse. The tremors subside when the puppy is sleeping. Mentally an affected puppy is otherwise fine.

Myelin insulates and protects nerve cells, and if a puppy is deficient in this fatty protection around nerve cells, signs of tremors will result. In most breeds the condition is inherited as a simple autosomal recessive gene.

A dog of any breed can develop hypomyelination; however, certain breeds appear to be predisposed to the condition. Among the gundog breeds these include the English and Welsh Springer Spaniel, Weimaraners, Golden Retrievers and Hungarian Vizslas. In Golden Retrievers, hypomyelination involves the peripheral nervous system, rather than the central nervous system, so they exhibit all the signs of hypomyelination seen in other breeds, but don't actually shake. The condition also starts slightly later in Golden Retrievers, between five and seven weeks of age.

There is no effective treatment for shaking puppy syndrome, but fortunately most affected puppies will eventually recover, and appear relatively normal by the time they are one to one and a half years of age. Some dogs retain a mild hind-limb tremor for the remainder of their lives.

CEROID LIPOFUSCINOSIS

Neuronal ceroid lipofuscinosis (NCL) is an inherited disease of dogs characterized by progressive unsteadiness and blindness. The genetic defect results in material known as 'ceroid- or lipofuscin-like lipopigments' forming within nerve cells in the brain and the retina of the eye. Among gundog breeds it is reported in the English Setter, but it also occurs in other dog breeds as diverse as the American Bulldog, the Tibetan Terrier, the Border Collie and the Dachshund.

Clinical signs usually start to become apparent by two to three years of age, often as the dog having poor sight in low light conditions and seemingly disorientated. As the disease progresses, more obvious signs occur and can include behavioural changes, where the dog may show aggression or anxiousness or disinterest, blindness, unsteadiness both standing and walking with uncoordinated muscle movements, a loss of coordination, dementia, and partial seizures. Affected dogs will typically adopt a wide stance when standing, with occasional muscle twitching. A definitive diagnosis requires DNA testing of buccal swabs.

There is no known treatment, and most affected dogs are euthanased within twelve months of first showing clinical signs.

FUCOSIDOSIS

Fucosidosis is a relatively uncommon hereditary disease that occurs in the English Springer Spaniel. It causes a variety of neurological signs that progress over a period of several months. The dog's balance and movement are particularly affected, and are most evident when it is walking on a slippery surface or attempts movements such as turning. In addition, affected dogs lose weight and may suffer from swallowing difficulties, and sometimes they regurgitate their food.

The disease affects young adults, usually between eighteen months and four years of age, and is caused by the absence of an enzyme called alpha-L-fucosidase. When this enzyme is absent, more complex compounds build up in the cells, particularly cells in the lymph nodes, liver, pancreas, kidney, lungs and bone marrow. However, it is the accumulation in the brain and nerve cells that is most important, giving rise to the clinical signs and eventually resulting in death.

Fucosidosis has what is known as an autosomal recessive mode of inheritance. A dog needs to inherit the defective gene from both its dam and sire in order to be affected, which is one reason why the disease is relatively rare. Unfortunately carriers, which show no signs of the disease, can be much more common. A DNA test is available to use in the English Springer Spaniel.

SKIN DISEASES

ELBOW HYGROMA

A hygroma is a non-painful, fluid-filled swelling surrounded by a thick, fibrous capsule that develops under the skin and is caused by repeated trauma to an area over a bony prominence, often as a result of lying on a hard surface. Most commonly hygromas are seen on the outside of the elbow in larger, short-haired breeds of dog.

Among the gundog breeds, Labrador Retrievers appear particularly prone to developing elbow hygromas. The elbow isn't the only site where these swellings develop – they can also occur on the hip and hock.

Initially they are small, soft and fluctuant, but they may become quite large, up to two inches in diameter, or very hard. They may be present for the whole of the dog's lifetime, causing no problems at all. In some instances, however, hygromas can become infected, when they are painful and sometimes warm to the touch, and may discharge serosanginous fluid from a number of draining tracts. In such instances hygromas will require some form of veterinary intervention.

Hygromas are often associated with a more sedentary lifestyle, and as a consequence some dogs only develop them in old age. The reason they tend to be more common in larger dogs is that more weight is placed on the bony area having contact with the hard surface. Technically they can be prevented by providing the dog soft bedding to lie on; however, for many gundogs this may be impractical, and many dogs will either habitually destroy such bedding material, or will simply choose to lie on a firmer surface in preference to a softer bed.

If the hygroma becomes particularly large and problematic, bandaging the elbows can help prevent the condition worsening, or your vet may recommend draining the fluid. Drainage is only a temporary solution, of course, and will often need to be repeated, thus increasing the risk of introducing infection. An alternative form of treatment is to remove the hygroma in its entirety. Unfortunately quite a large area of skin will usually require removal, and skin grafts may be required. The dog may also have to wear a splint whilst the wound heals and to protect the leg during recovery.

Note: It is always a good idea to move dogs recovering from illness, injury or surgery so that they don't persist in lying on one side, increasing the tendency for a hygroma to develop. Get the dog up and moving around occasionally, or at least alternate the side that it is lying on several times during the day.

INTERDIGITAL CYSTS (FURUNCLES)

So-called interdigital cysts are painful nodules located on or near the web of a dog's paws between the toes. They can occur singly, or as multiple lesions affecting more than one foot. Interdigital cysts seem to occur more frequently in dogs that have short bristly fur between the toes, such as Labrador Retrievers, which can easily become ingrown causing infection, swelling and irritation.

The cause of these interdigital comedones and follicular cysts is unknown, but most likely involves some form of damage to the tissues of the toe, resulting in blocking or narrowing of the opening of hair follicles, and hence the retention of the follicular contents. They can also be caused by foreign material that becomes embedded in the paw, typically grass awns, splinters and thorns. A parasitic mite infestation (demodectic mange) can also cause interdigital furunculosis, when multiple swellings may be seen affecting more than one foot.

They appear as reddish-purple, shiny swellings around 1–2cm in diameter. They are often fluctuant, and may rupture when palpated and exude a bloody material. Interdigital furuncles are most commonly found on the dorsal aspect (top) of the paw, but may also be found ventrally. They cause irritation and the dog may constantly lick its paw, making it more susceptible to infection.

Interdigital furuncles or comedones are often associated with deep bacterial infection, and if so there may be several nodules with new lesions developing as others resolve. A common cause of recurrence is the granulomatous reaction to the presence of small particles of hair (keratin) in the tissues of the toe. If the cause is foreign material, this will frequently migrate causing recurring lesions as it tracks up the foot.

Treatment

Successful treatment will be dependent on the immediate cause, but it will be helpful to prevent the dog licking its foot, and to bathe it in a warm solution of either table salt, Epsom salts, or an antiseptic solution such as chlorhexidine. This will remove bacterial and fungal material that could cause further infection, it will also be soothing to the sore, itchy feet, and it can help bring foreign material or ingrown hair to the surface and encourage the cyst to burst. Dissolve about a cupful of salt or Epsom salts in approximately two gallons of water, and if necessary stand the dog in a bath so that he/she can soak all four feet at once. Do be sure to rinse and dry the feet afterwards, because moisture makes the pads more attractive to infection.

If the cyst bursts, examine the site for any foreign material, and if you can, remove it with blunt-ended tweezers. The dog will most likely resent this, so get someone to hold and restrain it for you, and if necessary use a muzzle. If there is pus the cause will most likely be infection, so keep bathing the foot in antiseptic as previously described until the wound heals over.

If the cyst recurs despite your efforts it is best to take the dog to see your vet. He may wish to examine the lesion more closely, which often requires an anaesthetic, when the cyst can be opened up and the area explored to see if there is further foreign material, or to attempt to flush out small hair particles and suchlike. Afterwards the vet is likely to bandage the foot and prescribe a course of antibiotics. Because of the deep-seated nature of this type of infection, a more prolonged course of treatment may sometimes be necessary.

RINGWORM

Ringworm, contrary to what the name suggests, has nothing to do with worms but is a fungal skin infection particularly affecting the hair follicles. The fungi involved are called dermatophytes, which literally means 'plants that live on the skin' – and essentially these fungi feed on dead skin and hair. Ringworm is not species specific, and can be transmitted from animal to animal and from animal to man. It is also highly contagious, so be aware that if your dog has ringworm it is possible for you to contract the infection.

Dermatophytes are ubiquitous. Under certain conditions they can live in the soil, and as affected cattle will scratch themselves on gateposts and fencing, it is easy to see why dogs exercising in the countryside can be especially susceptible. The infection will be more apparent in younger dogs and puppies because their immune systems have not yet fully developed. The disease usually starts out as a small reddened circle (or ring, hence the name), and will usually result in the loss of the hair within that ring. Other diseases can start out in the same way – demodectic mange can also present as reddened bald circles – so appearance is not diagnostic, and as with many other skin conditions, ringworm can be very difficult to diagnose. Infected lesions fluoresce under ultraviolet light, so your vet may try to confirm the diagnosis using what is called a Wood's Lamp, or by taking samples of skin or skin scrapings for analysis.

Ringworm itself is not particularly 'itchy', however, the resulting skin lesions or sores can become infected, and the resulting skin infection can be especially itchy, which in turn causes the dog to scratch even more.

Treatment

Treatment is effective, and typically comprises a course of an antibiotic known as griseofulvin, so your vet is likely to prescribe a course of tablets to be given for a number of weeks. As with all antibiotics, it is important to complete the course of treatment even though the infection may appear to have cleared up well before you finish the tablets.

'PUPPY DERMATITIS'

'Puppy dermatitis', or 'juvenile staphylococcal pyoderma', is a condition that quite commonly affects young dogs of twelve to sixteen weeks of age, and particularly younger puppies. It presents as small pustules on hairless parts of the body, particularly over the abdomen, and especially those areas that can become soiled with urine once the bitch stops cleaning up her puppies, such as around the vulva in bitches and the prepuce in dogs and the inside of the thighs. It can also occur on the muzzle and under the chin. The small pustules, little pus-filled 'blisters', can erupt and coalesce, but although some dogs lick and occasionally scratch these lesions, they tend

to cause little or no discomfort. This is one of those conditions that seems to worry the owner more than the dog.

Bacteria called *staphylococcus aureus*, a very common bacterium that as a 'commensal organism' causes little or no problem whatsoever, can often be cultured from these lesions. Occasionally it may be necessary for your vet to administer an antibiotic, usually as a cream or ointment to be rubbed on affected areas, but as no more than a mild skin condition, it will usually clear up spontaneously. The puppy eventually develops its own natural immunity to these bacteria, and although antiseptic bathing lotions and soaps can help speed recovery, many puppies and young dogs will simply 'grow out' of the condition.

'PUPPY HEAD GLAND DISEASE'

This is a somewhat uncommon but sometimes severe condition variously referred to as 'puppy strangles', 'puppy cellulitis', 'juvenile cellulitis' and probably more correctly termed 'juvenile dermatopathic lymphadenitis'. It is a disease of young dogs occurring most frequently in puppies aged less than four months, but in more unusual cases has also been seen in older juvenile dogs under twelve months of age. Golden Retrievers, Gordon Setters and Labrador Retrievers are the gundog breeds that seem predisposed to this condition, although it has been described in a variety of other breeds. A familial history is present in some cases, suggesting a hereditary component, and occasionally whole litters may be involved.

The disease is essentially a pustular dermatitis, and in the early stages the signs could be confused with those of puppy dermatitis. However, in this case the signs are progressive and the disease is much more severe.

In the early stages the skin over the muzzle, lips and inside the ears will often be swollen, and small papules appear in these areas. Similar lesions may also appear on the feet, and less commonly the abdomen, chest, vulva, prepuce, or around the anus. These papules look like little pimples and typically fistulate, drain, and become crusty. A marked pustular otitis externa (an inflammatory ear disease) is common, and

A Labrador Retriever puppy with skin lesions typical of puppy head gland disease.

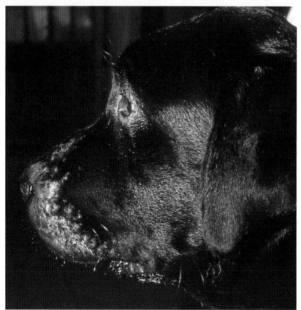

Despite effective treatment this Labrador Retriever was still left with extensive scarring after recovering from head gland disease.

the ears frequently become thickened and oedematous. Commonly there will be an associated enlargement of the regional, submandibular and prescapular lymph nodes, which can be seen and felt as swellings under and just behind the jaws, and in front of the shoulders, respectively. The puppy may have difficulty eating and swallowing because of the enlarged lymph nodes. Lameness is often reported, and as the condition worsens, it will become lethargic and unwilling to walk or stand.

The cause remains unknown. The disease is believed to be immune related and caused by some dysfunction in the immune system, because of the immediate, often dramatic response to corticosteroid treatment, and there is likely to be some hereditary component because of the breed and familial predisposition that is often reported. Whilst there may be some secondary bacterial infection, particularly as lesions erupt and discharge, which will require antibiotic therapy, a primary cause due to viral or bacterial infection can be ruled out because microscopic examination of papulopustular lesions shows granulomatous inflammation with pus but no microorganisms present, and carefully performed cultures from these lesions are negative.

Puppies suffering this disease can become quite sick, and for them the condition can be life-threatening. Even if they recover, if left untreated, serious scarring and permanent hair loss can result. Affected puppies must therefore be treated immediately by a veterinary surgeon, because as previously indicated the condition responds to corticosteroids. Glucocorticoids in relatively large doses are the treatment of choice, and when the puppy's condition has resolved, these drugs must be withdrawn slowly under veterinary supervision in decreasing doses over a period of weeks. Early and aggressive therapy is indicated, and if there is evidence of secondary bacterial infection, your vet will usually prescribe antibiotics as well.

BURNS

Gundogs specifically are at no greater or lesser risk of injury from burns than any other type of dog, but some consideration, certainly of appropriate first aid measures, needs to be included here for completeness. A burn is an injury to the skin caused by the following:

- Dry heat such as fires and contact with hot surfaces
- Corrosive chemicals, particularly strong acids and petroleum products
- Electricity or radiation
- Excessive cold, which can cause frostbite, especially to the extremities such as the feet, tail and ear tips in extreme weather conditions

A scald is an injury caused by moist heat, typically boiling water, but the distinction is of little practical interest since treatment will generally be similar. The clinical signs are also similar, and initially comprise redness and heat, swelling and pain, and later the loss of hair and a leathery appearance to the affected skin surface.

Burns and scalds are extremely painful, and any such injury, if extensive, should be treated by a veterinary surgeon. Nevertheless some useful first aid measures include:

- Cooling the affected area as quickly as possible
- Keeping the dog warm once the initial cooling is completed
- Dressing the wound as necessary

Cold water is best, gently hosed on to and over the affected area. Applying ice packs is less effective since only a limited area of skin can be cooled, and pressure is thereby applied on a wound that is already extremely painful and sensitive.

It is usually difficult to keep the patient warm without heating any burnt areas (which will cause the animal considerable pain). Consequently it is better to conserve heat by wrapping unaffected areas in dry blankets and shielding the dog from draughts.

If it is practical, dressing a burn wound will prevent any further fluid loss, protect the damaged tissues from further injury, and prevent the animal contaminating the wound by licking it. The heat that causes a burn will destroy most skin bacteria, so burn wounds and scalds present as sterile wounds and a dressing will assist in reducing any subsequent infection risk.

Always wear gloves when treating chemical burns. Flush away as much as possible of the chemical contamination. If caused by a known alkali, such as caustic soda or quicklime, prepare and mix equal quantities of vinegar and water and use this solution to flush the wound. If it has been caused by a strong acid, such as battery acid, use a concentrated solution of bicarbonate or soda (washing soda). However, the success of treatment will depend on quickly flushing away as much of the contaminating chemical as possible, and prompt use of a hosepipe will usually suffice.

The most serious complication of electrical burns is electrocution; however, electrical burns are rarely extensive. The most common circumstance is a puppy or adolescent dog that has chewed through a household cable. This typically leaves a longitudinal wound across the tongue.

Many burns and scalds may not be immediately obvious, and only become apparent later when hair is lost over the area of the injury, or affected skin takes on a characteristic leathery appearance. Always suspect scalding as the cause of a skin wound that resembles an inverted pear drop, where boiling water or some other hot fluid has dropped on the skin and then run vertically down the dog's coat.

ACRAL MUTILATION SYNDROME

Acral mutilation syndrome (AMS) is a relatively rare autosomal-recessive genetic disease that affects the sensory nerves of the feet and results in progressive self-mutilation. Among gundogs, the disease has been reported in German Short-Haired Pointers, English Pointers and English Springer Spaniels. Affected dogs present as over-grooming and licking their pads and paws to the point that there is skin loss and bleeding. These dogs can be identified soon after birth by a lack of sensory nerve reflexes – they won't withdraw the foot when pinched. Affected pups are often smaller than unaffected littermates, and breeders are likely to report how these pups constantly lick and bite at their paws, so there will be swollen reddened paws, nail loss, and in severe cases, paws may be lost through chewing and there can be painless fractures.

Mildly affected dogs can be treated with anxiolytic drugs such as diazepam, and be made to wear Elizabethan collars, but many cases rapidly deteriorate and require euthanasia.

IDIOPATHIC CUTANEOUS AND RENAL GLOMERULAR VASCULOPATHY (CRGV)

Otherwise known as 'Alabama rot', CRGV was first reported in the 1980s as affecting racing greyhounds in the USA. More recently, between December 2012 and March 2013, a very similar disease was recognized as affecting dogs walked in the New Forest. Since then it has been reported in a number of areas of the UK, including Surrey, Dorset, Cornwall, Kent, Greater Manchester, Yorkshire and the Border Counties. At the time of writing the cause of the disease remains unknown. In the USA, CRGV only affected greyhounds, and some genetic link was suspected; however, the disease in the UK has no such familial predisposition, and a variety of dogs has been affected.

Affected dogs present with skin lesions and acute kidney failure. The skin lesions typically present as a focal swelling, a patch of red skin or a defect in the skin (like an ulcer) around 1–4cm in length, generally, but not exclusively, below the stifle or elbow. They can also be found in the mouth, or on the tongue.

Over the subsequent two to seven days, affected dogs can develop clinical signs of kidney failure, which can include vomiting, reduced appetite and tiredness. Although the majority of affected dogs have died or been put to sleep due to acute renal failure, aggressive veterinary treatment has enabled a proportion of dogs to recover. Microscopic examination of the kidneys revealed changes almost identical to those reported in greyhounds affected by Alabama rot (CRGV) in the USA.

The key points to understand are that the total number of cases reported in the UK has been very low as a proportion of the total dog population, and that both skin lesions and kidney failure in dogs are much more likely to be due to other causes.

Without knowing what causes this disease, it is difficult to advise on prevention. Washing the dirt and mud off your dog immediately after it has been walked or worked, especially in woodland, would seem sensible, and as early recognition and aggressive management of this disease are crucial, speak to your local vet if you are concerned about your dog.

EYE CONDITIONS
CONJUNCTIVITIS

Also known as red eye or pink eye, conjunctivitis refers to inflammation of the sensitive lining inside the eyelids and covering the outer surface

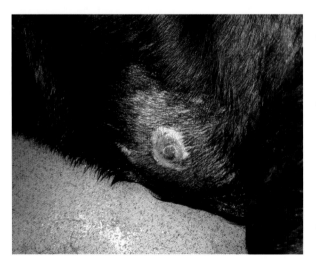

Cutaneous and renal glomerular vasculopathy (CRGV), or 'Alabama rot'. Although this particular dog did not go on to develop the disease, this suspected case serves to illustrate the type of skin lesion commonly found and associated with the disease. GILLY NICKOLS

of the eyeball. The conjunctiva has a rich blood supply, so when irritated it goes red and becomes inflamed and thus painful. Conjunctivitis is one of the most common eye disorders in dogs.

Signs include a reddening of the conjunctiva, excess tears, swelling of the eyelids and pain, causing the dog to squint and paw at its eyes. It can occur in either one or both eyes. If untreated, conjunctivitis can extend to lead to permanent damage of the cornea (the transparent front of the eye) and other ocular structures.

There are many causes of conjunctivitis, including trauma, allergies and foreign bodies, and infection that may be due to bacterial, viral or other similar microbiological causes. Certain breeds are predisposed to developing this condition, particularly those prone to either entropion (where the everted eyelid exposes the conjunctiva to insult) or ectropion (where the in-turned eyelid causes the eyelashes to brush against the sensitive conjunctiva and cornea).

Treatment

Successful treatment relies on identifying and resolving the underlying cause, and unless you can see an obvious, easily rectifiable cause, a thorough ophthalmic examination by your veterinary surgeon is to be recommended. In most cases, topical, broad-spectrum antibiotics in the form of prescription eye drops will resolve conjunctivitis caused by bacterial infection in dogs. Topical steroid eye drops may be indicated to reduce the inflammation, however never use steroids in an eye unless directed by your vet. If eye drops are not effective and a more chronic condition develops, further investigation is likely to be indicated, to include referral to a specialized veterinary ophthalmologist.

ECTROPION

Ectropion is an eye condition where one or both of the lower eyelids roll outwards. Ectropion appears to be a genetic predisposition in some breeds. It can also be caused by trauma, marked weight loss, or loss of facial muscle tone around the eyes in old age; it can also follow on from other eye conditions, such as infection. Develop-

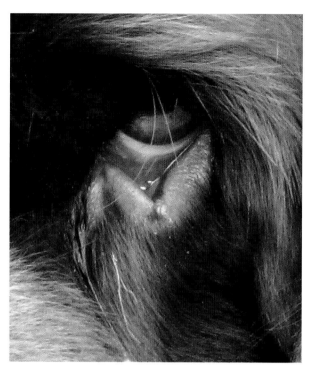

A Sussex Spaniel with entropion. In this instance the dog is not clinically affected, but the exposed conjunctiva is obviously prone to insult.

mental or inherited ectropion is most frequently seen in younger dogs. Acquired ectropion can obviously occur at any age, but may be more common in older dogs. One or both eyes can be affected.

Affected dogs have droopy lower eyelids. Since ectropion exposes the sensitive conjunctiva on the inner surface of the eyelid, it will cause watery eyes, swollen or red conjunctiva, and facial hair staining from an overflow of tears. Recurrent eye infections are common in affected individuals.

Treatment

The disorder can be treated. Eye drops or other lubricants, such as eye ointments, may be prescribed for mild to moderate cases to help keep the eyelid well lubricated. If there is secondary infection then eye drops or ointments containing antibiotics can be substituted until the infection clears. Surgery may be necessary in more severe cases, which, if left untreated, might progress to cause increasing pain and permanent eye damage. One of several surgical procedures can be used to correct ectropion, including shortening the affected eyelid to tense the skin and evert the drooping lid.

ENTROPION

Entropion is the inversion, or rolling inwards, of all or part of the edge of an eyelid. The effect is to cause hairs along the eyelid to come into contact with the eye, particularly the conjunctiva and cornea (the transparent front of the eyeball), creating frictional irritation and discomfort; this can severely damage these sensitive structures. Entropion is a painful condition.

Entropion can be developmental/congenital, when it is referred to as primary entropion, or acquired, when it is called secondary entropion. There is a genetic predisposition to developmental entropion in some breeds; where it is congenital, this will be apparent soon after birth, once the puppy's eyes open. It can also be acquired as a result of trauma, inflammation or infection, and as the facial skin becomes more lax in old age.

Entropion usually affects both eyes. It can affect the upper eyelids, the lower eyelids, or

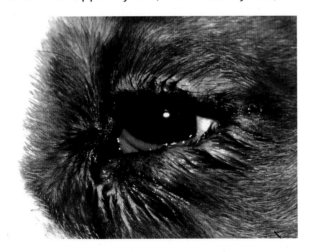

Entropion affecting the lower eyelid: the lid is inverted, and hair rubs on the sensitive cornea, causing pain and resulting in excess tear production. In this case early surgical correction was successful in effecting a long-term improvement.

both, although generally it is more common as a lower lid defect. Signs include excessive production of tears, squinting, eye redness and pain. Entropion is likely to be a hereditary abnormality in facial conformation; selection for one facial characteristic results in the development of entropic eyes as an unintended consequence. Whilst much more common in breeds with flat faces, short muzzles and heavy facial skin folds, it occurs sporadically in gundogs. In Clumber Spaniels, the working varieties without the heavy facial folds, appear to be less affected.

Treatment

Entropion is extremely painful. Severe developmental entropion will not improve without treatment, and the signs of entropion will worsen with time. If left untreated, entropion can lead to severe scarring of the cornea, erosion, ulceration, rupture and eventually blindness. The goals of treating this disorder are to relieve chronic irritation. Surgical correction is normally the best option, and involves everting the eyelid margin away from the eyeball by removing a slice of the inverted eyelid and pulling together and stitching the exposed skin edges. Surgical correction is often best carried out once the dog is mature and its facial conformation and the eyelids themselves are fully developed. Consequently treatment can include a temporary correction, especially in puppies, as well as permanent correction once adult conformation is achieved. The underlying problems, such as corneal abrasion, corneal ulceration and conjunctivitis, will then resolve.

DISTICHIASIS

Distichiasis is another eyelid condition where in this case small hairs, called cilia, originate from abnormally positioned follicles just behind – that is, inside – the eyelashes. The condition is congenital – present at birth – although the cilia may not be immediately apparent or cause problems until the dog is juvenile. It is probably hereditary, and although all breeds can be affected, among gundogs it is more common in the Golden Retriever.

These aberrant hairs impinge on sensitive structures in the eye, particularly the conjunctiva and cornea, causing discomfort, and consequently the dog has a tendency to squint, produce excess tears, and be prone to conjunctivitis. The condition can be particularly uncomfortable once the cornea is involved and becomes inflamed.

Treatment

Involves removing the abnormally growing hairs, either by periodically depilating the hairs under sedation and local anaesthesia, or by operation, using either electrolysis to remove individual hairs, or surgically removing the affected strip of tissue from just behind the eyelid.

CORNEAL ULCERS

Corneal ulcers are deep abrasions of the clear, transparent part of the eyeball, known as the cornea. Corneal ulcers are painful, and affected dogs will squint, have swollen, cloudy or watery eyes, rub at their faces, and avoid bright light.

There are many causes, but trauma, or direct damage to the eye surface is probably the most common. This can be caused by a cat scratch, or a foreign body such as a stick or thorn, injuring

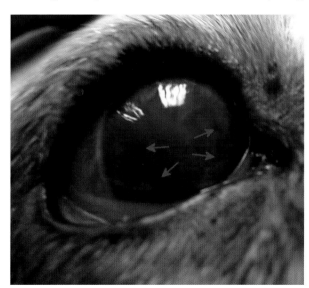

A healing corneal ulcer. The cornea has no blood supply, so healing relies on temporary vascularization (arrowed), whereby small vessels migrate into the affected part of the cornea from the surrounding conjunctiva.

the cornea, or something like a grass awn entering the adjacent conjunctival sac. Ulcers are especially common in highly excitable dogs that have little fear of entering and hunting through thick covert. In serious and more complicated cases, the corneal ulcer can become deeper and may eventually rupture, leaking pus and blood from the eyeball. Corneal ulcers can predispose to deep bacterial eye infections, which can cause permanent scarring to the otherwise transparent cornea, and sometimes lead to permanent blindness.

If you notice the signs listed above, or otherwise suspect your dog may have damaged the front of its eye, always have it checked by your vet, who may in some cases wish to refer it to an eye specialist for treatment.

Treatment

Simple, superficial corneal ulcers are normally treated with topical broad-spectrum antibiotic and/or antifungal eye drops or ointments to manage infection, together with topical medication to help reduce pain. Sometimes the vet may choose to stimulate the healing process by cauterizing the ulcer.

Deeper corneal ulcers and those slow to heal or complicated by secondary infection usually require surgical intervention to save the eye. Depending upon the cause of the ulcers, topical treatments may be tried before surgery. There are a number of surgical techniques, and more are being developed all the time. Generally these procedures involve covering and protecting the ulcer by some form of corneal or conjunctival graft over that area. Surgery will be followed by treatment with antibiotics, medication to reduce pain, and possibly soft contact lenses and topical tear supplements.

HORNER'S SYNDROME

Horner's syndrome has three component signs that manifest more or less simultaneously, affecting only one eye. The signs are:

- Drooping of the upper eyelid and a loss of tone in the lower lid

- Constriction of the pupil (a condition referred to as 'miosis')
- A sinking of the eyeball back into its socket, and a consequent 'prolapse'/elevation of the third eyelid, which becomes reddened as a consequence

These signs together result from some interference to the integrity of the sympathetic nerve supply to various facial muscles, part of the autonomic nervous system that controls functions that we perform automatically, and which we are not usually conscious of performing (such as breathing, blinking and the movement of our intestines).

The precise cause of a dog developing Horner's syndrome varies; anything that impinges on the particular autonomic nerves supplying the eye and its surrounding muscles can be a factor, and sometimes the cause may not be obvious (when it is termed 'idiopathic'). Frequently trauma anywhere along the nerve that tracks down the spinal column in the neck, emerges between vertebrae under the forelimb, up the side of the neck, through the inner part of the ear, and then up to around the eye, can lead to Horner's syndrome. Examples include cervical spinal disc prolapse, blunt trauma to the neck, and an infection deep inside the ear, when it is often associated with the animal holding its head down on the affected side.

Incorrect use of a 'choke lead', which tightens and in so doing traumatizes the neck muscles and the associated nerve running up the side of the vertebrae, has a relative common association.

The likelihood and rate of recovery will obviously be dependent on the underlying cause, and it is best to take the dog to your vet so that he or she can make a thorough examination. Clearly some of the potential underlying causes, such as cervical vertebral disc disease and deep-seated ear infection, need appropriate treatment.

What is known as 'idiopathic' Horner's syndrome, where the precise cause cannot be determined and so it is essentially a cosmetic condition, is a relatively common cause and is particularly prevalent in Golden Retrievers. Idiopathic Horner's syndrome will usually resolve spontaneously, but over a number of weeks, although it may take up to eight months.

'CHERRY EYE'

'Cherry eye' is a condition which usually develops during the first year of life. It involves the third eyelid or nictitating membrane. All dogs have a third eyelid or nictitating membrane that normally lies hidden by the lower eyelid. Tear glands are located around the cartilage connections of the nictitating membranes, and these so-called Harderian glands provide a major source of tear film and eye lubrication. However, if the fibrous tissues that hold the third eyelids to the surface of the eye become weakened, the tear glands can prolapse or evert over or around the third eyelid. The mass will remain unless the condition is corrected, and will appear as if the dog has a 'cherry' sticking out of its eye (which is why most people refer to the condition as 'cherry eye').

The precise cause is unknown; however, it appears to have a genetic component involving weak connective tissue around the third eyelid. Inflammation as well as tissue hypertrophy (an increase in the size produced solely by enlargement of existing cells, rather than by new cellular growth) may also play a role in the development of cherry eye. While cherry eye can affect one or both eyes, it doesn't normally happen in both at the same time. Affected dogs are uncomfortable because the eye becomes dry, and there is swelling, irritation, inflammation and pain. The dogs are likely to paw at their eyes and rub their faces on flooring or furniture to try and relieve the discomfort.

Treatment

Prolapse of the gland of the nictitating membrane or third eyelid should be treated as quickly as possible. The condition itself is not particularly dangerous, but the longer the third eyelid gland is out of place, the more inflamed, irritated and possibly infected it may become. At one time, the treatment of choice was to remove the prolapsed gland; however, we now know that removing the gland will cause the dog to suffer from severe dry eye, because that gland is responsible for much of normal tear-film production.

More recently, surgical repositioning rather than removal of that gland has become the treatment of choice. Many different surgical repositioning techniques have been reported, and vets can determine which technique to use, usually considering the ease of the procedure, its potential effect on future tear production, the chances of re-prolapse, and the expected cosmetic results. Any of the repositioning techniques, performed properly, should result in a cosmetically acceptable outcome with a very low chance of recurrence.

Note: Some dogs are born with visible third eyelids along the lower portion of their eyes. These are commonly referred to as 'haws'. The existence of haws is not the same thing as cherry eye, and is almost always only of cosmetic rather than medical concern.

HEREDITARY CATARACT

Young dogs may suffer two types of inherited cataract. Developmental or congenital cataracts develop before the puppy is born and should be detectable by ophthalmoscopic examination once the eyes are open, certainly by at least eight weeks of age. Dogs of those breeds that suffer juvenile cataracts, on the other hand, are born with normal lenses which then proceed to degenerate over time so that, depending on the type of cataract and the breed of dog involved, the cataract may be seen any time from as young as eight weeks to as old as seven or eight years of age.

Hereditary cataract in the Welsh Springer Spaniel is apparent in very young dogs, typically those less than twelve months of age. At the time of writing it is thought to have been eliminated from breeding stock in the UK as a result of eye testing and only breeding from clear dogs.

Labradors suffer hereditary cataracts which usually, but not always, become apparent between one and three years of age. The cataract affects the back of the lens, and doesn't necessarily cause complete blindness. The mode of inheritance of hereditary cataract in the Labrador Retriever is either due to a dominant gene, with what is known as 'incomplete penetrance', or to a recessive gene. Although the cataract is not always apparent in younger dogs they may still be carrying the gene, and are still capable of passing on the condition to their offspring. Current research aims to identify the gene or genes responsible, and thus develop a DNA test that should enable the genetic status of Labradors to be established for HC, and allow responsible breeders to avoid producing affected puppies. Until then we must continue to rely on clinical eye testing to identify the defect, and attempt breeding from only clinically 'clear' dogs in the hope that the cataract won't develop later.

HEREDITARY RETINAL DISEASE

The retina is the light-sensitive layer at the back of the eye. It is composed of two principal types of photoreceptive nerve cells, the rods and cones, each responsible for detecting and responding differently to light of various wavelengths, which is then processed in the brain to enable the dog to appropriately distinguish all the various things that it sees.

Behind part of the dog's retina lies another layer of pigmented and highly reflective cells that form what is known as the tapetum. The tapetum reflects incoming light back to the retinal nerve cells lying above, thus increasing their sensitivity in the central, tapetal part of the retina. This structure is responsible for the illuminous phenomenon seen at night when light shines into the eyes of animals with a tapetal fundus; it is particularly obvious in the cat.

There are various forms of inherited retinal disease recognized in some of the gundog breeds. Those most commonly recorded will be described.

Progressive Retinal Atrophy (PRA)
PRA is a term loosely used to describe a variety of retinal degenerative diseases that produce similar clinical signs. The condition was called 'night blindness' in the past, as this is one of the

commonly presenting signs. Although PRA can be both acquired and inherited, most people will use the term to refer to the inherited form of the disease. Inherited PRA will affect both eyes similarly. As our knowledge of the inherited form of the disease increases, however, it becomes appropriate to refer more accurately to the particular type of disease, described below, that is found in each of the respective breeds that are affected.

Generalized Progressive Retinal Atrophy (GPRA)

GPRA is an all-encompassing term for a number of inherited retinal diseases seen in many breeds of dog. In the UK we see two principal types of GPRA: rod/cone degeneration, and rod/cone dysplasia. Clinical signs and ophthalmoscopic findings are similar in both dysplastic and degenerative GPRA, with the exception of a late-onset generative form in which the ophthalmic changes are apparent in a different part of the retina. The age of onset is variable, but generally the dysplastic form of GPRA appears earlier than the degenerative form. GPRA is recognized in the Irish Setter, the Chesapeake, Golden, Labrador and Nova Scotia Duck-Tolling Retrievers and both Cocker and English Springer Spaniels. Another, second form of GPRA in Irish Setters is also being investigated as being potentially inherited in the breed.

Owners first recognize a loss of night vision, especially when their dog is negotiating unfamiliar territory. The disease will progress until there is visual loss in all lighting conditions, and the dog will go blind. At this stage the dog will have large, dilated, unresponsive pupils so that the reflective part of the retina at the back of the eye appears much more obvious. In time, secondary cataracts appear, which although appearing only as focal or radical opacities at first, will progress to being total, rendering the dog to all intents and purposes, completely blind. Because GPRA itself results in irreparable loss of vision, cataract surgery will not restore sight in affected dogs.

GPRA is inherited as a simile autosomal recessive gene. This means that to be affected, a dog must inherit a copy of the defective gene from both its parents. If one or other carries the defective gene and the other is 'clear', the dog will be clinically normal (as of course will dogs whose parents are both 'clear'). As various genetic defects in single genes responsible for causing the various forms of GPRA are identified, DNA tests become available. Those that have been developed at the time of writing are listed in the table.

DNA Tests available for GPRA in Gundogs

Gene Mutation	Breed
prcd	Portuguese Water Dog
	Chesapeake Bay Retriever
	Golden Retriever
	Labrador Retriever
	Nova Scotia Duck-Tolling Retriever
	Cocker Spaniel
rcd-1	Irish Setter
	Irish Red and White Setter

Retinal Pigment Epithelial Dystrophy (RPED)

Central progressive retinal atrophy, or retinal pigment epithelial dystrophy (RPED) is recognized in the Golden and Labrador Retriever and the English Springer Spaniel. Although in some dogs changes in the retina can be detected as early as twelve months of age, it is more commonly reported as starting at around eighteen months of age. The disease is caused when pigment containing nerve cells of the retina fail to break down materials formed when they respond to light. This material accumulates within the cells, and in turn causes the rods and cones of the retina to degenerate.

In contrast to GPRA, owners of dogs affected with RPED first report an inability to work in bright light, whilst in dim light the dog's vision appears to be adequate. Later, however, as the disease becomes more advanced, dogs with RPED will start to show poor vision in dim light.

Although the effects of RPED in working dogs are serious, unlike in GPRA, these dogs do not go totally blind (some peripheral vision is retained), nor do they develop cataracts. The mode of inheritance of this disease is more complex than in GPRA, and environmental factors such as feeding a poor diet and levels of vitamin E seem to influence the extent to which the disease manifests itself in different dogs.

RETINAL DYSPLASIA

Retinal dysplasia comprises a number of congenital conditions that result in abnormal development of the retina, the light-sensitive layer at the back of the eye, during gestation whilst the puppy is being formed in its mother's uterus. Not all forms of retinal dysplasia are hereditary; infection with canine herpes virus, for instance, can lead to retinal dysplasia.

Defective retinal development results in various anomalies that can be apparent when the retina is examined by specialist instruments called ophthalmoscopes. Folds, rosettes and ridges in the surface of the normally smooth retinal surface, as well as detachments of all or part of the retina from the underlying eyeball, can each be recognized depending on the form the condition takes.

There are two distinct forms of hereditary retinal dysplasia: multifocal retinal dysplasia, and total retinal dysplasia.

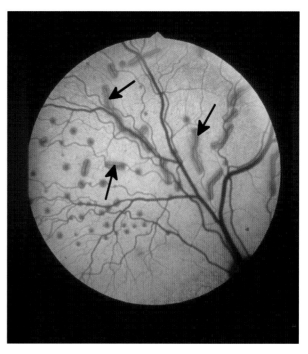

Characteristic signs of multifocal retinal dysplasia. Vermiform ('worm-like') greyish streaks in the retina (arrowed) are apparent where the retina is thrown up into folds.

Multifocal Retinal Dysplasia

This condition is recognized in the English Springer and American Cocker Spaniel, and the Labrador and Golden Retriever. It is characterized by the appearance of retinal folds and rosettes, the former appearance resulting from linear ridges in the retina, thrown up where abnormal growth has occurred, and the latter comprising discrete areas of variable numbers of retinal cells, rather than the smooth homogeneous distribution in the normal retina. Multifocal Retinal Dysplasia is currently under investigation as a hereditary disease in Sussex and Field Spaniels.

Total Retinal Dysplasia

This condition comprises either embryonic non-attachment or detachment of the retina. Among gundogs, TRD is only recognized in the Labrador Retriever, which suffers three forms of retinal dysplasia:

Form 1 retinal dysplasia comprises complete detachment of the retina. Puppies are blind from birth, and the condition is often associated with other ocular abnormalities such as microphthmus, where the eye is smaller than usual, and cataract.

Form 2 retinal dysplasia is reported in the USA, where retinal dysplasia accompanies other skeletal defects in growth.

Form 3 retinal dysplasia comprises multifocal retinal dysplasia, as described previously.

Retinal dysplasia is inherited as a simple autosomal recessive gene in all the breeds studied, with the exception of the disease reported in the USA among Labrador Retrievers, where it is associated with skeletal defects; here the inheritance is thought to be more complex.

PRIMARY GLAUCOMA OR GONIODYSGENESIS

Glaucoma is increased pressure within the eye, known as intraocular pressure, or IOP. The front of the eyeball, the part that lies in front of the lens, is filled with a clear fluid called aqueous fluid. Unlike tears, which bathe the outside of the eye, aqueous fluid is produced by cells within the eye, and exits through a drainage angle situated inside the eye, which runs all around and just behind the periphery of the cornea. Maintaining a normal IOP requires a balance between the rate of production of aqueous fluid, and the rate at which it is drained through the drainage angle. Should the drainage angle become partially blocked, IOP will increase, and the result is glaucoma.

Primary glaucoma is an inherited condition in which the drainage angle, which normally comprises a meshwork of tiny ligaments resembling a sieve, doesn't form properly. Aqueous fluid cannot escape as quickly as it should because this tissue is not as 'open' as it should be to facilitate its passage. This condition is described as primary angle-closure glaucoma, and in the UK it is recognized in the American and English Cocker Spaniel, the English and Welsh Springer Spaniel, and the Spanish Water Dog. The disease is also under investigation as an inherited angle-closure condition in the Hungarian Vizsla and the Golden Retriever. An open-angle form of inherited glaucoma is also recognized, although not, to date, to affect any gundog breed. A late-onset form is also being investigated in Welsh Springer Spaniels; these are dogs that, when previously tested as younger dogs, appeared to have had normal drainage angles.

Glaucoma is a very painful condition, and raised IOP affects the optic nerve at the back of the eye, which quickly degenerates. Consequently acute glaucoma causes pain and a risk of the dog becoming permanently blind.

Glaucoma can also arise as a consequence of another condition that indirectly obstructs the drainage angle. It can become obstructed by pus and cellular material produced as a consequence of some inflammatory disease within the eye, or it can become partially obstructed by the displaced lens in cases of lens luxation.

Treatment

Primary glaucoma is a condition of middle age and occurs in both eyes, although one eye is usually affected before the other. Typically it arises quite suddenly and often too late to save the sight in the affected eye. Left untreated, the affected eye will gradually soften under pressure and enlarge until the raised IOP is alleviated; the eye will then become less painful. Consequently most affected eyes require enucleation (removal of the eye) once the disease is diagnosed, and medical treatment is normally directed at attempting to control pressure and preserve sight in the other eye. Treatment will normally be prescribed to influence the production of aqueous fluid, and try and open up the drainage angle. This may include the use of miotics, drugs that constrict the pupil and hence open up the angle, and carbonic anhydrase inhibitors that tend to slow down the production of aqueous fluid.

There are several surgical procedures available intended to facilitate drainage from the anterior chamber of the eye, but unfortunately the response to surgery has been variable and not always successful. In short, there remains no effective cure for primary glaucoma.

The mode of inheritance of primary glaucoma has still to be determined. It is unlikely to be a single disease entity, but the clear breed and line predisposition would indicate an underlying genetically determined cause. Currently control of the disease relies on clinically screening dogs prior to breeding, and avoiding breeding from affected dogs.

EAR CONDITIONS

OTITIS EXTERNA

The opening to a dog's ear is very unlike ours, and the anatomy of the ear canal tends to make the dog more prone to ear problems. As you can see in the accompanying diagram, the canine ear canal descends vertically before turning in at right angles and continuing horizontally before

Dogs tend to get water down their ears whilst swimming, especially those that enthusiastically enter water for a retrieve, as shown here.

ending at the eardrum or tympanic membrane. This particular anatomical configuration tends to make the dog prone to having foreign bodies, notably grass awns, enter the vertical canal, where they cause irritation.

This arrangement also impedes drainage, and wax and other detritus can consequently build up where it acts as a focus for infection. The situation is made worse if the canal happens to be particularly narrow. Check your dog's ears regularly, and if you detect any abnormal odour, excess wax or discharge, clean the outer ear using a little olive oil or a proprietary human ear cleanser. Never attempt to clean further down the vertical canal than the part that you can easily visualize, otherwise you risk poking foreign material further down the canal, where it becomes more difficult to remove. Never try to treat your dog's ears if you cannot see the problem and feel confident that you can rectify it.

If you suspect your dog has an ear problem and there is no obvious cause, always ask your vet to examine the ears, when he can use a special instrument called an otoscope to inspect lower down the vertical ear canal. In addition a vet is likely to have special forceps which he or she can pass down the otoscope to grasp and withdraw any foreign material that has entered the ear.

AURAL HAEMATOMAS

Aural haematomas are warm, painful or non-painful swellings under the skin of a dog's ear flap resulting from the accumulation of blood. They are not particularly uncommon, and occur when a dog shakes its head vigorously and persistently scratches at its ears in an attempt to relieve the irritation caused by an ear infection or something similar – a grass seed down a dog's ear can cause intense irritation. Other causes for a dog scratching or shaking its head are infestation by fleas, mites, ticks or lice, and foreign material stuck inside the ear. Puncture wounds of the ear flap can also cause haematoma if the skin wound seals quickly but blood continues to seep under the skin.

Aural haematomas are caused by bleeding from one or more terminal branches of the auricular artery, which provides the blood supply to the ears. Trauma to the ear leads to inflammation and breakdown of the auricular cartilage, and rupture of the fragile superficial blood vessels in the ear flap. As blood leaks out, it becomes trapped between the skin and the ear cartilage, causing the focal swelling known as an aural haematoma.

Treatment
If left untreated, aural haematomas will frequently result in scarring and deformity of the affected ear flap, commonly called a 'cauliflower ear.' The best course of treatment is to drain the haematoma surgically. Sometimes vets will opt

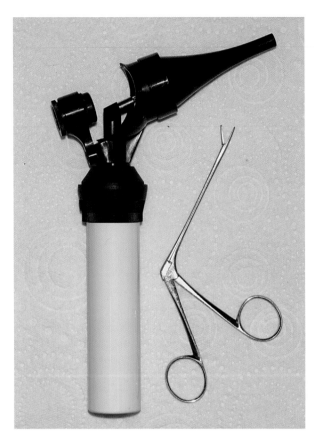

A veterinary otoscope and fine forceps. The instrument can be used to identify small foreign bodies, such as grass awns, deep down in the external ear canal. Fine forceps can then be passed down the otoscope, to grasp and withdraw the offending item.

to delay surgery to allow the traumatized blood vessels to stop bleeding and for the clot under the skin to start to resolve before scarring sets in.

The procedure involves making a skin incision over the haematoma and flushing the site thoroughly. Special surgical sutures are used to bring the affected tissue layers into direct contact and eliminate the pocket formerly filled with blood, and a temporary drain is inserted to allow continuous drainage so the haematoma doesn't reform as the wound heals. Of course, in addition the underlying cause has to be identified and eliminated, otherwise without alleviating the dog's discomfort, self-trauma and the haematoma will

recur. With correct surgical treatment the likelihood of a full recovery without recurrence is excellent.

DISEASES OF THE DIGESTIVE SYSTEM

GASTROENTERITIS

Gastroenteritis is a common condition, but one where early recognition and treatment are pivotal to returning the dog to normal health. The term 'gastroenteritis' refers primarily to inflammation of the stomach and intestines. The term 'gastritis' refers to inflammation of the stomach alone and is characterized by intermittent vomiting. Dogs are 'ready vomiters', meaning that any foreign item or material entering the stomach is likely to be immediately returned, a reaction which seemingly represents part of the species' natural protective mechanism. Inflammation primarily affecting the large bowel (the colon) is referred to as 'colitis'.

Gastroenteritis can have numerous causes, the most common being a reaction to new foods, foreign substances or medications, but it can also be caused by bacterial, viral or parasitic infections, and as a sign associated with other medical conditions. It often involves abdominal discomfort or pain, diarrhoea and/or vomiting. The vomit may contain foamy, yellowish bile, especially after the stomach has been emptied. Many owners will observe 'dry heaving' or 'gagging' after their dog eats or drinks.

Characteristically there will also be large volumes of diarrhoea produced three to six times a day. The diarrhoea may have a 'soft ice cream' consistency, and is often pale in colour. Many dogs will be tender when picked up around the abdomen, or will resist handling of the stomach and hindquarters. Most dogs affected with gastroenteritis will appear less active and have a decreased appetite. A low-grade fever is common.

Dehydration can occur quickly if the vomiting and diarrhoea persist for more than twenty-four hours. Furthermore, if the dog drinks to quench its thirst, that water will be returned along with gastric fluid from the stomach. The net result is an escalating loss of body fluid and a worsening of the dehydration. This is why withholding food and water is essential in the early stages, followed by offering 'little and often' so that the fluid balance can be gradually restored.

To determine what is causing the vomiting, diarrhoea, lethargy and other associated clinical signs, a good medical history is really helpful; key information to share with your vet would be the following:

- What you normally feed, how much and how often; more specifically what the dog ate or drank within the past forty-eight hours, including any new foods, treats or rewards that may have been given
- Any recent exposure to pesticides, medications, cleaning agents or any other new materials in your home environment, and any recent exposure to a new animal or person
- Any previous episodes of vomiting and diarrhoea (including their cause and treatment), in fact, any illness within the past month and any chronic illness that the dog may suffer

A thorough physical examination will establish evidence of dehydration, abdominal pain or tenderness, bloating or gas, swellings, or any other physical abnormality. Don't be surprised if some laboratory tests are recommended; there are many causes of vomiting and diarrhoea in dogs, and diagnosing gastroenteritis is often a question of elimination. Some other, more serious causes that the vet might need to rule out include systemic infections such as pneumonia, septicaemia, urinary tract infection, meningitis, foreign bodies or other obstructions, an intussusception (the telescoping of the intestine upon itself, causing a complete or partial obstruction), tumours, poisoning, or toxicities and pancreatitis.

Treatment

The principal treatment for gastroenteritis comprises the following:

- Rehydration and restoration of the blood electrolyte balance (especially sodium, potassium and/or chloride). Depending on the degree of dehydration, this fluid replacement therapy may be administered by mouth, subcutaneously (under the skin), or by means of an intravenous drip
- Food (and usually water) is withheld during the initial stages of treatment, and then slowly reintroduced. A bland diet fed in small, frequent feeds is generally recommended: give easily digestible food such as fish or chicken, white meat rather than red meat, and mixed with rice (say) rather than feeding dry dog biscuit. Your vet can always advise you on how best to feed the dog as an aid to speed recovery
- Antibiotics are not normally prescribed these days unless diagnostic testing suggests a bacterial infection. Antidiarrhoeal agents will, however, be more commonly used, and drugs that influence intestinal motility (activity) will only be prescribed if the likelihood of an intestinal obstruction, or indeed any mechanical and/or anatomical issue, has been eliminated

GASTRIC DISTENTION/ VOLVULUS SYNDROME

Gastric distention ('bloat') and volvulus are two related conditions that together represent one of the few really life-threatening emergencies in dogs, and which require immediate veterinary intervention. Distention occurs when the dog's stomach becomes over-distended with fluid and/ or gas, and volvulus is when the then unbalanced stomach rotates longitudinally on its axis, thus twisting the entrance to the stomach and the relative position of the distal stomach to the intestines. The dog is unable to evacuate its stomach: attempts to vomit fail, and the stomach contents cannot pass on to the intestines. Consequently the stomach becomes more and more distended, and as the stomach distends, the dog goes into severe shock.

Large, deep-chested breeds are at greatest risk, especially following vigorous exercise after consuming a large meal. Breeds such as Irish Setters and Curly-Coated Retrievers are most prone to gastric distention and volvulus, as well as, but more so than, Labrador Retrievers, German Short-Haired Pointers and Golden Retrievers. Signs vary: typically the dog is restless and panting, it attempts to vomit unsuccessfully, and either has, or looks to have, a distended abdomen, which it resents being touched. The gums are pale and the heart rate goes up, and eventually the dog will collapse and die of shock.

If the dog develops volvulus, attempts must be made to pass a tube down into the stomach to evacuate the contents. This will normally require the vet to operate and attempt to rotate the stomach back into its normal position whilst simultaneously treating the dog for shock. This is very much easier said than done, because when the stomach rotates it takes a number of associated organs, especially the spleen and its attachments, with it. To make matters worse, because of all that is going on, there is pressure on the chest and lungs and so the risk of anaesthesia becomes greater.

Even if the operation is successful, a very high proportion of dogs suffer a recurrence. Many vets try to help prevent a recurrence by stitching the stomach to the wall of the abdomen once it is repositioned, thereby helping to prevent the stomach flopping over again should it become distended.

Total prevention is not always possible because the anatomical structure of these breeds makes them more susceptible, but to help reduce the risk it is advisable to feed two to three smaller meals each day, rather than one large daily feed. Feed 'moist' feeds, and not a dry diet – soak dry feeds by adding water prior to feeding, and feed

these diets as a mash. Prevent the dog drinking large quantities of water, especially before and after meals, feed off the floor, and certainly avoid strenuous exercise after meals – wait until the dog has had one to two hours to digest its meal before taking it out training or working.

PHARYNGEAL FOREIGN BODIES

The one significant hazard associated with dogs playing with sticks and balls is the risk that, in trying to catch the item, either the ball becomes lodged at the back of the dog's throat, or the stick is snatched, breaks, and a portion becomes lodged across the hard palate between the top molar teeth. In both cases the dog becomes frantic in its attempts to dislodge the item, which, depending on its relative size, can be remarkably difficult to remove. Such incidents may require the dog to be restrained under general anaesthesia so that the object can be grasped, sectioned, or otherwise withdrawn.

Balls are particularly problematic in this respect, and can represent a life-threatening emergency, since a ball that just passes through the jaws into the back of the throat acts as a valvular obstruction to the airway. The dog is able to gag whilst conscious, which pushes the ball forwards a fraction and momentarily clears the airway so it can gulp in air. However, as soon as it is anaesthetized the gagging reflex is lost, and unless the ball can be withdrawn quickly, the dog will start to suffocate. It can sometimes be extremely difficult to get a firm enough grip of the ball to be able to pull it out through the jaws, and for this reason many vets advise against allowing dogs to play with balls.

This shouldn't necessarily put you off using tennis balls to train dogs to hunt and retrieve: the risk is of allowing the dog to play with any balls in general – and never encourage dogs to jump

Feeding bowls such as the one illustrated here can help prevent a dog 'bolting' its food. These may be beneficial in breeds predisposed to volvulus.

to catch a ball. Simply be aware of the hazard and use balls sensibly. An accident with a tennis ball used properly for training purposes rarely, if ever, happens.

ANAL GLANDS

Each time a dog passes a large firm stool it voids a small amount of foul-smelling serous or pasty liquid that coats the stool and is believed to play some part in territorial marking behaviour. This fluid is secreted by numerous small anal glands positioned just inside the anal sphincter, and passes into two anal sacs, one on each side of the rectum. If the dog's stools are soft or small the sacs may not empty completely, and if this continues they can fill up, become uncomfortable for the dog, and if left untreated become impacted or even infected.

Most dogs will try and relieve this discomfort by licking or biting their rear end, or dragging their bottom along the floor ('scooting'). Many owners mistake this behaviour as a sign of worms, but it is much more likely that the dog's anal glands need emptying. Note that whilst we commonly refer to this situation as having to 'empty the dog's anal glands', technically it is not the glands themselves, but the two sacs that fill up with fluid and require emptying. Other signs that may indicate that the dog's anal sacs may be full include the following:

- A strong, unpleasant fishy smell on your soft furnishings or coming from your dog
- The dog licks its backside, after which there is a strong fishy smell on its breath
- Pain in the area, particularly if there are fistulous tracts that discharge on each side of the anus, which is likely to indicate that the anal glands may have become infected

With a little practice and patience you can empty your dog's anal sacs yourself (see Chapter 2), but the smell of anal gland fluid is so unpleasant that many people prefer to take their dog to the vet or to a local dog groomer to have its glands emptied. If you take your dog to the vet, he or she may be able to advise on how to prevent or reduce the problem, usually by attending to the dog's diet, and most vets will be willing to show you how to empty the glands yourself.

If the situation cannot be easily resolved, and the situation becomes problematic and difficult to control, your vet may have to operate to remove the anal glands and the associated anal sacs. This is quite a difficult operation to perform, and since it involves some disruption of the normal anatomy to locate and remove the glands, there can be subsequent complications. There can be risk of faecal incontinence, or if the dog is left with local scar tissue after the operation, it may strain unduly when subsequently passing faeces.

MISCELLANEOUS CONDITIONS

PYOMETRA

Pyometra, or cystic endometrial hyperplasia, is a relatively common chronic inflammatory condition of the bitch's uterus (womb), characterized by an inflammation of the uterine wall and an increase in the size and activity of the glands lining the womb. This condition frequently leads to a degeneration of uterine muscle, enabling bacteria invading from the vagina to proliferate in the uterus at the end of oestrus.

Toxins released from the infected, inflamed uterus cause the bitch to drink much more than usual and consequently to pass more urine; many will show a persistent bloody vaginal discharge, and haemorrhage is quite common within the uterus. If left untreated, the bitch can become quite ill, and if ultimately neglected, the disease would be fatal. A bitch that is drinking a lot, urinating large amounts frequently, and has recently been in season, is likely to be suffering from pyometra, especially if you see evidence of a foul-smelling, bloody vaginal discharge. Diagnosis is based on the presenting clinical signs, along with X-ray examination and ultrasound.

The most effective treatment is to spay the bitch, an operation known as ovariohysterectomy. Surgery may be postponed if the bitch is particularly ill so that she may have supportive treatment to improve her condition so she is better able to tolerate the anaesthetic prior to undergoing the operation. Some vets will prescribe drug treatment for earlier, less severe cases of pyometritis, or if the bitch presents as a poor anaesthetic and surgical risk.

EXERCISE-INDUCED COLLAPSE (EIC)

EIC generally renders the dog unsuitable as a working gundog, although it may be perfectly suitable to be re-homed as a pet, provided it receives no strenuous exercise. Affected dogs collapse soon (five to twenty minutes) after the onset of exercise, and their collapse is characterized by profound weakness in the hindquarters.

EIC is what is known as an 'autosomal recessive gene', which means that both sets of parents have to carry the disease to produce a proportion of affected puppies. Only dogs with the EIC gene from both its parents will be clinically affected; those that are genetically 'clear', or 'carry' only one copy of the gene, will be clinically unaf-

fected. Carriers won't show the signs, but can, of course, still pass on the defect to their offspring if bred to another carrier or an affected dog. Although first recognized in the USA, the disease is not confined to American lines because now that there is a DNA test available, EIC has been identified in retrievers in the UK and other European countries.

DWARFISM

Pituitary dwarfism is essentially a lack of the growth hormone that regulates growth, and is caused by an underlying defect in the pituitary gland, which lies at the base of the brain. It can also result from the presence of a cyst or benign tumour in the pituitary gland, which can also adversely affect the production of growth hormone. Pituitary dwarfism is well recognized as being inherited in German Shepherd Dogs, and is known to occur in a variety of gundog breeds, including the Weimaraner and Labrador Retriever. The precise mode of inheritance is unknown.

It is estimated that a large proportion of Labrador Retrievers in the UK could be carriers of exercise-induced collapse, and the screening of breed stock using the DNA test is to be strongly recommended.

Non-familial dwarfism in a Welsh Springer Spaniel. Dwarfism can have a variety of causes and is not necessarily inherited, but all result in stunted growth and usually, but not always, other abnormalities.

Affected dogs appear to be normal at birth, but there is a noticeable change in growth rate by the time they are two to three months of age. In addition to size and growth, other signs will become apparent as the puppy gets older:

- Gradual hair loss or alopecia
- A soft, woolly coat
- Hyperpigmentation, seen as a darkening of the skin
- Small testicles
- Small stature compared to littermates
- Delayed eruption, or absence of the permanent teeth
- An altered bark
- Infertility, often in both males and females
- Anoestrus (absence of heat in bitches)

Affected dogs will require treatment and special care if they are to survive. Typical treatment might comprise growth hormone injections, cortisone replacement therapy, if there is a defect in the function of the adrenal glands, and thyroid hormone supplementation if there is underproduction of thyroid hormone.

Skeletal Dysplasia 2 (SD2): This is a form of genetic dwarfism that is recognized primarily in working lines of Labrador Retrievers. Unlike pituitary dwarfism, SD2 results in what is best described as a 'disproportionate' dog with shortened front limbs – though as far as we currently know, it is not otherwise affected with any other health problems, such as secondary arthrosis. The mutation that causes SD2 in Labrador Retrievers is inherited as an autosomal recessive trait. This means that dogs must inherit the mutated gene from both its parents to be affected. Dogs that carry only one affected copy of the gene inherited from one of its parents, along with one normal copy inherited from the other, are carriers but are clinically unaffected; as of course are dogs with two copies of the normal gene.

OculoSkeletal Dysplasia: This condition has been recognized mainly in field trial strains of Labrador Retrievers in the USA for a number of years; at the time of writing it has not been reported in Labrador Retrievers in the UK. Retinal dysplasia involves the abnormal development of several structures of the visual system. Labradors with the more severe form of retinal dysplasia may also suffer from skeletal dysplasia or dwarfism. In this condition the gene causing retinal dysplasia, which has a dominant mode of inheritance, causes skeletal dysplasia, when it apparently acts as a recessive gene.

The mode of inheritance can be explained if we consider N to be the normal gene and Rd the gene of retinal dysplasia. If both parents have the N gene, their puppies will have normal eyes and a normal skeleton, but if one parent has the N gene and the other the Rd gene, their offspring will develop milder forms of retinal dysplasia; retinal folds will be seen on ophthalmoscopic examination and they will have a normal skeleton. If, however, both parents have the Rd gene, their puppies can suffer dwarfism as well as more severe forms of retinal dysplasia – that is, eye problems – including blindness as well as skeletal problems.

PYRUVATE DEHYDROGENASE PHOSPHATASE 1 DEFICIENCY

PDP1 is an inheritable enzyme deficiency identified in Clumber and Sussex spaniels. The PDH complex is responsible for helping the body expel waste products from metabolism. When this complex does not function properly, the dog suffers extreme exhaustion after very limited exercise. PDP1 deficiency can lead to an early death in affected dogs.

Typically the condition will only become apparent once a dog starts lead exercise, because previously affected pups seem to limit their activity. Affected individuals start to stagger, then have difficulty moving after going for a walk; the dog recovers, but thereafter has limited exercise tolerance.

PDP1 deficiency is caused by a genetic defect, a simple autosomal recessive. This means that a dog must have two copies of the defective gene, one from each parent, to be affected. Dogs with only one copy are unaffected carriers, but can produce affected pups if mated to another carrier. Carriers lead normal, long and healthy lives, and can be safely bred from as long as they are mated to 'clear' dogs.

HEREDITARY NEPHRITIS

Also known as 'juvenile nephritis' or 'juvenile nephropathy', this is a kidney disease that affects English Cocker Spaniels, Cocker Spaniel crosses and possibly other spaniel breeds, and is inherited as an autosomal recessive disease. It has been estimated that around 11 per cent of English Cocker Spaniels in Europe are carriers of the disease. Carriers show no signs of the disease, but can pass on the condition to affected puppies in later generations. A DNA test has been developed to identify and distinguish between affected dogs, unaffected dogs carrying the mutation, and normal unaffected dogs.

The first signs are often seen at around three or four months of age when affected puppies fail to put on weight as they should, drink more than usual, and urinate frequently, passing very dilute urine. Some owners won't necessarily recognize that the puppy is urinating more than normal, but simply report it to be slow and difficult to housetrain. Blood samples taken at this time will often show early indications of kidney dysfunction.

As the juvenile dog matures, the kidneys become more and more dysfunctional, because they fail to develop in line with the rest of the body. Other signs will then start to be seen, including poor appetite, loss of weight, lethargy, vomiting and pale gums. Pale gums are due to anaemia because kidney failure depresses the production of red blood cells. Although the progression may be slowed by veterinary treatment, kidney failure is ultimately fatal, and affected dogs rarely survive beyond the age of one to three years.

PHOSPHOFRUCTOKINASE (PFK) DEFICIENCY

PFK deficiency is an inherited enzyme storage disease causing abnormalities in red blood cells and muscle cells. It occurs in English Springer Spaniels as a single autosomal recessive trait. A genetic screening (DNA) test is available for PFK deficiency that can determine whether a dog is affected, is an apparently unaffected carrier, or is normal.

PFK is a major regulatory enzyme found in all cells of the body. The enzyme stimulates the conversion of sugar into energy essential for normal cell function. PFK deficiency can present as anything from mild to life-threatening illness. Clinical signs include the intermittent production of dark urine (ranging from orange to dark coffee-brown), and in severe cases, pale gums (anaemia) or jaundice (yellowing of skin and gums), with a high temperature and poor appetite.

The characteristic dark-coloured urine commonly develops following strenuous exercise, extensive panting or prolonged barking. The condition is well recognized in the USA. Clinical signs may be particularly noticeable in field trial and active working dogs, where weakness, exercise intolerance, muscle cramps, poor performance or even outright refusal to move, may be observed. The signs usually resolve within hours or days, and can be avoided by managing the dog's activity and stress levels to prevent the development of severe anaemia; however, this is normally impractical if the dog is to be worked in the field.

VON WILLEBRAND'S DISEASE

Von Willebrand's disease is the most common inherited bleeding disorder; it occurs in a variety of breeds including Golden Retrievers, German Short-Haired Pointers, German Wire-Haired Pointers, and Chesapeake Bay Retrievers. When blood clots, a cascade of biochemical reactions must occur in a specific order, and for a clot to form, all the factors involved in the cascade must be present, fully functional and in the correct amounts.

In this disease, the factor known as 'von Willebrand's factor' (vWF) is either not present or defective. The condition is similar to haemophilia in humans. There are three types of von Willebrand's disease: in Type 1, von Willebrand's

factor is functional but not present in sufficient amounts to cause blood to clot properly; Type 1 is the most common form of von Willebrand's disease in dogs. Type 2 is characterized by von Willebrand's factor that does not function properly; and in Type 3 there is almost no von Willebrand's factor present.

Signs of von Willebrand's disease are prolonged or excessive bleeding. This can obviously be seen when performing surgery and when a dog becomes injured, but may also be apparent when a bitch is in season, or when nails are clipped. In some cases spontaneous bleeding will occur from the gums or nose. Signs can also range from mild bleeding, with bleeding times only being extended slightly, to severe, where bleeding cannot be stopped.

A diagnosis of von Willebrand's disease can be made by taking a small blood sample and performing what is known as an ELISA assay, which tests for plasma von Willebrand's factor, or by a buccal mucosal screening time. In many cases this condition is not suspected, and only becomes apparent – though it must be confirmed – when the affected dog experiences a bleeding episode during surgery or following a road traffic accident.

For breeds with a high risk of von Willebrand's disease, genetic testing can be performed to determine if a dog is clear of the disease, a carrier of the disease, or affected by the disease. There is no cure, and if a dog has this condition, the owner should take what precautions he can to ensure the dog does not injure itself – and with care, there is no particular reason why affected dogs should not be worked, unless they are severely affected and bleed spontaneously. If an injury should occur, then take your dog to a vet immediately, calling ahead to inform them that it has the condition, so that by the time you arrive they should have made suitable preparations to help stop the bleeding.

5 CARE OF THE OLDER DOG

Like people, dogs go through the various life stages from growth, through maturity, to ageing. Ageing is a gradual process, and old age comes at different times in different breeds and in different individual dogs. The larger breeds tend to age earlier and their life expectancy is generally less. A robust, healthy dog will probably age later than a dog that experienced a poor start to life. As a dog ages, important bodily functions start to slow down or malfunction as its organs start to deteriorate and its senses decline, leading to impaired vision, hearing, taste and smell, and its energy levels begin to diminish.

SIGNS OF AGEING

It's not often easy to tell when a dog first enters old age. You may notice he has slowed down since last season, or that he may not be marking birds as well as before, or that he is stiff each morning and maybe sleeps more deeply than usual. Certainly the day your dog remains fast asleep and does not leave his bed when you call his name first thing in the morning, is the time to realize that he is no longer as young as he used to be, and maybe this is the time to think about giving him the appropriate attention.

Be vigilant, recognize the signs outlined below, and admit to the fact that your dog is getting old, because significant progress has been made in preventive veterinary health care and the treatment of senile disease in companion animals is at a point where pets are living longer. With a little care and comfortable accommodation, there is no reason why most gundogs these days can't remain fit for some work, as well as comfortable and content, through their later years.

Typically the first sign of ageing is a general decrease in activity level: a tendency to sleep longer and more soundly, less enthusiasm in going for long walks and undertaking strenuous exercise, along with some loss of interest in what's going on in and around the home. Hearing loss is a frequent consequence of ageing. You may notice that not only is your dog sleeping more than usual, but that he is less easily aroused by sudden or unusual sounds.

There can also be some deterioration in sight, although dogs can compensate for these conditions, and you may need to be quite perceptive to identify the deterioration. Partial or even total blindness may not be noticed if the

Just as in humans, grey hairs start to appear as a dog ages, particularly around the face and muzzle.

dog is in familiar surroundings and has learned to adjust as his eyesight gradually fails. See how well he copes in unfamiliar surroundings, and note how well he marks both on very bright days and towards the end of the day as the light fades.

Extremes in temperature affect ageing and older dogs to some degree. Your dog may no longer want to sprawl out on the concrete path in the height of summer, or spend time outside the kennel in the depth of winter. When he is indoors you might notice that he is careful to lie on carpet or a rug, and not on the cold tile floor.

Older dogs will often start to suffer a little discomfort and stiffness in their joints. You may notice that he has a bit of trouble getting up after lying down for a while, and occasionally is a little stiff-legged after being out for a long walk.

Skin and coat changes occur. The skin loses pliability and becomes drier, and the coat may no longer maintain its previous lustre. Wounds heal more slowly, any allergies sometimes worsen, and non-malignant growths, such as warts, may appear and small fatty lumps start to occur on or under the skin.

As ageing advances, major organs such as the heart, liver and kidneys lose their efficiency, and the immune system is less able to fight off infection. Bladder control may be affected, and the muscles decrease in size and become generally weaker.

HEALTH PROBLEMS IN OLDER DOGS

OSTEOARTHRITIS

Osteoarthritis (OA) is a progressive, non-inflammatory deterioration of the cartilage surrounding the joints; it is otherwise known as degenerative joint disease (DJD). It is not to be confused with arthritis, the medical term for inflammation of the joints. Osteoarthritis is the term referring to a form of chronic joint inflammation caused by permanent deterioration of joint cartilage. It is one of the most common conditions affecting older dogs.

The signs of DJD can vary. Typically the dog exhibits a decreased level of activity, occasional lameness, and a stiff gait that is often worse with

exercise. These signs may get worse with exercise, long periods of inactivity, or in cold weather.

DJD in dogs may be caused by abnormal development of the hip or elbow joint (hip or elbow dysplasia), dislocation of the kneecap (the patella) or the shoulder joint, and osteochondritis dissecans (OCD), a condition in which the bone and cartilage develop abnormally so that a flap of cartilage develops within the joint. Another factor that predisposes to the onset of DJD is

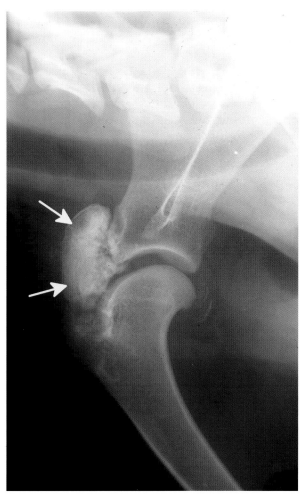

An X-ray photograph of severe degenerative joint disease, in this case associated with osteochondritis dissicans in the shoulder joint. Osteoarthritic changes have resulted in abnormal, new bone development (arrowed), particularly in front of the shoulder. This disrupts the normal smooth articulation of the joint, causing pain and decreased movement ('flexibility') in the joint.

obesity, as excess weight increases stress on joints. Dogs with diabetes, or following prolonged steroid treatment, as well as dogs with hyperlaxity (excessive looseness of the joints) may also be at higher risk of DJD.

Treatment

There is no effective cure for degenerative joint disease, although surgery for many of the orthopaedic conditions that predispose to osteoarthritis may significantly slow the progression of the disease. These surgical procedures include reconstructive surgery of the stifle joint for instance, as a treatment for ruptured anterior cruciate ligament, or joint removal or replacement as a treatment for hip dysplasia. Surgical removal of the bone or cartilage fragments within the joint capsule is indicated to treat osteochondritis dissecans.

Once osteoarthritis is established, treatment is typically directed at alleviating pain and providing supportive therapies to help maintain joint function and the dog's quality of life. This can take a variety of forms, and it is not uncommon to recommend various combinations according to the needs of the specific patient.

Prescription Medications

Vets will normally prescribe specific medications to help manage your dog's arthritis. These medications are fast acting, and can be very effective. Unfortunately many of the more effective drugs are not without risks. Fortunately new compounds or modified forms of these drugs are being continually developed, primarily to improve their effectiveness and reduce the incidence of unwanted side effects. In most cases the pain associated with osteoarthritis is such that the risk of adverse side effects does not justify withholding drug treatment. The following types of drug might be recommended for an arthritic dog:

Non-steroidal anti-inflammatory drugs (NSAIDs): These drugs reduce inflammation, decrease pain and improve mobility. Some veterinary NSAIDs in common usage are Metacam, Rimadyl, Previcox and Ketofen.

Corticosteroids: For example, prednisone or dexamethasone may be used instead of NSAIDs. Steroids have potent anti-inflammatory properties, but their use for treating osteoarthritis has largely been superseded by NSAIDs due to the unavoidable long-term effects of steroid use.

Analgesics: These are specific pain-killing drugs, and include products such as gabapentin or tramadol. These may often be prescribed in conjunction with (say) an NSAID, and there is an increasing interest in using two or more of these and other analgesics simultaneously, since the combination can often result in more complete pain control with less risk of side effects.

Joint Supplements

There is a variety of proprietary supplements available that will not ease the pain and discomfort of DJD directly, but work to slow disease progression. There is less risk associated with the use of these products than with prescription medications, but before using them it is still wise to seek advice from your vet, who might suggest the best treatment options and discuss the indicated drug combinations.

The most commonly recommended supplements include glucosamine, chondroitin, and long-chain omega-3 polyunsaturated fatty acids, particularly eicosapentaenoic acid (EPA). MSM

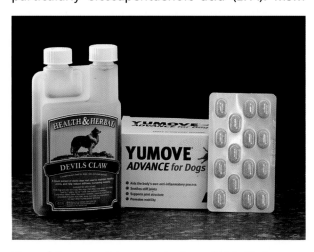

Two of the proprietary products available that can help in the treatment of degenerative joint disease in dogs.

(methylsulfonylmethane) may be beneficial, but probably only in the early stages of the disease. These are referred to as nutraceuticals, and comprise naturally occurring compounds or foods that have the ability to affect health.

Alternative Therapies

Acupuncture involves the therapeutic use of tiny needles in specific points on the body. This can be an extremely effective treatment for a number of diseases, and arthritis is no exception. Positive results from acupuncture are often seen immediately, and can increase with ongoing therapy. Acupuncture should always be performed by a person certified as competent in veterinary acupuncture.

There are also numerous herbal treatments available; traditional Chinese veterinary medicine (TCVM) can be especially helpful. Although owners have reported positive results with these therapies, any reported improvement is typically subtle, and sometimes only recognized after long-term use.

Physiotherapy

Physiotherapy designed to maintain or increase joint movement is very beneficial. Various motion exercises can be used including swimming, other forms of water therapy such as the use of an underwater treadmill or exercising in a resistance pool, and physical massage. Exercise intended to improve muscle tone is also beneficial, and cold and heat therapies, such as the application of heat pads, can help ease arthritic pain. Some of these exercises can be performed at home, and the physiotherapist will be able to show you how.

Exercise and Weight Management

Exercise is important, but should be low impact to avoid further stress on damaged joints – walking more with the dog on the lead and allowing only mild controlled cantering, as opposed to letting him have his head and engaging in strenuous exercise, might be appropriate for working dogs suffering signs of arthritis.

Weight management is critical. Implement a weight reduction programme as necessary, and closely monitor the dog's bodyweight – don't rely purely on body condition scoring if your dog develops osteoarthritis, and adjust his or her calorific food intake accordingly.

Stem Cell Therapy

Stem cell therapy is a promising new form of treatment for canine (and equine) joint conditions. The idea is to harvest particular undifferentiated cells (stem cells or embryonic stem cells: cells in the form that existed during early embryonic development in the womb before they went on to become specialized muscle, nerve or bone cells, for instance) and then implant these within damaged tissue where they might replace the diseased cells with new, healthy tissue. Research is ongoing, and any treatment that is offered is typically in the early development phase; nevertheless as time passes this may well be an option that your vet might find being offered at specialist treatment centres.

DENTAL DISEASE

Dental conditions are amongst those most commonly diagnosed in older dogs. As dogs age, their teeth become stained and tartar deposits accumulate, particularly at the margins of the teeth and gums. As a consequence, the gums will tend to retract, exposing the tooth in its socket to

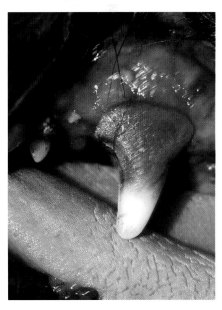

The typical appearance of tartar that accumulates on dogs' teeth. Here, an excessive amount of tartar has built up on the teeth, which will require dental treatment.

147

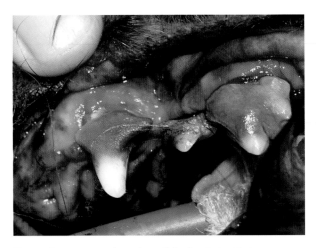

Tartar has accumulated on this dog's teeth to the point that periodontal disease is developing, especially visible here around the gum margin of the tooth on the right.

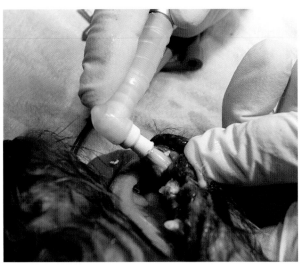

There is greater emphasis these days on preventative veterinary dental medicine, and wherever possible, dental treatment is aimed at prophylaxis – preserving, rather than having to extract teeth once dental disease has become established. This dog's teeth are being polished following the removal of excess tartar.

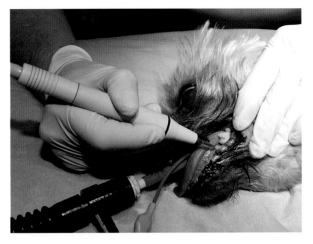

A dog's teeth being cleaned using an ultrasonic tooth scaler.

further wear and infection. Left untreated, such periodontal disease can lead to pain and tooth loss.

If you can brush or very gently scrape your dog's teeth it may help, and special dental treats can assist in reducing tartar. Ultimately, however, your dog is likely to need appropriate dental cleaning under anaesthesia at the local veterinary surgery, when any other treatment that the teeth and gums require can be more easily given.

This is one very good reason to take an older dog for regular veterinary check-ups, since preventative dental care is much more likely to be successful if it is carried out before severe periodontal disease has a chance to develop.

CHRONIC KIDNEY DISEASE AND RENAL FAILURE (CKD, CRD, CRF)

The kidneys have several important functions. They primarily act as a filter, removing waste products generated from the breakdown of food, old cells, toxins or poisons and many drugs. These wastes are removed from the bloodstream by the kidneys and are excreted with water as urine. Kidneys also regulate the amount of water in the blood by varying the amount of urine produced. The kidneys help regulate blood pressure, as well as calcium and vitamin D, and produce a substance that assists the formation of red blood cells. The consequences of kidney disease and kidney failure are therefore wide-ranging and serious.

Causes of CRD, CRF and CKD

Chronic renal disease (CRD), chronic renal failure (CRF), and chronic renal insufficiency refer to the same condition: a disorder caused by the gradual failure of the kidneys or the long-term consequences of severe acute renal failure. Chronic kidney disease (CKD) is defined as kidney disease that has been present for months to years. CKD is not a single disease: it has many different causes, and by the time the animal shows clinical signs, the cause of the disease may no longer be apparent – indeed, often the cause of CKD is unknown.

Some potential causes of CRF include:

- The normal ageing process, in which kidney function gradually deteriorates
- Congenital defects (birth defects affecting the kidneys)
- Chronic bacterial kidney infection, which may also be associated with kidney stones (pyelonephritis)
- Diseases associated with the immune system (such as glomerulonephritis, systemic lupus)
- The consequence of acute kidney disease that severely damages the kidneys, for example antifreeze poisoning

CKD is progressive and irreversible; it is important to understand that this disease cannot be cured, and that kidney failure carries a poor prognosis (the chances of recovery are low). The primary goal of treatment is to alleviate those signs of the disease that most compromise the animal's quality of life. Depending on how quickly the disease progresses, dogs with chronic renal failure may live anywhere from weeks to years.

Signs of Kidney Disease

The most commonly observed signs of chronic renal disease are an increased water intake (polydipsia) and urine output (polyuria). Other signs may include lethargy, a poor appetite, weight loss, vomiting, diarrhoea, bad breath, weakness and exercise intolerance.

To diagnose kidney disease, your vet will need to make a physical examination, when he may find signs of dehydration and may, depending on the size and type of dog, be able to feel (palpate) the size and shape of the kidneys. In more advanced cases there may be signs of anaemia. The vet is likely to want to carry out laboratory tests to confirm the diagnosis and estimate how far the disease may have progressed. For this purpose he or she is likely to take a blood sample, and if you have a sample of your dog's urine at the time of examination, this can be useful.

Treatment

Dogs diagnosed with less severe chronic renal failure may be treated at home with medications and dietary changes.

Kidney Diets

A vet will usually prescribe a so-called kidney diet that contains less protein as compared to other diets, and a source of protein that is of higher quality. It is primarily protein that is converted to waste products, which the kidneys remove in the urine. The lower the quantity and the higher the quality of that protein, the less waste is created for the kidneys to eliminate.

Protein is used by the body to repair cells and tissues that are continually regenerating, so a dog needs some protein in its diet, but by feeding a lower amount of a higher quality protein in a diet that contains appropriate amounts of

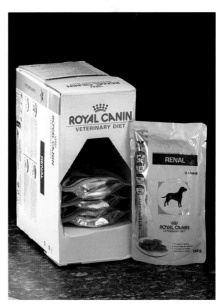

An example of a proprietary renal diet specially formulated so that it is suitable for feeding to dogs with chronic renal disease (CRD).

fats and carbohydrates, the dog can use the protein for replacing cells and tissues, and the fat and carbohydrates for energy. Kidney diets will also contain different levels of other substances, which may otherwise be too high or too low for patients with CKD, such as salt, phosphorus, potassium, magnesium and B vitamins.

Unfortunately many affected dogs find these 'renal' diets less palatable than the conventional diets they are accustomed to eating. Dogs with CKD that are still eating well are more likely to accept the change in diet than those that are very ill and refusing most foods. Changing to a kidney diet in the earlier stages of the disease is often beneficial, and enables the less palatable food to be introduced gradually. Substituting increasing amounts of the new diet while reducing the amount of the current diet over several weeks will also enable the kidneys to adapt gradually to the different types and levels of dietary constituents.

If a dog refuses to eat one of the specially formulated proprietary 'renal' diets, it may be necessary to review the type of feed the dog is accustomed to eating in order to ascertain if it could be modified to make it more suitable. Proprietary complete feeds are typically supplemented so that the required levels of essential nutrients are achieved, and consequently the final product may contain excessive amounts of those elements that need to be restricted for dogs with CRD. One effect of renal dysfunction, for example, is a tendency towards high blood pressure, and feeding a diet with high sodium content will be deleterious.

When dogs are normally fed raw ingredients, it is possible to have representative samples of their current feed analyzed to see how it compares to the levels of essential ingredients provided in a specially formulated kidney diet, and if necessary it can be adjusted accordingly. A diet low in phosphorus is usually important in renal disease, and if the diet is too high it is possible to feed phosphorus binders in the diet that will effectively lower the level absorbed by the dog.

Alternatively, there are recipes available on the internet with details of suitable ingredients that can be fed to dogs with renal disease. It is likely that a dog would prefer some of these if it finds the proprietary formulated products unpalatable.

Other Treatments

Medications may be prescribed as appropriate to control certain aspects of the condition, such as nausea, inappetence, and mineral and electrolyte imbalances.

Dogs diagnosed with moderate to severe chronic renal failure may require subcutaneous fluid therapy, along with regular follow-up monitoring by your vet. The frequency of these visits will depend on the severity of the dog's disease and its response to treatment.

Dogs with severe chronic renal failure will normally require hospitalization. Treatment might include the administration of intravenous fluids (especially if the dog has stopped drinking or is otherwise dehydrated), nutritional support, and appropriate medications. Laboratory tests will often be carried out to monitor the condition of the patient and as indicators of improvement during hospitalization.

Complications associated with chronic renal failure include uremia, stomatitis (an inflammation of the stomach lining), mouth ulcers; gastroenteritis (inflammation and ulceration of the stomach and intestines), anaemia, urinary tract infections; and high blood pressure.

OBESITY

As discussed in Chapter 2, overweight dogs are susceptible to numerous secondary problems, particularly joint disease, diabetes, heart disease and respiratory illnesses. Obesity is becoming more and more prevalent among the pet population, and many pet owners are now less likely to be aware that their pet is overweight because overweight pets tend to represent an apparent norm. Working gundogs are generally much fitter and in better bodily condition than their pet counterparts, but as they age, and particularly once they are retired from active work, the risk of obesity remains.

An older, heavier Labrador still active enough to enjoy picking up game.

Exercise, and especially appropriate control of calorie intake, are both critical to managing a dog's weight. Regular gentle exercise is beneficial even for older dogs with health issues. Older dogs are typically less active, have a lower metabolism, and consequently have different calorific requirements. Fortunately proprietary 'senior' diets are now becoming widely available as convenient for feeding to older dogs. So regular monitoring of bodyweight, body condition scoring (*see* Chapter 2), along with a change to feeding an appropriate amount of a 'senior' dog diet, is definitely to be recommended for ageing gundogs.

BEHAVIOURAL PROBLEMS

Just as puppies can suffer a variety of behavioural problems, either because they have not learnt or been taught the 'rules' of appropriate behaviour, so many older dogs can also suffer behavioural issues. In the case of the older dog, however, it is usually because, for some reason or other, they are unable to follow those previously learnt rules. Some of the more common behavioural problems include vocalization, aggression, separation anxiety, inappropriate soiling, and cognitive dysfunction.

Vocalization

Stress in an older dog is often manifested as barking, howling or whining. This is commonly a strategy to gain their owner's attention, especially if for some reason the dog feels neglected by, or is physically unable to get to, their owner. The dog will then attempt to get the owner to come to them. It can also be a sign of cognitive dysfunction (*see* below).

If your dog does start vocalizing as it gets older, wherever possible try to determine the cause. Some deaf dogs, for instance, will bark, although others may simply withdraw. Never try to correct the behaviour because all you will be doing is 'rewarding' the dog, by giving it attention. It is much better to ignore the dog and use some other form of correction strategy. Try throwing a tin containing coins of stones towards – *not* at – the dog without it seeing you, or create some other loud, unexpected noise as a distraction.

If increased vocalization is a means of getting attention, think about how much time you spend with your dog, and maybe increase the duration and/or type of attention you are giving. Make sure you initiate the extra time spent with your dog. Don't start a session when the dog is exhibiting the problematic behaviour: it is better to ignore it and come back later when it is quiet.

Aggression

Older dogs can occasionally become more aggressive. If this is the case, do try to determine the cause. It may be a response to pain, for example to arthritis or dental problems. Chronic low grade pain can be particularly debilitating, and may cause dogs to become irritable and more aggressive. Medical conditions that cause a loss of visual acuity or a hearing deficit can result in a dog being more easily startled and reacting accordingly, especially if it cannot easily withdraw from the stimulus. Aggression can also be a sign of cognitive dysfunction.

Where several dogs are maintained in the same household, and especially if they are grouped in kennels, changes in their social hierarchy – especially the challenge to an older, 'dominant' dog by the presence of younger individuals – can lead to increased aggression, particularly among bitches. Some of this behaviour represents no more than a natural dynamic social interactive behaviour pattern within the 'pack', and if that is the case, the behaviour should rarely, if ever, result in any injury being inflicted or sustained.

Be on the lookout, however, for escalating uncontrolled aggression where normal, typically submissive behaviour patterns are either not displayed, or are ignored or interrupted (often by inappropriate owner intervention). In such circumstances, dogs are much more likely to inflict and sustain serious injuries, and more importantly, other members of the group are more likely to contribute to the confrontation.

Separation Anxiety

Separation anxiety is one of the most common behaviour problems seen in older dogs. The older dog often has a decreased ability to cope, especially when separated from its owner – typically it becomes very anxious when its owner is about to leave, and when left becomes destructive, barks or howls incessantly, may urinate or defecate and/or salivate profusely, and will often be overly excited when the owner returns. There are a few techniques that might be used to help avoid or overcome the problem of separation anxiety in older gundogs:

- Assuming your dog is trained to 'stay' or respond to the 'down' command, use and/or reinforce this command so your dog learns to relax in this position for extended periods while you are present. He will then be more likely to relax while you are gone, and you can progressively extend those periods. Always leave and return to your dog calmly – any emphasis on leaving, or undue fuss on returning, will simply reinforce the behaviour
- Start with very short departure periods. Find out how long you can leave your dog before he gets anxious: it may only be for a minute or two, but start with that. So, leave him for a short period, then return, and if he has remained calm, reward him without making a big fuss about it. Gradually increase the time he is left, always returning before the dog becomes anxious, and reward him for staying calm. This is likely to be a slow process, and it may take weeks or months to resolve the problem, so be prepared and remain patient, because it is important
- Change your departure cues and/or change your routine so the dog does not know you will be leaving. Pick up the car keys, for instance, and then go and sit in a chair and read the paper; at the weekend, get up and dress as if you are going to work, but stay at home.
- Anxiety tends to be self-perpetuating, so if you prevent anxiety from occurring before and at the time of your departure, the dog may remain calm after you leave. Associate your departure with something positive. Give your dog a treat to take his mind off your leaving. Make sure his environment is comfortable, that the room is neither too hot nor too cold, that he has a comfortable bed, and maybe some background noise such as the radio playing 'easy-listening' music. Some dogs will be more relaxed if they can see what's going on outside, whilst others may become more

anxious. Some older dogs are better behaved if left in an outdoor kennel, whereas others settle much better when they can stay in the house. Determine what is best for your dog
- If you have to leave your dog for extended periods, consider arranging for someone to come and let it out to exercise. Older dogs, especially, may need to go outside more often to urinate and defecate, and if they are given this opportunity they may be less anxious. It will also help break up their day, meaning they are left alone for shorter periods.
- Try crating your dog. Many dogs feel safe in a crate, and being in a crate helps to reduce their destructive tendencies

If your dog continues to suffer separation anxiety, discuss the problem with your vet, who may refer you to an appropriate consultant behaviourist. Anxiolytics – anti-anxiety medications – are sometimes required to break the cycle of anxiety that the dog associates with separation from its owner. However, medication alone will not solve the problem, so be prepared to work with your vet or behaviourist to develop a plan that works best for you and your dog.

Inappropriate Soiling
Dogs that have been properly housetrained and 'clean' for years occasionally start having 'accidents' as they get older. This is rarely a simple behavioural problem, and an older dog with a house-soiling problem should be examined by a vet. Medical conditions that can cause this change in behaviour might include diabetes mellitus, bladder stones or infections, inflammation of the prostate, and kidney or liver disease. Medical conditions that cause pain, or make it difficult for the dog to go outside to eliminate, can also contribute to the problem.

When having the dog examined, be prepared to outline a detailed history so the vet can better understand the problem: for instance, the colour and amount of urine (or stool) passed, the frequency at which the dog needs to eliminate, changes in eating or drinking habits, any postural change while eliminating, and whether the 'accidents' only occur when you are away.

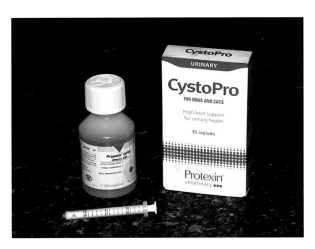

A variety of products is now available to treat urinary tract disorders. Propalin, one of the drugs shown here, is indicated for sphincter mechanism incontinence (SME), which is fairly common in spayed bitches of certain breeds (mostly tail-docked breeds). The incontinence may develop a long while after spaying, causing the dog to dribble or leak urine, often while asleep.

Both cognitive dysfunction and separation anxiety may result in the dog defecating and urinating when separated from its owner(s). Once an accurate diagnosis can be established, any medical and behavioural condition contributing to the house-soiling problem can then be treated appropriately.

Cognitive Dysfunction
This syndrome as recognized in older dogs appears to affect them in much the same way that Alzheimer's disease affects humans. It is known variously as cognitive dysfunction, canine cognitive dysfunction (CCD) or 'cognitive dysfunction syndrome' (CDS). Research shows that many older dogs with these geriatric behaviour problems have lesions in their brain that are very similar to those seen in patients with Alzheimer's. In many dogs affected with cognitive dysfunction, there is a specific protein (B-amyloid) that forms plaques inside the brain. It is likely that these plaques contribute to the cell death and shrinkage of the brain characteristic of animals with cognitive dysfunction. In addition, many of

153

the substances that transmit messages within the brain appear to be altered, which could also lead to abnormal behaviours.

Signs of canine cognitive dysfunction include the following:

- Less inclination to retrieve or hunt on command, or otherwise respond to (say) the whistle
- Confusion or disorientation: the dog may lose its way in otherwise familiar territory, or get 'trapped' in corners or behind obstacles
- Pacing, especially whilst awake all night when previously it would have slept soundly, or some similar change in sleeping pattern
- Inappropriate soiling, for a dog that was previously house trained: it may not signal that it needs to go outside, and may consequently urinate or defecate where he or she would never have done previously
- Decreased activity
- Decreased attentiveness and increased vocalization; a dog may sometimes be found 'staring into space' or 'howling at the moon'
- Not greeting friends or family members
- Displaying signs of anxiety and increased irritability

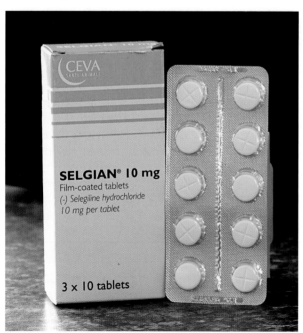

SELGIAN® 10 mg
Film-coated tablets
(-) Selegiline hydrochloride
10 mg per tablet

3 x 10 tablets

One of the most challenging aspects of dealing with canine cognitive dysfunction is helping owners recognize and accept that the changes in their dog's behaviour are more than just normal ageing changes. Clearly from what has been described previously, in order to diagnose CCD, other behavioural problems and medical conditions will first need to be ruled out; thus decreased activity may be due to pain, for example from arthritis, while inattentiveness may result from visual or hearing deficits. Any dog showing signs of cognitive dysfunction will require a thorough physical examination, appropriate laboratory tests, and possibly specialized tests in order to eliminate these other conditions and enable cognitive decline to be established as a potential problem.

Sometimes if there is no other obvious cause, the response to treatment can be useful as an indication of cognitive dysfunction. The use of a drug called 'Selegiline' or L-Deprenyl, (Anipryl), although not a cure, has been shown to alleviate some of the symptoms of CCD – and of course, if the dog responds, it will need to be treated daily for the remainder of its life. Other management techniques may include the use of antioxidants or 'senior' diets, and in addition, dogs with CCD should continue to receive regular exercise and some form of positive mental stimulation.

If the response to Selegiline is inadequate, or if the dog is unable to take selegiline for other medical reasons, behavioural enrichment and a diet rich in antioxidants have also been found to be beneficial – and both treatments in combination are more effective than either one or the other alone. An antioxidant-enriched diet would contain higher levels of vitamins such as vitamin C and vitamin E, and fatty acids such as DHA, EPA, L-carnitine, and lipoic acid. It might also comprise fruits and vegetables – such as carrots and/or spinach – that contain antioxidants.

Behavioural enrichment can be as simple as spending more time stroking, grooming and interacting with the dog. Regular walks taking

Selgian can sometimes help treat the signs of cognitive dysfunction and other behavioural disorders in dogs.

It may be a good idea to start attending training sessions again with an older gundog. Use different exercises to reinforce compliance with previously learned commands, since the purpose of the exercise is to have the dog use its brain, not to try and 'teach an old dog new tricks'.

a variety of different routes that provide auditory, visual and particularly olfactory stimulation would be useful; the intention is to provide mental stimulation as much as physical exercise.

Behavioural Counselling
If you suspect an older dog is experiencing behaviour problems, discuss the situation with your vet, or consider being referred to, or otherwise taking advice from, one of a number of vets who are now experienced and trained in behavioural counselling. The latter, in particular, have the advantage of being able to prescribe treatments that might include the use of drugs not licensed for use in animals, but which would be used to treat the same or similar conditions in humans. Thus there

could be numerous ways of helping your dog lead a happier and healthier life in his senior years. So consult your vet if there is any reason to be concerned about an older dog's behaviour, no matter how trivial. When there is a problem, whether it is cognitive dysfunction or some other condition, generally the earlier the intervention, the more successful the outcome will be.

SENILE OCULAR DISEASE

Nuclear Sclerosis of the Lens
Nuclear sclerosis of the lens is considered a normal ageing process, and rarely causes any significant impairment to a dog's vision. The lens, although transparent, is made up of many

Nuclear sclerosis is apparent as a slight cloudiness in the centre of this lens.

Senile epithelial degeneration, in this case leading to a bluish translucent appearance at the front of the eye, caused by fluid accumulating within the normally transparent cornea.

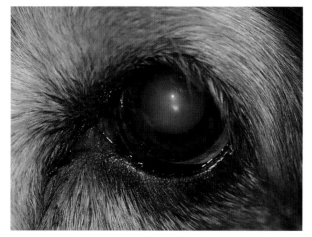

As nuclear sclerosis advances and becomes more dense, owners are sometimes concerned that their dog is developing cataract.

thousands of tiny fibres that together provide its form and intricate, complex structure. The dog continues to lay down lens fibres as it grows, and this process continues through to old age. The lens is fully developed at quite a young age, and thereafter, since there is no further increase in its overall size, as more fibres are laid down they become more and more compressed. This tends to influence the translucency of the lens, and as more fibres are accommodated, the lens in older dogs will appear slightly more 'cloudy'.

The process is gradual, but it will reach a stage where this cloudiness becomes so obvious that many owners become concerned that their dog is developing cataracts. Your vet will be able to differentiate this normal change in lens translucency, which has little or no effect on vision, from a true cataract that affects transparency and therefore will impair vision.

Senile Endothelial Degeneration (SED)

SED affects the inner lining of the cornea, the transparent 'window' at the front of the eye. To keep the cornea clear, this lining contains thousands of tiny 'pumps' that pump fluid in and out of the cornea, maintaining a balance between the fluid inside the eye and the amount of fluid in the cornea. As dogs age, the number of 'pumps' tends to decline, making the process less efficient until eventually in some dogs the ability of the endothelium to maintain this fluid balance becomes critical: water then starts to accumulate in the cornea, causing a cloudy appearance known as 'corneal oedema'.

The cornea is extremely delicate, and SED tends to render the surface prone to damage – there is a tendency for the surface to 'blister', and if the blisters burst, this leads to ulceration and secondary infection. The signs of SED need to be distinguished from other, more serious eye diseases, such as glaucoma – an increase in pressure inside the eye – and uveitis, an inflammation of those parts of the eye that contain most blood vessels, particularly the iris, the coloured part in front of the lens that opens and closes regulating the amount of light entering the back of the eye. Your vet may need to refer you to a specialist to determine the cause of the problem, and if it turns out to be SED, to recommend treatment.

Treatment can comprise simple 'conservative' treatment, where typically eye drops or ointment containing 5 per cent sodium chloride are administered two or three times daily to help reduce the amount of fluid. In more advanced cases, and depending on the age of the dog, a surgical procedure may be required.

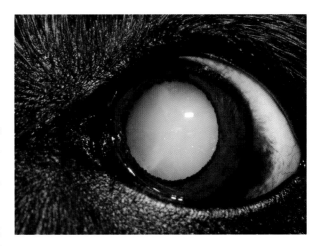

A mature, total cataract in a Labrador Retriever. These are relatively common in older dogs, either showing up quite suddenly or developing relatively slowly. DENISE MOORE

Cataract

The term 'cataract' refers to cloudiness or opacity of all or part of the lens in the eye. In dogs, cataracts typically have a strong hereditary component, although other common contributing causes include diabetes, an injury to the eye, and especially any penetrating injury to the eye. Some cataracts would appear to occur spontaneously for no apparent reason. Unlike a nuclear sclerosis, which is a natural ageing change in the lens, cataracts are brought about by a change in the protein composition, or a disruption in the arrangement of the fibres of the lens, and always interfere with vision and can cause blindness.

Cataracts are not painful, and most dogs adjust remarkably well to visual deficiencies and will soon learn to negotiate obstacles such as furniture in familiar surroundings; it's been said that a dog relies on its sense of sight about as much as we rely on our sense of smell. Most cataracts are treatable with surgery as long as they are diagnosed early enough in the course of the disease. The dog's sight can be restored following surgery, and it can resume working providing there is no concomitant retinal disease. Surgery typically involves either the total removal of the opaque lens, or removal and replacement of the

affected lens with a prosthetic lens implant. Vets would normally have to refer owners to a veterinary ophthalmologist for these procedures to be carried out.

HYPOTHYROIDISM

Hypothyroidism occurs most commonly in medium to large breeds of gundogs, and usually in middle-aged dogs. Breeds most commonly affected include the Golden Retriever, the Curly-Coated Retriever and the Irish Setter. Thyroid hormones affect the function of many parts of the body and pay a major role in metabolism. Hypothyroidism, a low production of thyroid hormones usually caused by inflammation or shrinkage of the thyroid gland, is the more common. Dogs with overactive thyroid glands are rare, and when it occurs the condition is usually associated with cancer of the thyroid gland. In some breeds, such as the Curly-Coated Retriever and Welsh Springer Spaniel, there is evidence of a familial, inherited form of thyroiditis, inflammation of the thyroid gland, that results in hypothyroidism.

However, as any dog ages, its production of thyroid hormones gradually drops. This not only means that the dog will have less tolerance to cold, due to a reduced function of the thyroid and adrenal glands, but that the thyroid is producing a less than adequate amount of thyroid hormones, principally thyroxine, and consequently can develop signs of hypothyroidism.

Unfortunately the most common signs of the disease tend to occur gradually, and many – including lethargy, obesity, reduced exercise tolerance and dragging the feet when walking – can be misinterpreted as signs that the dog is simply ageing. There are, however, other visible signs that characterize the disease, especially those related to the skin; these include:

- Thinning of the coat and hair loss (alopecia)
- The coat regrows unusually slowly after trimming
- Wounds are slow to heal
- Chronic skin infections
- Itching
- Frequent ear infections

There are also others, such as occasional gastrointestinal problems, decreased mental abilities and personality changes, which help indicate that the dog may be developing hypothyroidism.

Treatment

Treatment comprises giving oral replacement hormone for the rest of the dog's life. Initially thyroid hormone is usually given twice daily, but once hair growth resumes and the dog's general demeanour is restored, some dogs can be maintained on once daily medication. Vets will most likely prescribe a thyroid hormone supplement, the dosage depending on the severity of the condition, and there are two general forms of thyroid medication. Most hypothyroid dogs will respond to levothyroxine or L-thyroxine (T4), but a few dogs are unable to convert this form of thyroid hormone to the more active form (T3), and require T3 medication. It normally takes four to six weeks before hair regrowth becomes apparent. Thereafter, blood levels of T4 are often monitored regularly in order to adjust the dosage more finely. With continuing treatment the prognosis for a dog with hypothyroidism is excellent.

CANCER

Cancer in dogs is a common disease often associated with older dogs; however, it is not simply an age-related phenomenon. Genetic factors, such as mutations in the tumour suppressor gene, have also been reported to exist in dogs, and may be involved in the apparent predisposition of some breeds of gundog to cancer – although cancer can develop spontaneously in any breed. Cancer is more correctly termed 'neoplasia', and cancerous masses are often referred to as 'neoplasms' or 'tumours'. A very simple definition of a tumour is 'a mass of purposelessly proliferating cells'.

Sadly, dogs are susceptible to many of the same cancers as seen in humans. Bone cancer, lymphoma and melanoma are just a few of the neoplasms commonly diagnosed in dogs. Fortunately, alongside the significant advances in human cancer treatment, rather than simply being euthanased, more and more dogs are being treated for cancer than in the past. Early detection and diagnosis, however, remain the key to dogs surviving cancer.

It is beyond the scope of this book to describe each and every one of the many types of cancer that can affect dogs, but some of the more notable tumours diagnosed in gundogs are described here.

Mammary Tumours

Mammary tumours are the most common cancers found in the female dog, and some 40–50 per cent can be malignant, so these tumours should be seen by a vet as early as possible. Spaying bitches at an early age can reduce the risk of mammary tumours, but the procedure does have some disadvantages (see Chapter 1); otherwise, however, the incidence is not directly related to neutering. Several of the spaniel breeds have been reported to have an increased incidence of mammary neoplasia. Mammary gland tumours have also been observed in male dogs, but the incidence is 1 per cent or less.

There are numerous different types of mammary tumours, although the majority are malignant adenocarcinomas and carcinomas. The growth

A well defined mammary tumour.

muscle. These tumours are rarely metastatic, but can invade local muscle. They occur most commonly on the body, although they have been reported elsewhere. Very large lipomas can become so big that they overgrow their blood supply, and tissue in the centre of the mass dies (becomes necrotic); this results in the release of toxins from the dead tissue, causing the dog to become ill.

Clinically, these tumours vary in size from small pedunculated subcutaneous swellings to large solitary tumours weighing up to 1kg or more. They are commonly diagnosed in dogs over ten years of age, and are rarely life-threatening. Surgical excision is usually curative, although because of a potential greater risk of anaesthesia and surgery, small tumours are often left untreated unless they otherwise cause health concerns or are aesthetically unpleasant for the owner.

and development of mammary gland neoplasms appears to be dependent on female hormones, because the incidence increases as the number of oestrous (heat) cycles increases, and the rate of growth of tumours in some individual dogs can be influenced by the phase of their heat cycle. Mammary carcinomas may exhibit rapid growth, doubling in size within a few weeks. However, the size and appearance of these neoplasms can vary greatly.

Clinically affected dogs present with single or multiple nodules within their mammary tissue, and the associated lymph glands may also be swollen due to secondary spread of the tumour (metastasis). These nodules are present in less than 50 per cent of dogs with mammary neoplasms.

Although chemotherapeutic drug regimes are available for dogs with mammary cancer, treatment usually involves surgical excision, and provided there has been no secondary metastatic spread, the prognosis (the outcome for the dog) is usually good. There is little benefit, in terms of tumour remission, in spaying the bitch at the time of the mastectomy surgery.

Lipomas

Lipomas are relatively common, slow-growing, canine neoplasms; they occur primarily immediately under the skin, in fat and subcutaneous

Osteosarcoma (OSA)

Osteosarcoma is a rapidly growing, destructive neoplasm of bone that accounts for 80 per cent of all malignant bone tumours in dogs. OSA is most common in older dogs and the larger breeds.

OSA can occur in the spine as well as in long bones, although it originates most commonly in the extremities of the long bones. It forms in the central cavity of the bone, penetrates the surrounding cortex, and then extends into the space beneath the fibrous tissue that coats the outside of bone, called the periosteum. The periosteum is rich in nerve fibres, and because OSA causes the periosteum to tear away from the underlying bone, osteosarcomas are typically very painful cancers. Clinical signs include lameness, limb swelling and pain.

OSA spreads (metastasizes) rapidly via the bloodstream, and the lung is the most common site for secondary tumours. Other secondaries might be found in the liver and kidneys, and adjacent bones, though rarely. Vets will usually X-ray and scan other parts of the body to try to ensure there has been no metastasis before recommending treatment. Unfortunately even after the amputation of the affected limb and/ or chemotherapy, and radiation therapy for spinal OSA, survival has been generally poor. More recently, however, chemotherapy administered after amputation has seemed to help to control metastatic disease, and may increase survival time significantly. It is believed that dogs between seven and ten years of age have greater survival times than younger and older dogs.

Testicular Tumours

There are a number of testicular tumour types in dogs, and more than 30 per cent of dogs diagnosed with testicular cancer have more than one primary testicular tumour, however sertoli cell tumours are the most commonly encountered. It is particularly common in dogs with retained testicles (cryptorchidism). Among gundogs, Weimaraners appear to have an increased risk of developing primary testicular tumours.

Clinically affected dogs usually present with vague symptoms, including weight loss, hypotension, caudal abdominal pain and a palpable abdominal mass. Other symptoms include bilaterally symmetrical hair loss, increased pigmentation of the skin, and enlarged mammary glandular tissue (gynecomastia). They may even produce

milk and have an atrophied (withered) penis. Castration, or otherwise the removal of only the affected testicle, is the most common treatment. Chemotherapy and radiation treatment seems to be of limited value.

CARING FOR THE SENIOR DOG

REGULAR VETERINARY CARE

Regular veterinary care is really important for older dogs. Appropriate vaccinations, and regular worming and flea treatments, remain just as important during a dog's later years, when its immune system tends to be slower to respond. Older dogs should be weighed regularly and suitable adjustments made to their diet to maintain a healthy bodyweight, avoiding any tendency to lay down fat. Obesity has serious medical implications. Regularly weighing your dog will also determine if it is starting to lose weight, in which case a blood and/or urine sample might be analyzed to rule out certain diseases or enable early, more effective, intervention if they occur. Some veterinary surgeries run special nurses' clinics where older pets can have a regular check-up.

Routine dental care from your vet is very important, since older dogs are more prone to gum disease and plaque build-up. In addition to regular visits to your veterinary practice, it is always a good idea for you to check your dog's teeth and gums regularly yourself.

SENIOR DOG DIETS

Diets for the older dog are specially formulated to provide a proper balance of the nutrients it requires, typically with a rather different fat:protein ratio compared to a standard adult dog food. These diets include high quality, easily digestible protein sources, which become

Older dogs represent an increasing proportion of the pet population, and consequently a growing consumer share of the total pet-food market. Feed companies respond by constantly striving to improve their senior dog diets.

The owner of this old Labrador provides plenty of soft bedding in the back of the vehicle so his dog is able to snuggle down, nice and warm, especially after spending the day picking up.

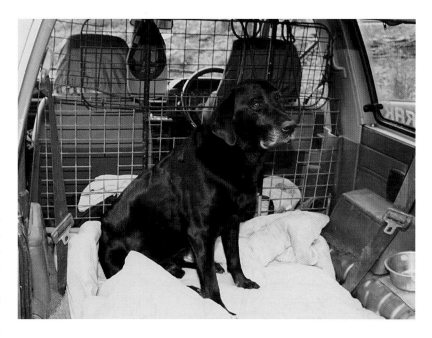

more important with ageing in helping to maintain overall body condition. A good senior diet should also include more easily digested forms of carbohydrate for energy, essential minerals to support ageing joints, and vitamins, along with protein, to help support the ageing immune system. Increasingly, proprietary senior dog foods will contain additional beneficial ingredients, for example glucosamine to help maintain healthy joints.

If your older dog appears reluctant to eat, check with your vet that there is no underlying medical cause for what you might otherwise dismiss as being 'fussy eating'. As with feeding puppies, it can be beneficial to offer an older dog its daily food ration in smaller amounts two to three times a day – little and often – rather than as one substantial meal, as smaller meals are easier to digest. Varying the form of the meals can also provide the dog with varying textures and flavours, and warming the food, or feeding an otherwise dry diet as a mash, can release tasty smells to encourage the appetite of an older dog.

HOME COMFORTS

Home comforts, such as providing a soft bed, make a considerable difference to your dog when he is older and suffering sore joints. Ideally position the bed somewhere quiet, where he can retreat as he wants, in a place that is free of draughts, maybe next to a radiator in winter. Arthritic joints make jumping especially uncomfortable, so you may need to help lift a spaniel in and out of the car, or provide a ramp for a larger dog such as a Labrador. Always make sure that food and water are within easy reach, and not somewhere, for example, that requires the dog to negotiate steep steps, or go up and down stairs to get a drink.

BATHING AND GROOMING

Bathing and grooming an older gundog periodically is to be recommended because it will remove dead coat as well as keep the skin clean and healthy; older dogs tend not to groom themselves as they did when they were younger. Ask your vet about a good quality dog shampoo; many human shampoos are unsuitable as they tend to remove natural protective substances from a dog's coat. If your dog has a long coat, and particularly if it is well feathered, especially over its ears, you may need to consult a dog groomer to trim excess coat and remove any matted fur to make it more comfortable.

Nails that were previously worn down by an active gundog can become more overgrown with age and a less active lifestyle. Longer nails change the angle at which the toe meets the ground, and this can become uncomfortable for the dog. Alternatively they start to become misshapen, or at worst grow back around towards the pad. Ask your vet or one of the veterinary nurses to trim your dog's claws regularly if you are unable to do this yourself.

STAYING ACTIVE

Staying active is essential. Diet is important, but so is regular exercise, and a consistent daily exercise routine will help maintain an older dog's physical, mental and emotional health, and provide with it a reassuring framework to maintain an active lifestyle. If necessary speak to your vet about an appropriate diet and exercise plan for your dog, which takes into account any underlying conditions such as osteoarthritis. Acknowledge failing senses: any loss of sight and hearing may mean your dog sleeps very deeply and doesn't hear people approach, especially from behind. Make sure that all the family are aware, particularly the children so they know to be quiet around the dog, and how it might react if it is suddenly startled.

As important as physical fitness is an older dog's mental aptitude. Maintain a regular routine, but don't let this become too repetitive or boring for your dog. Introduce variety as a means of mental stimulation, and try to utilize small changes to challenge the dog's mental agility. It does no harm to start taking an older gundog back to training classes. Stimulate an old dog using positive reinforcement training techniques. Your 'reward' for his good behaviour provides him a form of emotional support by reinforcing the owner/dog bond that is so fundamental to the relationship between man and dog. Train your dog to complete each exercise correctly, and use the opportunity to correct small faults that may have developed over the years – all this will provide him with mental stimulation.

Try to be sensitive to the physical changes, and consequently also the psychological changes that may be taking place as your dog gets older. Working an older dog is likely to require a little more patience on your part, but your commitment to

Older age need not necessarily represent a barrier to a working gundog's abilities. This is Reuben Corbett's Ft. Ch. Oakvalley Black Jack, who was made up to field trial champion at nine years of age, just before this photograph was taken.

maintaining his role will really help promote his quality of life during these senior years.

In conclusion, caring for an older dog can be very rewarding. Veterinary care and small management changes can make a tremendous improvement in your older dog's quality of life, and ensure a continuing partnership for many years to come.

APPENDIX: BREED PREDISPOSITION TO HEREDITARY AND OTHER DISEASES

(Sources: Dog Breed Heath Information website, KCABS and BVA/KC/ISDA health testing schemes.)

Labrador Retriever

The Labrador Retriever.

Hip dysplasia
Elbow dysplasia
Multifocal retinal dysplasia
Total retinal dysplasia
Hereditary cataract
Generalized progressive retinal atrophy
Centralized progressive retinal atrophy
Centronuclear myopathy
Exercise-induced collapse
Macular corneal dystrophy
Nasal parakeratosis
Cystinuria
Narcolepsy
Haemophilia B
Dwarfism with retinal dysplasia
Atopy
Hepatitis (autoimmune liver disease)
Epilepsy
Cruciate ligament disease
Cancers (in particular mast cell tumours; osteosarcoma; melanoma; soft tissue sarcoma; brain tumour)
Osteochondritis dissecans
Tricuspid valve malformation
Patellar luxation
Laryngeal paralysis and other neuropathies
Hypoadrenocorticism
Hyperadrenocorticism
Hypothyroidism
Primary seborrhoea

Golden Retriever
Hip dysplasia
Elbow dysplasia
Multi-focal retinal dysplasia
Hereditary cataract
Congenital hereditary cataract
Generalized progressive retinal atrophy
Centralized progressive retinal atrophy
Goniodysgenesis/Primary glaucoma
Multifocal retinal dysplasia
Muscular dystrophy (may be more relevant to US dogs)
Degenerative myelopathy
Ichthyosis (ICT-A)
Atopy
Cruciate ligament disease
Cancer (malignant hystiocytosis; haemangiosarcoma; osteosarcoma; lymphoma; melanoma; mast cell tumour; soft tissue sarcoma; thyroid; trichoepithelioma)

The Golden Retriever.

Idiopathic epilepsy
Osteochondrosis dissecans
Heart disease: sub-aortic stenosis; pericardial effusion
Entropion/ectropion
Hypothyroidism
Horner's syndrome
Acral lick dermatitis
Uveodermatological syndrome (autoimmune disease)
Extraocular myositis (autoimmune disease)

English Springer Spaniel
Hip dysplasia
Goniodysgenesis/primary glaucoma
Multifocal retinal dysplasia
Generalized progressive retinal atrophy
Centralized progressive retinal atrophy
Retinal pigment epithelial dystrophy
Fucosidosis
Phosphofructokinase deficiency
Acral mutilation syndrome
Otitis externa
Immune mediated conditions (particularly atopy, haemolytic anaemia, trombocytopenia, masticatory muscle myositis)
Ehlers-Danlos syndrome
Idiopathic epilepsy

The English Springer Spaniel.

Cancer (mammary tumours; anal sac adenocarcinoma; histiocytoma; basal cell tumours; trichoepithelioma)
Endocrine conditions (particularly hypothyroidism, hypoadrenocorticism, hyperadrenocorticism)
Chronic hepatitis (autoimmune liver disease)
Incomplete ossification of the humeral condyle

Cocker Spaniel
Hip dysplasia
Generalized progressive retinal atrophy
Centralized progressive retinal atrophy
Goniodysgenesis /Primary glaucoma
Progressive retinal atrophy
Multiocular defects
Persistent pupillary membrane
Familial nephropathy
Adult onset neuropathy
Acral mutilation syndrome
Atopy

The English Cocker Spaniel.

Cancer (anal sac adenocarcinoma; mammary carcinoma; perianal gland tumours; histiocytoma; oral melanoma; plasmacytoma (coetaneous))
Otitis externa and media (ear disease)
Chronic pancreatitis
Distichiasis
Immune-mediated thrombocytopenia
Immune-mediated haemolytic anaemia
Hypoadrenocorticism
Intervertebral disc disease
Keratoconjunctivitis sicca
Heart disease (patent ductus arteriosus, dilated cardiomyopathy)
Chronic kidney disease
Patellar luxation
Epilepsy
Systemic lupus erythematosus
Acral mutilation syndrome

German Short-haired Pointer
Hip dysplasia
Progressive retinal atrophy

von Willebrands disease type 11
Cone degeneration
Lupoid dermatosis
Junctional epidermolysis bullosa
Atopy
Idiopathic epilepsy
Entropion
Cherry eye
Osteochondritis dissecans
Panosteitis
Acral mutilation syndrome
Heart disease (subaortic stenosis)
Cancer (mammary carcinoma; nasal carcinoma)
Hemivertebrae
Haemophilia
GM2 gangliosidosis
Myasthenia gravis
Epidermolysis bullosa
Polyarthritis/meningitis syndrome (autoimmune disease)
Cutaneous lupus erythematosus (autoimmune disease)
Muscular dystrophy

German Wire-haired Pointer

The German Wire-Haired Pointer.

Hip dysplasia
von Willebrands disease (vWD) type 2
Haemophilia B
Exercise-induced collapse
Atopy
Idiopathic epilepsy
Entropion
Osteochondritis dissecans
Hypothyroidism
Cataract
Heart disease, dilated cardiomyopathy

Hungarian Vizsla

The Hungarian Vizsla.

Hip dysplasia
Progressive retinal atrophy (none recorded in the UK to date)
Goniodysgenesis/primary glaucoma
Cerebellar ataxia
Atopic dermatitis
Sebaceous adenitis
Polymyositis (autoimmune disease)
Myasthenia gravis
Haemophilia A
Idiopathic epilepsy
Entropion

Flat-Coated Retriever
Hip dysplasia
Hereditary cataract

The Flat-Coated Retriever.

Goniodysgenesis/primary glaucoma
Generalized progressive retinal atrophy
Cancer (malignant histiocytosis; soft tissue sarcoma)
Juvenile kidney disease
Patellar luxation
Cruciate ligament disease
Autoimmune thyroiditis
Gastric dilatation and volvulus
Laryngeal paralysis
Renal dysplasia
Epilepsy
Entropion/ectropion
Distichiasis

Chesapeake Bay Retriever
Hip dysplasia
Elbow dysplasia
Hereditary cataract
Generalized progressive retinal atrophy
Degenerative myelopathy
Exercise-induced collapse
Cruciate ligament disease
Osteochondrosis dissecans
Cancer (melanoma)
Epilepsy

The Chesapeake Bay Retriever.

Curly-Coated Retriever

The Curly-Coated Retriever.

Hip dysplasia
Elbow dysplasia
Progressive retinal atrophy
Exercise-induced collapse
Glycogenosis (GSD) type 111a
Entropion
Distichiasis
Epilepsy
Gastric dilatation and volvulus

Cataract
Alopecia (seasonal hair loss from flanks)
Canine follicular dysplasia (hair loss)

Nova Scotia Duck-Tolling Retriever

The Nova Scotia Duck-Tolling Retriever.

Hip dysplasia
Elbow dysplasia
Progressive retinal atrophy
Collie eye anomaly/choroidal hypoplasia
Degenerative encephalopathy
Systemic lupus erythematosus (autoimmune disease)
Meningitis
Polyarthritis
Hypoadrenocorticism
Cleft palate
Hypothyroidism
Multisystemic autoimmunity
Idiopathic epilepsy
Distichiasis

Irish Water Spaniel
Hip dysplasia
Breed health survey results (Kennel Club/British Small Animal Veterinary Association 2012) indicate that the most commonly reported conditions comprise skin diseases, reproductive conditions, cystitis, bladder stones and ear problems.

The Irish Water Spaniel.

Welsh Springer Spaniel

The Welsh Springer Spaniel.

Hip dysplasia
Goniodysgenesis/primary glaucoma
Hereditary cataract (believed to have been eliminated from the UK population)
Idiopathic epilepsy
Atopic dermatitis
Entropion
Distichiasis
Otitis externa
Cancer (basal cell tumour (trichoblastoma))
Immune-mediated haemolytic anaemia

Clumber Spaniel

The Clumber Spaniel.

Hip dysplasia
Elbow dysplasia
Pyruvate dehydrogenase phosphatase 1 deficiency
Exercise-induced collapse
Entropion and Ectropion (central lower lid ectropion, and entropion at the eyelid margins)
Kerratoconjunctivitis sicca
Hypothyroidism
A relatively high percentage of births by caesarean section

English Pointer
Hip dysplasia
Progressive retinal atrophy
Heart disease (aortic stenosis)
Cancer (various forms)
Allergic skin disease
Hypothyroidism
Idiopathic epilepsy
Wobbler syndrome
Osteochondritis dissecans
Ectropion
Cataract
Deafness

English Setter
Hip dysplasia
Elbow dysplasia
Progressive retinal atrophy
Neuronal ceroid lipofuscinosis
Atopy
Malassezia dermatitis
Osteochondritis dissecans
Symmetrical onychomadesis
Ectropion
Deafness
Panosteitis
Cancer (trichoepithelioma; lymphoma)
Lysosomal storage disease
Pancreatic disease
Hypothyroidism

Irish Setter
Hip dysplasia
Generalized progressive retinal atrophy
Generalized progressive retinal atrophy (late
    onset)
Canine leukocyte adhesion deficiency
Atopy
Acral lick dermatitis
Hypothyroidism
Cancer (osteosarcoma; trichoepithelioma; pan-
    creatic; lymphoma)
Idiopathic epilepsy
Uveodermatological syndrome
Entropion
Gluten sensitivity enteropathy
Haemophilia
Immune-mediated haemolytic anaemia
Heart disease (persistent right aortic arch; tricus-
    pid valve dysplasia)

THE CONTROL OF HEREDITARY DISEASE IN GUNDOGS

The Inheritance of Genetic Disease and the Impact of Inbreeding

A dog's genome (the sum of its genetic material) is the complete set of its DNA, which will include all its genes. Genes are made up of DNA (deoxyribonucleic acid), which can be used to make proteins. These proteins represent the building blocks which together are required to assemble the dog and then maintain it through life. Each cell in the dog's body that has a nucleus will have a copy of the entire genome.

Importantly, each dog has two versions of every gene, one that it inherits from its mother and one that it inherits from its father. A copy of these variant genes is made by each parent when they produce sperm or eggs, respectively. A sperm or an egg differs from all other cells insofar as they contain only one copy of each parental gene. The respective single-copy genes are combined when a sperm fertilizes an egg and are so passed on to the puppies. When their genes are copied to produce the sperm and eggs, however, errors can occur, creating mutant genes (incorrect copies).

Dogs that inherit such a mutant (faulty) gene will make a copy of the error and can pass it on in turn to their descendants. The impact of such an event will depend on the type of error made; a mutant gene may have no apparent effect, or alternatively it could cause a serious health problem. Since each dog inherits two versions of every gene – one copy from each parent – some health conditions may only appear if one of the two copies has an error, while others can only occur if both copies of the same gene have the error.

A health condition that occurs when a dog has only one copy of a faulty gene (inherited from either its dam or its sire) is known as an 'autosomal-dominant condition'. Many of the more severe autosomal-dominant conditions are generally not passed on to any further generations because the affected dog is often too ill to reproduce, or dies before it reaches sexual maturity. For this reason autosomal-dominant conditions are usually quite rare.

A health condition that can only occur when a dog has two copies of a faulty gene (inherited from both its dam and its sire) is known as an autosomal-recessive condition. Dogs with only one copy of the mutant gene are said to be carriers, and normally display no signs of the disease (although they can still pass on the gene to their offspring). The mutant genes for autosomal-recessive conditions can be the most difficult to deal with because they can be passed on from generation to generation without being noticed or identified. Providing a dog also has a healthy copy of the gene functioning normally, the mutant gene may never be noticed.

Simple inherited disorders occur from a mutation of a single gene and represent a significant proportion of the known inherited diseases in the dog. Some inherited conditions, however, are more complex and are caused by a number of genes that act together, contributing to the disease. When a single gene causes disease, dogs are either normal or similarly affected. In more complex inherited conditions, affected dogs don't necessarily show signs to the same degree; some may be only mildly affected, whereas others may be much more severely diseased. Hip dysplasia is a good example of an inherited disease with a complex mode of inheritance.

Usually in a randomly bred population where every individual has a similar chance of reproducing and contributing to subsequent generations, there is no way of knowing these mutant genes exist. We have no way of recognizing what disease they cause until they are expressed in a dog that perchance inherits two copies – one from each parent.

The more closely related that parents are to one another, the more likely they are to share similar genetic material. This is what tends to happen when we selectively breed animals – choosing to breed only from dogs that share a common desirable attribute. Whilst this similar genetic material could be genes associated with positive traits, it could also include faulty genes. The more closely related that dogs are, the higher the risk is that they are both carriers for the same autosomal-recessive conditions. Should these two dogs be mated, then there is a risk that the puppies will inherit a copy of the faulty genes from both parents and will therefore be affected. This risk of producing dogs affected by inherited health conditions therefore increases with the degree of inbreeding.

Furthermore, as the number of these smaller inherited conditions increases, they can have an accumulative effect, leading to a decrease in the general health of the dog, otherwise known as inbreeding depression. This can lead to reduced litter sizes, increased puppy mortality, reduced fertility and a shorter lifespan.

PHENOTYPIC TESTS

The BVA/KC Hip Scoring Scheme
In this test a dog's hips are X-rayed and submitted for examination by a panel of formally appointed experts, who score the hips according to agreed criteria. Each hip is evaluated by two experts, who score nine anatomical features of the hip and score each hip out of a total of 53. The two hip scores are then added together to give an overall total hip score. So a dog's hip score can range from 0 to 106, and the lower the hip scores, the better the anatomy of the dog's hips.

In breeds where significant numbers of dogs have been through the hip scheme, it is possible to calculate a breed mean hip score, which gives a feel for the average score within that

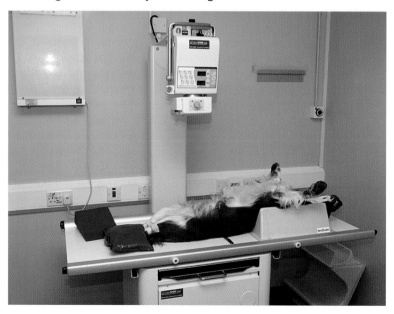

A dog being X-rayed for the purpose of hip scoring under the BVA/KC scheme.

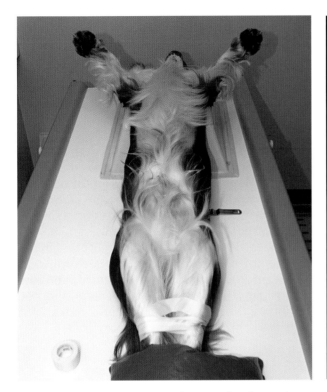

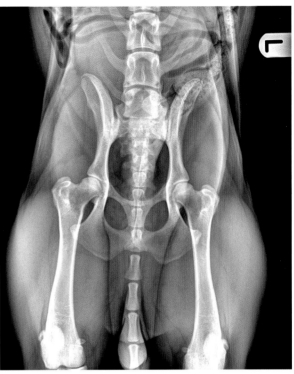

For the BVA/KC hip-scoring scheme a dog has to be positioned carefully. Here, the dog is lying in a frame that ensures the chest is upright and the pelvis is level. The hind legs are extended and taped together to ensure that the radiographic image of the hip joint can be properly evaluated and correctly scored

A hip X-ray taken for the BVA/KC hip scoring scheme. Radiographs submitted for evaluation must include the dog's unique KC registration number and microchip number; for reasons of confidentiality these have been deleted from this particular image.

breed. The X-ray appearance can be used by the vet to advise the owner on ways to reduce the impact of disease in an affected individual, and the score(s) can be used to help breeders select less severely affected dogs for breeding.

The BVA/KC Elbow Grading Scheme

This scheme is similarly applied to X-rays taken of the dog's elbows. In this case the X-ray appearance of each elbow is graded by two panel specialists from 0–3 depending on certain observable criteria: the lower the grade, the better the anatomy of the elbow. In this scheme, if the dog has two different elbow grades, the higher of the two is used as the dog's elbow grade.

Breeders are advised to use only unaffected dogs for breeding, and the grade will usually

determine if an individual dog is likely to subsequently become lame as a result of elbow dysplasia. Surgery to ameliorate the signs of disease can also be attempted in higher graded dogs. The grading scheme is particularly helpful to owners and breeders alike. Not only will it determine if a dog is suitable for breeding, but the result obtained is likely to determine if an individual dog is likely to require subsequent veterinary treatment, or, if suitable for work, if it warrants investment in the time and cost of training.

The BVA/KC/ISDS (International Sheep Dog Society) Eye Scheme

This scheme requires dogs to be examined by a member of a specialist panel of veterinary ophthalmologists who examines the eyes looking for characteristic signs of breed-specific inherited eye conditions. These conditions are categorized as two lists: Schedule A conditions and Schedule B conditions. Schedule A contains all the known inherited eye diseases, and the breeds that are currently known to be affected by these conditions. Schedule B lists breeds and conditions where further investigation is urged. Specialist panelists, appointed by the BVA, can examine any individual dog for clinical signs of these diseases. Unfortunately many of these inherited eye diseases are not present from birth, and breeders especially are advised to have their breeding stock examined throughout their dog's life.

One of the specialist veterinary ophthalmologists appointed by the BVA examines a dog for the BVA/KC/ISDS eye scheme.

DNA Testing

A gene is the basic physical and functional unit of heredity. Genes are made up of DNA (deoxyribonucleic acid). DNA has a complex, double-helix structure rather like a coiled ladder that is able to replicate itself. A gene is simply a small part of this complex double helical structure.

By comparing the DNA from dogs affected by genetic disorder with DNA from normal individuals, the difference (the defective gene) can be established and analyzed. A DNA test can then be developed that identifies other cells that have that same defective gene. Since those cells will

each have two copies, one inherited from each parent, the DNA test will also determine whether one or both copies are defective. DNA tests look at the dog's genotype as distinct from its phenotype. They tell us whether the dog has inherited a genetic condition and the likelihood of passing on that condition to any progeny.

To submit material for DNA testing we usually collect either a small blood sample or a buccal swab, a sample of cells taken on a small brush rubbed just inside the cheek. Samples are sent to a reference laboratory, usually the laboratory that first developed the test. Testing typically takes about a week.

DNA tests are only available for a limited number of diseases, and a DNA test will only reveal information about the particular disease being tested for, not each and every inherited condition. Nevertheless, more and more DNA tests are continually being developed.

THE BENEFITS OF TESTING

Despite the fact that the BVA/KC schemes have rarely eliminated hereditary conditions among our gundog breeds, over the years they have generally reduced the incidence and overall severity of a number of serious breed-predisposed conditions.

The hip and elbow schemes were quite ambitious in attempting to address what we now understand are two quite complex inherited orthopaedic conditions. Hip and elbow dysplasia are likely to be polygenic (caused by more than one gene acting together) and influenced by a variety of extrinsic factors such as diet and exercise. Nevertheless using test results for hip dysplasia and knowing the genealogy of closely related dogs in these respects – that is, knowing the scores of parents and other closely related dogs – statistical analyses can now be made to determine the likelihood of an individual dog passing on the condition to its progeny.

The results of these analyses, called EBVs ('Estimated Breeder Values') are now published by the UK Kennel Club for KC-registered dogs and are freely available on-line via the 'Mate Select' programme. Mate Select also allows you to calculate the degree of inbreeding, or 'Coefficient of Inbreeding' (COI), for puppies that could be produced from a hypothetical mating.

EBVs have been successfully applied for many years in improving production among food-producing farmed livestock, and we have every hope that similar use can be made to improve pedigree dogs. The more dogs there are that have been scored in a dog's pedigree, the greater the confidence in the accuracy of the EBV. Consequently it is now, more than ever, important that owners and breeders continue to support the BVA/KC schemes and submit their dogs for testing.

EBVs are only available for breeds with a large number and wide spread of tested dogs. Among gundogs, at the time of writing, EBVs are available for the English Setter, Flat-Coated Retriever, Golden Retriever, Gordon Setter and Labrador Retriever.

DNA tests are normally applied to simple inherited conditions. Most inherited condi-tions use this type of inherence; only relatively few of those identified so far have a more complex mode of inheritance. Using these tests it is possible to determine if a particular dog is 'clear' or affected by the disease, or whether it is a symptomless carrier of the disease that can nevertheless, potentially, pass on the condition to its offspring. A list of breed-specific official Kennel Club DNA testing schemes and dogs tested under these schemes can be found on the KC website.

DNA tests used in these schemes can accurately identify clear, carrier and affected dogs, and can be used by breeders to effectively eliminate undesirable disease genes in their stock. By publishing these results, on the UK Kennel Club website for instance, it also allows breeders to have a better understanding of which genes a dog may pass on to its offspring, giving them the information required to avoid producing affected puppies. Making informed decisions from health test

CANINE GENOTYPE BREEDING CHART

Expected results from mating DNA tested dogs

Bitch status	Stud dog status		
	Clear	Carrier	Affected
Clear	All puppies in litter will be will be normal/clear	50 per cent of litter will be normal/clear, 50 per cent of litter will be carriers	All puppies in the litter carriers
Carrier	50 per cent of litter will be be normal/clear, 50 per cent of litter will be carriers	25 per cent of litter will be normal/clear, 50 per cent of litter will be carriers, 25 per cent of litter will be affected	50 per cent of litter will be normal/clear, 50 per cent of litter will be affected
Affected	All puppies in the litter will be carriers	50 per cent of litter will be normal/clear, 50 per cent of litter will be affected	All puppies in litter affected

results enables breeders to adapt their breeding programmes and reduce the risk of this disease appearing in future generations.

It is important to remember that every dog is most likely already a carrier for many autosomal-recessive conditions. DNA tests are available for only a small number of the known mutations in dogs, but there are likely to be many more recessive mutations that we currently know nothing about. As well as taking into consideration health test results, the general health and performance of each parent, the inbreeding coefficient of the potential puppies that could be produced, as well as, importantly, the temperament of the dogs and their conformation, should be borne in mind when deciding on which dogs to breed from. It is also extremely important to consider the welfare impact of any particular inherited condition: diseases with a 'high' impact, having

severe consequences causing significant pain, suffering and lasting harm, are best avoided, whereas those with a 'low' welfare impact might be better tolerated.

A simple chart showing the outcome of various mating strategies that can be applied when deciding on mating tested dogs is shown on the previous page.

It can be seen that even if a dog is a carrier, it does not preclude its use for breeding, particularly within the numerically small breeds. As long as the gene is what's known as an 'autosomal recessive', mating carriers to 'clear' dogs will result in symptomless puppies, albeit they too will carry and pass on the gene to their progeny.

Health testing and the application of informed breeding strategies provides a means of controlling hereditary diseases and maintaining a healthier gene pool.

INDEX